SPECIAL VISUAL EFFECTS

SPECIAL
VISUAL
A Guide to
Special Effects
Cinematography
EFFECTS

Jack Imes, Jr.

PRENTICE HALL PRESS • NEW YORK

Copyright © 1984 by Jack Imes, Jr.

All rights reserved, including the right of reproduction
in whole or in part in any form.

Published in 1986 by Prentice Hall Press
A Division of Simon & Schuster, Inc.
Gulf + Western Building
One Gulf + Western Plaza
New York, NY 10023

Originally published by Van Nostrand Reinhold Company Inc.
Designed by Charlotte Staub

PRENTICE HALL PRESS is a trademark of Simon & Schuster, Inc.

Library of Congress Cataloging-in-Publication Data

Imes, Jack.
  Special visual effects.

  Bibliography: p.
  Includes index.
  1. Cinematography—Special effects.   I. Title.
TR858.I44   1984   778.5′345   84-2357
ISBN: 0-671-61194-1

Manufactured in the United States of America

10 9 8 7 6 5 4 3 2

First Prentice Hall Press Edition

Contents

Acknowledgments

The author would like to thank the many people who gave generously of their time to provide photographs, technical material, and personal replies to the many questions concerning special visual effects. For permission to reproduce pictures and illustrations of equipment and film project material, I thank the following individuals and companies: Apogee, Inc.; Cinetron Computer Systems, Inc.; Mitchell Camera Corporation; Bruner F. Barrie, Sculpture House, Inc.; Milton Laikin, Laikin Optical Corporation; J-K Camera Engineering; Charles Lipow, Inc.; Cinema Products Corporation; Samuelson Group PLC, London; Anivision, Ltd.; Neilson-Hordell, Ltd.; Alan Gordon Enterprises; Paul Mejias and Albert Mejias; Pioneer/Trebes; Susan Bickford, Digital Effects, Inc.; Michael Sigrist, Fries Engineering, Inc.; Steve Chamberlain, Arriflex Corporation; Joseph Vasata, Bolex, Inc.; Hubbard Hunt, Fax Company; Tiffin, Inc.; Marshall Stewart, Stewart Filmscreen Corporation; Robert Greenberg and Sandra Payne, R. Greenberg Associates; Bob Doub, R & D Latex Corporation; Windsor Hills Makeup Lab, Inc.; Anthony Zaza, Century Precision Optics; Continental Camera Systems, Inc.; Alcone Company; Tri-Ess Sciences; F & B Ceco, Inc.; Peter Regla, Elicon; Arthur Stroud, Photo-Sonics, Inc. (Acme Sales).

The author would like to thank Rick Catizone of Anivision for his photos of animation projects and for his general assistance in the Appendix discussion of the safe use of animation materials.

A thank-you to Robert Godlove of the Iowa City Photoworld for the loan of special lens equipment. To Tom Richards and the *Appleton Post-Crescent* newspaper for photos of the author and past favors. To Richard Jantz for photos and leads.

Finally, a general thank-you to my agent, Denise Marcil, for getting this project off the ground, and to my wife, Cynthia, to whom this book is dedicated, for her patience.

Introduction

If you have ever seen a motion picture, then you have seen the magic of special visual effects. In recent years a number of big-budget films have touted eye-dazzling images that could only have been created by . . . magic! The great mothership of Close Encounters, the little wizard called Yoda, the lost-and-found alien E.T., the soaring Superman—all were products of creative special visual effects. But the visual magic resulted from the combination of imagination with the technology of film.

No matter how imaginative the visual, special effects cinematography is the application of the basic tools of the trade: the camera and film. It is the known creating the as-yet-unknown, the final image that will be seen on the big screen. If the existing tools are not adequate for the imaginative concept of the script, then new tools are created. The 1933 production of King Kong brought the miniature rear screen technique to cinematic life; that same year the Invisible Man forced the optical printer into new visual territory. More recently, the computer camera reached fruition with Star Wars, and the front screen projection system enabled Superman to fly.

Even a traditional noneffects picture like the immortal classic Citizen Kane created film images that used the split screen and matte techniques in new ways for its time.

Special visual effects is an evolving art. The techniques of tomorrow are grounded in the innovations of today. In turn, the methods of the past form the foundation for current visual spectaculars.

I like special visual effects. At times, I think they are the best part of a movie. However, I also like to be fooled by a well-made visual effect—a shot that is a seamless fabric between what is real on the screen and what is a completely manufactured illusion. I appreciate a well-made effect even more because I know that so many parts go into its creation. The fact that you are reading this book indicates that you too are intrigued by how professional visual effects are created.

This book is an introduction to the tools and methods of special visual effects cinematography. It is designed to supply a working vocabulary for the effects seen on the screen. The chapters are organized to show a progression: how the effects shot is first planned, then visualized, put down on paper, then put on film. The chapters are written so that the basic terms of one chapter form the foundation for understanding the next. In reality, films are a combination of many techniques. Animation, puppets, paintings, and mattes can all be combined in a single frame. A clear grasp of the visual parts can lead to a full appreciation of the whole.

This book is limited to film production special visual effects. Video effects (except for computer animation, which is not really a *video* effect) and makeup effects are not explored. These two subjects deserve complete books in their own right.

The book concludes with chapter-related projects, fairly inexpensive ideas for using some of the basic tricks described. However, if you like effects work, you will be trying to do things long before you get to the end of the book!

Planning Visual Effects:
The Script and the Story Board

1

Special visual effects are the magical images that excite, enchant, and, more often, go unnoticed by the film audience. The best visual effect is one that fools the audience into believing that what they see is a perfectly natural event. A gigantic spaceship, a fire-breathing dragon, an exploding planet—all are memorable visual effects. The single image is often reinforced by dozens of carefully crafted and subtle lesser visuals. The result is a convincing illusion of reality on film.

Visual effects do not appear full-blown on the silver screen. The images the audience sees began as ideas in the imagination of the film writer or director. The ideas are transformed into simple words on paper, the *script*. Also known as a *screenplay*, the script of word-pictures is the common link to all the production stages of a film. In special effects work the script is essential to clarify what is required before thousands of dollars are wasted in misguided effort. To help the reader understand the script's role, this chapter presents the two basic script formats and the related form of visual script called the *story board*.

THE SCRIPT

A script contains the written descriptions of the film locations, story action, dialogue, and visual effects. It outlines the characters and dramatic structure. A well-written script uses a peculiar writing format to permit swift reading and later additions. The language style is often spare, nearly telegraphic. Unlike a novel's full-bodied prose, scripts intentionally leave plenty to the reader's imagination. The form follows its function, which is to serve as a set of general instructions to guide the director, actors, cameramen, and production technicians. The script is the blueprint for the construction of the film's images and sound.

Two types of script formats are most commonly used. Both tell the same story, but with slightly different approaches. The first, the *master scene* format, organizes the script descriptions and dialogue without any reference to specific camera angles. It is somewhat like a play in form and is used primarily for planning shot sequences in a scene. The *shot-by-shot* format is the one that shows the required camera angles for every shot. Although a film uses both types, a single script rarely mixes the two formats.

Master Scene Script

The master scene format arranges the scene action and dialogue under a simple descriptive heading of the scene location. No specific camera angle is indicated. For example, an interior scene of a room is written:

```
1      INT. PETE'S ROOM
```

A description of any scene action and the dialogue is then given.

The heading is numbered to help both the reader and film production personnel keep a proper scene identification and sequence. In practice a film is shot out of scene order. This permits an efficient use of actors, locations, and contract personnel within a limited number of shooting days. The scene number is essential in special visual effects work as well to keep track, since the scene shots are developed at different times in the production.

The following script is arranged in the master scene format.

```
Title: ALIEN ATTACK!

70    EXT. THE HARBOR

      The first cannon shell fired from the battleship
      strikes one leg of the huge Martian war machine.
      The second shell explodes uselessly on the
      machine's armored head. . . .

71    EXT. THE BATTLESHIP DECK

      The gun crew quickly prepares the cannon breech
      and fires again!

72    EXT. THE HARBOR

      The new round explodes without notice by the
      Martian walking machine.

        The Martians return fire, the single head gun
      shooting a brilliant beam of light!

73    EXT. THE BATTLESHIP DECK

      The alien ray slams into the deck, rips through
      the hull causing the ship to EXPLODE!
                                              CUT TO

74    INT. CONWAT TV BUILDING

      John Wilson has his portable TV camera working
      again. He aims his zoom lens through the blown-
      out window and focuses on the Martian war
      machine. He then sees the smoke and burning oil
      of the sunken battleship.
```

WILSON
(into mike)
. . . can't see anything . . . no
survivors . . . the ship's gone under
. . . the Martians are using their laser
beams to destroy everything in sight!

CUT TO

75   EXT. THE COUNTRYSIDE—A ROAD—DAY

A speeding car careens around a sharp turn in the
road, and then another.

76   INT. THE CAR

The driver, Jake Owens, tries to navigate the
bends in an unfamiliar road. His wife, Ann, is
next to him and has a bandage wrapped around her
hand. In the back seat is Phil Merton, blinded,
his eyes covered with a bloody, hastily tied
handkerchief.

ANN
Jake, slow down. I feel sick inside . . .
real bad . . . can't we stop for just a
little while?

JAKE
I can't. Too risky . . . maybe if we can
reach the mountains by nightfall we can—

He is cut off by Ann's sharp scream.

77   EXT. THE ROAD

A Martian war machine straddles the road ahead.
Jake's car veers off the road and into the nearby
woods. The Martian heat ray weapon fires and the
trees burst into instant flame. Within seconds
an inferno rages, trapping Jake's car.

CUT TO

In this brief excerpt, descriptions and dialogue advance the scenes,
with no instructions for camera placement. This type of script can
be used for photography setup if the director and cameraman (director
of photography) work out the camera angles at the time of shooting.
However, the master scene format is not detailed enough for the
other technicians working on the film. The *shooting script*, which is
the script in final form, is not done that way. Special effects people,
in particular, need a script geared to the exact camera view of every
shot in the scene. Since each special effects shot is made up of many
different optical elements, each filmed separately and later combined
as a single image, the script needs to be camera-view oriented. In
most cases the principal script used in effects preparation is the shot-
by-shot script.

Shot-by-Shot Script

As the term implies, each scripted scene is written as a series of camera view descriptions or *shots*. The result is a script most related to the edited film that will be seen by the theater audience.

The script format identifies each shot in the scene by a number, camera angle instruction, and brief shot description. For example, a description of a woman in an interior would be written:

```
1    MEDIUM SHOT—INTERIOR OF LEIA'S ROOM

     Any action and dialogue within the single shot.
```

As with the master scene format all descriptions are terse. The purpose of the script is to guide, not entertain. A common aid to brevity is to shorten the shot camera angles to an abbreviation, such as MED for a Medium Shot, or to use letters, such as MS or M.S. A listing of the conventional camera angles appears later in this chapter. However, the only hard and fast rule for shot terms is that they should be consistent within the entire script.

The following script is arranged in the shot-by-shot format.

```
     Title: ALIEN ATTACK!

25   LONG SHOT—THE FARMER

     standing at the edge of the huge meteorite
     crater, his flashlight beam stabbing into the
     thin mist.

26   LONG SHOT—CRATER INTERIOR (FARMER'S POV)

     still smoking with newly scorched earth and
     ashes of bushes as the farmer's beam searches
     out the weirdly shaped rock embedded at the
     bottom.

27   CLOSE SHOT—THE FARMER

     bewildered by the strange object from the sky.
     He glances down to his small companion, his dog
     T—BONE.
                    FARMER
     Ain't we dreamin', T—Bone?

28   MEDIUM SHOT—DOG (FARMER'S POV)

     bewildered as his human master. His sudden bark
     reveals his curiosity or lack of courage.

29   MEDIUM SHOT—THE FARMER

     starting cautiously down the crater slope.

30   CLOSE SHOT—METEORITE

     pulsating with an eerie light.
```

31 ESTABLISHING SHOT—ELSON AIR BASE

    as dawn brightens. The huge dish of the
    satellite tracking antenna looms above the
    nearby squat buildings. The following title is
    superimposed: ELSON AFB, TERROS RANGE, NEW
    MEXICO

32 LONG SHOT—COMPUTER CENTER INTERIOR

    as dozens of technicians monitor the maze of
    computer consoles. The CAMERA TRACKS two men who
    enter and go to a wall—size television computer
    display screen. The screen is alive with map
    diagrams. The two men, STROM and FRANKLIN, are
    in clear authority.

33 MEDIUM SHOT—STROM

    studies the screen.

                    STROM
                (to technician)
    Are you still getting the V—com signal
    transmission?

34 CLOSE SHOT—TECHNICIAN

                    TECHNICIAN
    It's weak, but we're still tracking on the
    recovery beam.

Script Terms

The simplified vocabulary used in scripts must be well understood
if the shots are to be visualized as intended. Terms such as Close
Shot, POV, Pan, and SFX describe the image seen in the writer's
imaginary camera viewfinder. They make a script easier to read by
other people involved in the film production. A working familiarity
with common shot terms is essential to translating word-pictures
into film images.

The basic notation for standard camera shots follows. Although
the specific composition of a shot is relative to each camera position,
the terms remain similar from film to film.

Add to this basic working vocabulary by reading scripts, either
borrowed from a script library or purchased from a movie store that
specializes in scripts, still photos, and posters. One such store is
listed in the Appendix of Suppliers. A repeated exposure to script
formats will add to the reader's facility with the practical terms of
camera placement, movements, shot transitions, and special visual
effects.

Script terms	Camera shot description
LS	A *long shot* gives the general view of a scene from a distant viewpoint.
ELS	When the long shot is really far away from the subject being photographed, then it is an *extremely long shot*.
ES	The first long shot in a scene is an *establishing shot* becauses it presents, or establishes, the place and time of the story scene.
CS CU	When the camera is quite near the subject, the shot is called a *close shot* or often a *close-up*.
ECU	A super-close camera shot is an *extremely close shot*.
MS	Halfway between a long shot and a close shot is the ordinary *medium shot*.
MCU (or MC) MLS	Of course, there can be slightly closer or slightly longer medium shots, called a *medium close-up* and a *medium long shot*.
FS	Sometimes a medium long shot is also called a *full shot*.

A shot can also involve some kind of camera movement during the filming. These movements can also be indicated in the script.

TILT	A *tilt* is when the camera pivots up or down.
PAN	A *pan* is when the camera swivels left or right. The term is short for a *panorama*, a complete view of a landscape.
DOLLY	A *dolly* is when the camera moves forward or backward. The term comes from a camera dolly, a platform with wheels that can be easily rolled through a scene.
TRACKING	A *tracking shot* is made by the camera following the subject of the shot wherever he, she, or it goes.

Sometimes a shot is described by the type of lens that will shoot the scene. Because various lenses have a certain look or angle of view, the script writer can specify what is visualized by lens terms.

WIDE SHOT	A *wide shot* is one that uses a shorter than normal focal length lens.
TELEPHOTO SHOT	A *telephoto shot* is one that uses a longer than normal focal length lens.
ZOOM	A *zoom* usually refers to zoom lens, which can change from a wide to telephoto focal length (or reverse) at any desired speed without moving the camera. The shot movement is made optically rather than physically. An actual camera movement would be written as a tracking or dolly shot.
TIGHT SHOT	Sometimes the script writer will just want a close framing of the subject and leave the actual camera shot to the director. In this case, the script writer wants a *tight shot*, or for the camera to *move in tight*.

Scripts also use a number of general terms for special effects and optical transitions between shots. These include:

A *fade-in* is a gradual transition from full black to full scene exposure.   FADE IN

A *fade-out* is the opposite number, usually to end a scene or the film   FADE OUT
entirely.

A *dissolve* is a short optical overlap transition between two shots. It   DISSOLVE
may be slow or fast as required for the visual rhythm of the film.

The *point of view* is when the camera pretends it is an actor and lets   POV or P.O.V.
the audience see a replaced actor's view of a scene.

Special effects or *sound effects* are indicated by a catch-all term accom-   SFX, SPFX, EFX, FX
panied by a brief note of what the effect is to be, as in "explosion."

The actors, male and female, are known as *live action*. The term is   LIVE ACTION
usually used to describe any footage with living creatures that will later
be printed with added backgrounds or special effects.

Animation is the special photography of puppets or cartoon drawings.   ANIMATION

If film is borrowed from a film library, the footage is known as *stock*   STOCK
film and saves the camera crew the expense of going on location to shoot
a volcano, flood, earthquake or other stock footage. Sometimes called
"canned shots."

THE STORY BOARD

In a script the shots are described in words to help create a strong
image in the reader's mind. The problem is that each person can
interpret the shot description in a slightly different way. Special
visual effects are the hardest to imagine since they do not exist in
a real sense, only on film. In order to create the same image in
everyone's mind, a form of visual scriptwriting is used by the director
and production personnel. This special script is called a *story board*.
It is simply an artist's drawing of how the written shot description
will look on film. An entire series of shot drawings serves to preview
the film before a single foot of film stock is exposed.

Story boards, sometimes called *visual continuity*, are used to plan
the unique aspects of a film story: camera movements, optical effects,
key dramatic images, and miniatures. However, story boards are not
usually required for standard feature films, since the photography
involved is fairly uncomplicated. The real strength of story boards
lies in commercials, animated films, and special visual effects. The
specific images in such films are often carefully designed and require
extensive coordination among the various departments responsible
for the individual shot elements.

After a script is approved for production, the film's *art director* discusses the shots with the film director and producer. During the meeting the art director creates simple *spot sketches* that capture the look, mood, and camera view that the film director wishes to achieve in actual photography. These simple sketches are later turned over to the *production illustrator*, sometimes called the *story board artist*, to be refined into a detailed story board presentation. Some directors who are handy with a pencil may produce their own spot sketches to clarify an idea or complicated visual sequence.

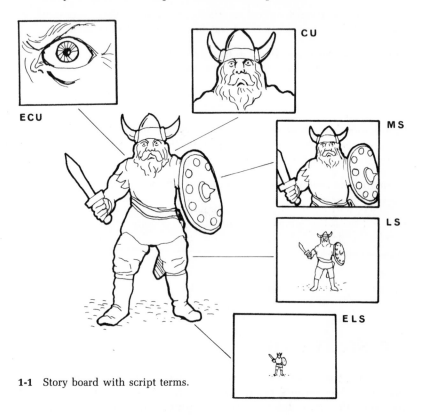

1-1 Story board with script terms.

Key Drawings

Spot sketches are only the first step in preparing the story board. Meant only as rough visual notes, spot sketches guide the production illustrator in making a more carefully rendered set of *key drawings*. A key drawing, based on several earlier spot sketches, shows a more detailed view of the master scene. Care is taken to indicate actor placement, set or location details, and any important lighting effects. The key drawing serves to present a visual summary of a dramatic highlight or climax in the master scene. No attempt is made to show a specific camera angle since the purpose of the key drawing is to present the main or "key" elements of the scene. Once a key drawing is prepared, it can then be used as the basis for planning the many camera shots that will form the actual master scene. Usually one key drawing per scene is enough to allow the production team members to see exactly what is visually required by the script.

Once the key drawings are approved, the production illustrator then creates the camera-view story board art panel drawings according to the director's instructions. Unlike the key drawings, these panels break down the scripted action and dialogue into specific camera angles. However, because the camera-view drawings are derived from the master scene's key drawing, the images are consistent in content and style.

Production Story Board

The final story board is made up of dozens or even hundreds of individual drawings assembled into groups identified by the associated scene numbers. The story board can then be reviewed by the key production personnel. To make viewing the many panels easier, the story board is often taped across walls or pinned to cork boards. The eye can travel easily from shot to shot and see the editorial pace of the intended action sequence. Photocopies of the story board are sent to the appropriate departments to establish a common standard for the model makers and all visual effects workers. Later, on location during photography, copies of the story board in ring binders aid in staging the live action elements of each shot.

The story boards are often changed by the director as work progresses. Reviews are frequently needed as the film's visual style is established. The original key drawings may generate any number of panels that are later discarded or extensively reorganized. Updated photocopies of all new panels are sent to all departments involved, which often generates abrupt comments from individuals laboring over complex but now obsolete shots.

Concept Story Boards

Selected key drawings are sometimes reworked into a highly refined set of art pieces known as a *concept story board*. Unlike the camera-oriented shot panels, the concept story board is primarily a device to sell the film idea to potential financial investors. It is a visual commercial to pitch the overall film concept. Full-color art instead of simple black-and-white drawings illustrates the script's dramatic high points and add vivid impact. Effective with nontechnical audiences, the concept story board—although it may contain excellent paintings—is not generally used to plan the actual shots themselves.

Story Board Format

The basic story board is a sketch bordered by a line that matches the camera frame proportion (*aspect ratio*). The drawing may be simple scribbles at one extreme, as in figure 1-2, or greatly detailed, as in figure 1-3, to show exactly what the finished shot will look like.

The drawing is made on stiff paper or bristol board with a soft-lead (B) pencil, pen and ink, ink washes, or dry-point markers. Color is not generally used except to accent a special detail in the artwork.

1-2   Story board rough.

159A ANGLE OVER FIREFOX AS CANARDS FOLD...

1-3 Detailed story board.

SHOT NO.

DESCRIPTION:

1-4 Simple story board frame.

The frameline border matches the proportion of the film format. Television story boards are likewise framed by the standard television screen border. Preprinted pads are available from suppliers to relieve the artist of the need to constantly redraw the border frame for each panel. An example of a simple story board frame is shown in figure 1-4.

In addition to the art, areas of the story board are set aside for the script shot number and for a brief description or action heading. Usually a camera shot angle is included to help explain the art. Dialogue or narrative captions are seldom used in feature film story boards. They are common in boards for commercials and animated films, where such lines underscore the visual action.

Story boards intended for special visual effects often require additional instructions to show how a shot is to be achieved. They can involve the use of miniatures, paintings, lighting, and special optical process photography. An example of a special effects panel is shown in figure 1-5.

SHOT NO. —	— OF —	FRAME COUNT —	PAGE NO. —
BACKGROUND —			ELEMENTS —
DESCRIPTION —		NOTES —	
DIALOGUE —			
OPTICAL —	PLATE NO. —	ANIMATION —	BOARD NO. —

1-5 Special effects panel.

A single shot may not require that all the block areas be filled in, but all the information needed to create a special visual should be included. In this way the instructions identify exactly what must be done by the model makers and optical personnel to schedule a shot for production.

MULTIPLE SHOT PANELS

Each camera story board panel is a single drawing of the intended camera shot of the scene action. However, a single drawing may not clearly explain the shot if several actions are to occur in sequence within a single camera shot. This limitation makes planning special effects sequences that involve both entry and exit of moving miniatures in a master scene awkward.

In such cases the production illustrator can create two, three, or more panel drawings to indicate the separate actions of elements within the shot. The panels are then kept together to give an easy visual analysis of what will happen in the flow of the shot action. The breakdown simplifies the planning of a complicated effects sequence within a single shot. Since no one initially knows exactly how the shot will be achieved, the extra panels clarify the separate elements needed to make the shot work. Another function of the subpanels is to indicate elements that move in and out of the shot frame at different moments in the action. Figure 1-6 shows how a series of panels would be numbered for multiple shot sequences.

To keep track of the extra panels, related shots are coded with a letter and the script shot number. Shot 5, for example, is a continuous shot that begins at 5 and ends at 5C. It is actually the cluster of shots indicated by the panels 5, 5A, 5B, and 5C. On film there is no break in the overall action, although the camera view may shift, elements may be maneuvered, and changes may be made within the shot. Because of the additional art panels required to display a complex special visual effect, the total number of story board shots can far outnumber the script shot count.

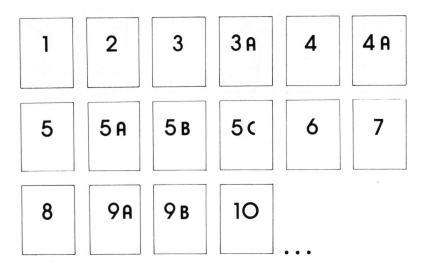

1-6 Panels numbered for multiple shot sequences.

PANEL CAMERA MOVEMENTS

The story board panel drawing represents the camera-lens view of the scene or subject. A stationary camera is implied. In practice, however, a film shot is often panned, tilted, or made with a mobile dolly-mounted camera. The story board must indicate any such camera moves (and any lens changes or zoom actions) in an easily understood way. The direction of the intended movement is usually shown by arrows. Figure 1-7 illustrates the basic graphics that show camera movements.

The arrows at the corners of the border frame represent a "third dimension" of camera movement into or away from the subject being filmed. They translate as a *dolly in* or *dolly back* from the action. The arrows can also indicate a lens zoom, an optical focal length change that simulates the physical movement of the camera on a dolly. The end-of-the-movement framing of the subject is approximated by a smaller frame drawn in a broken line. (An *out* movement would use the broken-line frame as the starting position.)

Pan and *tilt* movements are shown by combining two panels into a single graphic. The two sides, slightly offset, indicate the camera movement's start and stop positions. In practice the camera movement would span these two framings smoothly with no break in the shot or action.

If the composition of the shot requires an element to move into or out of the camera framing, a large arrow can indicate the required path. The arrow is drawn in a realistic perspective and shaded on one side to accent the outward or inward movement.

The use of directional arrows can be combined in a single panel or series of panels to display any required camera or subject movement. These graphic notations allow the story board to become more visually dynamic. More important, the "moving" story board can be studied by the production personnel in terms of actual camera actions. The panels permit decisions to be made on the basis of how the camera will move, and likewise the requirements of pacing those moves from shot to shot. In this way the story board does more than illustrate

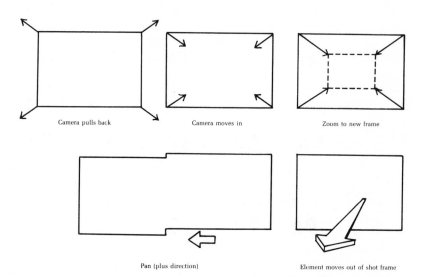

Camera pulls back   Camera moves in   Zoom to new frame

1-7 Standard panel moves.

Pan (plus direction)   Element moves out of shot frame

individual shots. When interpreted correctly, the collective panels provide a working diagram of the film's visual complexity, dramatic pacing, and action.

Examples of Story Boards

The story boards shown here were used to prepare the special effects for the film *Firefox*. The author wishes to thank Apogee, Inc., the special effects company that created the film's extensive visual effects, for use of the story boards and photos that appear in this chapter and elsewhere.

The story boards use many of the graphic techniques described in this chapter. A close study of each panel and sequence will demonstrate how a "movie on paper" can be presented in great detail. Many of the components of the individual shots, such as optical mattes, background projection, and motion-control, will be the subjects of the chapters to follow.

The climax of *Firefox* is an exciting high-speed chase between two sleek ultramodern (and fictional) aircraft, both of Russian design. The hero, Gant, is a crack American pilot smuggled into the Soviet top-secret airfield. Gant steals a prototype Firefox MIG 31 jet and heads toward the sanctuary beyond the Soviet border. He is hotly pursued by the only other Firefox, piloted by the Russian ace Voskov. The two aircraft streak at 3,000 mph, engage in acrobatic dogfights, and race toward the Soviet border.

In the film the two jets simulated real aircraft, although of imaginary design and capability. In reality both jets were nonflying detailed miniatures. All the *Firefox* aerial dogfights and complex flight manuevers had to be created in the studio by the Apogee visual effects team. The story board became an essential tool in the choreographing of the shot sequences, which required meticulous planning and coordination of the movements of the two jets and all camera movements.

A comparison of figures 1-8 and 1-9 shows how closely the story board art is followed in the composition of the jet in this frame blowup from the finished film. Note the arrow graphic for the aircraft's movement within the shot. In this board panel and in subsequent panels, the scene numbers of each shot are indicated in the upper left heading. Descriptions of the action and important effects are written along the bottom of the frame.

The double frame in figure 1-10 indicates a camera pan from right to left to follow the Firefox jet across the landscape. Note the "rooster tail" water spray caused by the jet's high speed. This effect requires a careful coordination of the jet's forward movement, the camera pan, and the special effects apparatus that will produce the spray.

Figure 1-11 is an *establishing shot*, which is usually a long shot. It merely presents or establishes a visual situation: a Firefox jet refueling in midair. Since no complicated camera or jet movements are called for and the flying direction of the two aircraft is obvious, the panel has no directional arrows or instructions.

Figures 1-12 through 1-39 represent an extended story board for an action scene from *Firefox*. The shots are in order according to the script to show the flow of the scene. Any panel omissions are shots dropped from the revised script used to shoot the film. The story

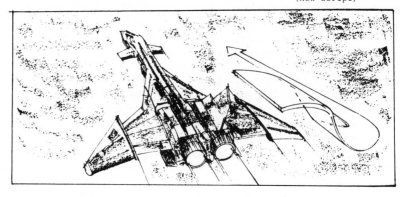

1-8 Story board art for shot.

DESCRIPTION: DIRECT POV ABOVE AND BEHIND FIREFOX.
FIREFOX SIDESLIPS DOWN TO 50 FEET ABOVE WATER.

1-9 Shot as filmed. (Courtesy of Apogee, Inc.)

SCENE: 207   page:114
                                                    (new script)

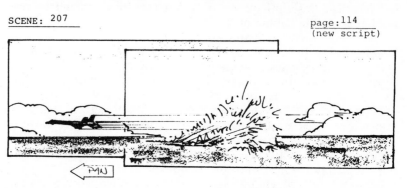

1-10 Double frame story
board.

DESCRIPTION: PANNING WITH FIREFOX, SUDDENLY IT BURSTS FORWARD
IN ACCELERATION: ROOSTER TAIL WATER EFFECT BEGINS IN FRAME AND
TRAILS FIREFOX AS THE PLANE ACCELERATES.

boards portray a scene in which Gant's Firefox is being hotly pursued by Voskov. The two jets race over frozen land and sea toward a massive wall of ice. In a dramatic chase, the two pilots maneuver at top speed through a narrow ice canyon, the jet sonic boom shock waves causing the ice walls to collapse. The use of story boards enables the production team to coordinate the miniatures and live-action elements of the shots. Without this kind of advance planning, the scene would have been nearly impossible to achieve on film.

SCENE: 252   page 139 (new script)

DESCRIPTION: ESTABLISHING SHOT OF VOSKOV'S FIREFOX LINKED UP
TO A REFUELING PLANE.

1-11 Establishing shot.

ITSA   TIGHT ON REAR VIEW SCREEN

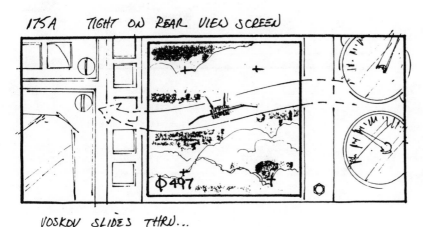

VOSKOV SLIDES THRU...

1-12 An interior shot of Gant's cockpit console. The large square is a television-like screen showing Voskov's Firefox approaching from the rear. Note the arrow showing Voskov's horizontal movement across the television screen alone and not the entire frame. The shot is from Gant's point of view.

1-13 This panel shows the simultaneous action of Voskov's Firefox, Gant's fired missiles, and moving clouds in the background to indicate Gant's follow of Voskov. The broken arrow indicates Voskov's travel, the border solid arrows the direction of the background movement. Two tiny arrows show the missiles' fire path.

194A   GANT'S P.O.V. AS MISSILES MISS VOSKOV

VOSKOV PULLS UP AND BEGINS HIS ROLL.

BACKGROUND
MOVING
DOWN

1-14 This panel is part of the scene sequence begun in Shot 195. The camera pan and movement arrows extend the frame. Note that the arrows for the jets are drawn to suggest the movement in depth—the jets fly from the distant background to the foreground.

SCENE: 195   page: 150 (new script)

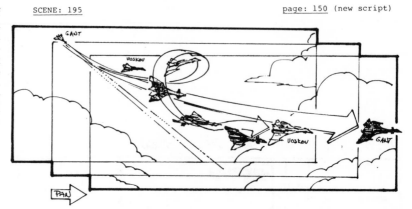

DESCRIPTION: WIDE SHOT PANNING WITH TWO FIGHTERS.

    1) GANT FIRES AND VOSKOV PULLS UP: THE
       MISSILES MISS AND GO OUT OF FRAME.

    2) VOSKOV ROLLS, DUPLICATING GANT'S PREVIOUS
       MANEUVER, AS GANT FLIES THROUGH.

    3) VOSKOV EXITS FRAME ON GANT'S TAIL.

188A

1-15 A shot from inside Gant's Firefox cockpit. Note that Voskov's jet flies into the shot from above the frame boundary. The sharp perspective of the arrow, matching that of Voskov's jet, implies a movement into the background, not simply down. Since Gant's Firefox is also in motion forward, the story board art portrays Voskov's jet racing ahead of Gant during his roll action.

ANGLE OVER GANTS SHOULDER. AS HE REACHES THE TOP OF HIS ½-CHILI-DOG ROLL, VOSKOV FLIES THRU UPSIDE DOWN "BELOW" GANT. GANT BEGINS TO ROLL BACK DOWN.

55 MISSILE DROPS FROM WING RACK, IGNITES AND FLIES

FORWARD; IT'S BACK BLAST WIPES OUT FRAME

1-16 Another arrow shot to show the movement of a missile fired from under a Firefox wing. In reality this wing and missile are large miniature mockups separate from the miniature of the Firefox jet—one miniature serves for both Gant and Voskov's jet, filmed twice and placed optically in a single shot frame.

Note the special action instructions for the missile miniature: the missile detaches from its rack, drops down as the engine fires up, then leaps forward with the backblast filling the shot frame.

THE STORY BOARD   **17**

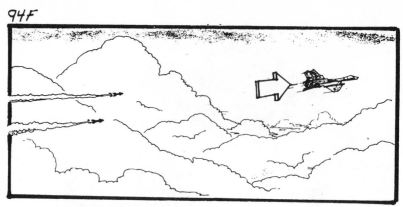

94F

WIDE SHOT: FIREFOX FLYING 3/4 AWAY FROM CAMERA (CLIMBING)
MISSILES FOLLOWING.

1-17 Note that in this panel the Firefox's direction is indicated both in the drawing (arrow) and in the shot caption.

165   VOSKOV'S FIREFOX FIRES MISSILE ...

SLIGHT PAN ON BACKGROUND, FIREFOX DRIFTING SLOWLY
BACK INTO FRAME AS IT FIRES.

1-18 A panel with simultaneous actions: (1) a slight background pan, (2) jet direction, and (3) a missile fired out of the frame.

171   FROM BELOW AS GANT CLIMBS: CANARDS FOLD OUT

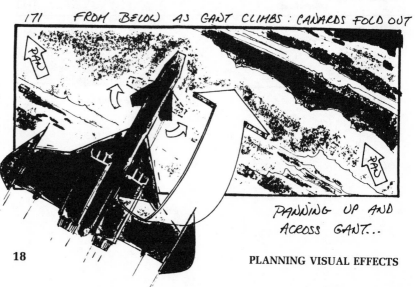

PANNING UP AND
ACROSS GANT...

1-19 Another shot with several actions at one time. Note the feature of the forward wing near the nose of the jet. The broken outline indicates the stop position of the small canard wings as they move into place. The Firefox miniature is designed to duplicate this action by pivot wing mounts inside the jet body.

PLANNING VISUAL EFFECTS

240 VOSKOV CHASING GANT TO CAMERA

VOSKOV FIRES TWO MISSILES — CONT'D

GANT PULLS UP AND MISSILES MISS, BUT GANT
STALLS AND BEGINS TO DROP, ROLLING TOWARD CAMERA.

1-20 Two related panels that depict a complex action sequence within a single shot. The separate actions of the two panels are timed to the movements of the jets. The arrow marked "CONT'D" means "Continued" and keeps the panel actions connected as a unit, rather than an *A* and *B* marking. (All Firefox photos courtesy of Apogee, Inc.)

198: TWO FIREFOXES COMING ¾ TO CAMERA... GANT ROLLS

TO CAMERA AND DIVES, STILL ROLLING... VOSKOV FOLLOWS
ROLLING AND DIVING...

1-21

THE STORY BOARD   **19**

199 PANNING DOWN WITH GANT IN A SPIN...

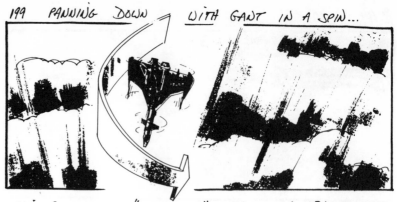

1-22 THIS IS A SLOW, "CONTROLLED" SPIN, MAYBE 3/4 OF A TURN.

201 INTERIOR COCKPIT ANGLE ON GANT...

VOSKOV

VOSKOV'S PLANE DROPS INTO SKY BEHIND GANT,
1-23 MANEUVERING FOR FIRING POSITION...

A 201 PAN DOWN ON BACKGROUND AS GANT RECOVERS...

PAN

PAN

1-24

202 3/4 ANGLE ON GANT... EVASIVE MANUVERING

VIGOROUS BACKGROUND PLATE.   1-25

203 INTERIOR VOSKOV'S COCKPIT...

ANGLE OVER VOSKOV'S SHOULDER AS HE PURSUES GANT...   1-26

204 VOSKOV FOLLOWING GANT OVER EDGE OF

ICE PACK , MANZUVERING... FURIOUSLY. THEY GROW FROM
TINY TO 1/2 FRAME   1-27

THE STORY BOARD   **21**

204A FOLLOWING VOSKOV, FOLLOWING GANT...

1-28   TOWARD THE ICE CLIFFS.

205   3/4 ANGLE ON VOSKOV... EVASIVE MANUVERING

1-29   VIGOROUS BACKGROUND PLATE.

205A   VOSKOV'S P.O.V. FIRING (TRACERS) AT GANT

1-30   HORIZON IS ROCKIN' & ROLLING ...

206. 3/4 ANGLE ON GANT... EVASIVE MANUVERING

VIGOROUS BACKGROUND PLATE.

1-31

206A   GANT'S P.O.V. :

HORIZON IS ROCKING & ROLLING

1-32

206B GANT'S REAR MONITOR ... VOSKOV FIRING

1-33

207

GANT ENTERS FRAME OVERHEAD, FOLLOWED BY VOSKOV...
MAKING EVASIVE MANEUVERS, THEY HEAD FOR ICE WALL.
<u>CAM</u>: TRUCKS INTO ICE WALL, BUT NOT AS FAST AS
1-34   THE TWO PLANES

A207. GANT, CHASED
BY VOSKOV,...

1-35   LOTS OF EVASIVE MANEUVERING

A 208   VOSKOV'S P.O.V. : ICE TRENCH

GANT (AHEAD) ENTERING TRENCH   1-36

216 TWO FIREFOXES ENTER FROM OVERHEAD GOING AWAY...

"SONIC DESTRUCTION" FOLLOWS FIRST FIREFOX
CAMERA PUSHING "INTO" TRENCH.   1-37

215 TWO FIREFOXES TO CAMERA; AND EXIT FRAME OVERHEAD

"SONIC DESTRUCTION" FOLLOWS FIRST FIREFOX
CAMERA IS PULLING BACK...   1-38

THE STORY BOARD   **25**

217 GANT'S REAR MONITOR ... VOSKOV CHASING HIM THRU

SONIC BOOM DESTRUCTION OF ICE TRENCH WALLS.

1-39   NOTE: FAST MOVE ON TRENCH.

SCENE/SHOT BREAKDOWN SHEETS

Once the story board and script have clarified the important visual elements of the film, the production team can begin the actual construction, photography and special effects work. Time and money are allocated to create specific images instead of being wasted on poorly visualized and irrelevant shots. After the story board is approved each scene is analyzed on a *breakdown sheet.* The numbered sheets list the physical requirements to create each shot of the scene. A typical sheet contains blocks for indicating costumes, props, cars, cast size, locations for shooting, special effects (smoke, sounds, rain), and miniatures. The breakdown sheets also include other important scene/shot information such as what kind of optical effects are needed, set and prop construction details, and special sound effects. Each department involved in the film's production tailors a breakdown sheet to fit its specific needs.

The script, story boards, and breakdown sheets are considered an essential part of the preproduction effort in films using special visual effects. Once the problems of an effects shot are worked out on inexpensive paper, the actual film production can begin. Miniatures are designed and fabricated, sets built, live action and animation footage shot, and optical lab work scheduled. Each visual effects shot is a custom-made team effort. A combination of optical techniques and tools is often needed to produce a final image. These techniques and tools are the topics of the chapters to follow.

The Basics:
The Camera, and In-Camera Special Effects

2

THE CAMERA

The device used to photograph a subject on film is the motion picture camera. Cameras are manufactured in a number of body sizes, film formats, and with features unique to each camera model. However, cameras intended for special effects cinematography fall into two categories: the *production camera* and the *process camera*. Both types work in combination to photograph the various elements that go into an effects shot assembly.

The production camera is used in the film studio or on location to shoot the original negative film of a subject, scene, or miniature. It produces the high-quality master footage, called the *first-generation camera original,* later used to make the duplicates for optical printing and projection. The production camera is designed to accept a range of lenses, motors for high-speed, sound-sync speed, or animation, and film magazine sizes. Figure 2-1 is an example of a 16mm production camera, the Bolex H16 Reflex. Other standard 16mm cameras include the Arriflex 16SR, Eclair NPR and ACL, Mitchell 16, and Photo-Sonics Action Master 500 (for speeds from 24 to 500 frames per second). Figure 2-2 is the Mitchell DSR-16 equipped with a 10 × 120mm zoom lens and 1200 foot (368m) film magazine. Thirty-five millimeter production cameras are illustrated here by the Mitchell S35R in figure 2-3, shown with a 25-250 zoom lens, and the CM35 FeatherCam in figure 2-4. The FeatherCam, made by Continental Camera Systems, is a versatile portable camera that weighs under five pounds (2.7kg) less lens and film, with a high-quality pin-registered film transport and through-the-lens viewing system.

Other 35mm cameras commonly used to shoot feature films include the Arriflex 35BL, Mitchell BNCR and Standard 35, and Panavision cameras.

Some special effects studios use large 65mm cameras to shoot the original negatives of miniatures and films for background projection. The 65mm negative provides an expanded negative frame approximately twice that of the standard 35mm frame. The larger negative also records more image detail for later printing stages. The final printed image also exhibits less inherited grain and loss of shadow and highlight details common when 35mm negatives are used.

A different type of camera that is now frequently used to photograph

2-1 The Bolex H16 Reflex.
(Courtesy of Bolex)

2-2 The Mitchell DSR-16.
(Courtesy of Mitchell Camera Corp.)

THE BASICS

2-3 The Mitchell S35R. (Courtesy of Mitchell Camera Corp.)

2-4 Continental Camera's FeatherCam. (Courtesy of Continental Camera Systems, Inc.)

THE CAMERA

29

2-5 35mm Model 6 Acme process camera with 400-foot magazine, stop-motion motor, and process lens. (Courtesy of Photo-Sonics, Inc.)

miniatures is the once-retired Vistavision format camera. This format runs standard 35mm film, but in a horizontal path across a widened camera aperture. The travel change produces a negative frame that extends over eight film sprocket holes instead of the usual four of standard 35mm camera apertures. The advantage of the Vistavision camera is that it is smaller and lighter than the bulky 65mm cameras, uses a smaller and less expensive film size, and shoots a large frame for high-quality negatives.

The process camera is specifically designed for use on an optical printer. The camera shoots exact duplicates (*dupes*, for short) of the production camera original for use as printing intermediates (for color printing), color separations, or for the production of sophisticated visual printing effects (high contrast, matte work, and the like).

The two standard process cameras are the Acme and the Oxberry camera models. Both are quite similar in design and function. Figure 2-5 shows the boxlike Acme camera, made by Photo-Sonics.

Process cameras are equipped for both manual and automatic operation of the shutter and motor drive. Many of the camera's film transport components are easily removed to exchange film format sizes in 35mm, double 35 (70mm), 16mm, and double Super-8 (16mm). The camera gate aperture is also modified by aperture masks conforming to the standard aspect ratios (Academy, wide screen, film strip, etc.). A comparison of the relative image area of standard aperture masks is shown in figure 2-6.

The optical system of the process camera is also designed for precision copy work. The lens, called a *flat field process lens*, produces

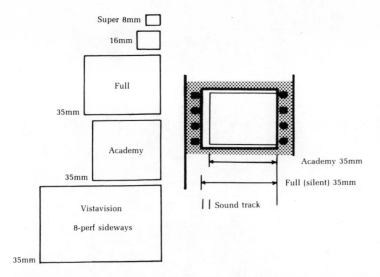

Super 8mm

16mm

Full

35mm

Academy

35mm

Vistavision

8-perf sideways

35mm

Academy 35mm

Full (silent) 35mm

Sound track

2-6 Relative image area of different film formats.

a sharp image across the entire aperture. When the process camera is used in an optical printer, the lens is mounted in a movable sliding track and positioned by a rack-and-pinion handwheel. Process lenses are also used in the photography of flat art such as animation artwork or matte paintings. The process lens is replaced with standard high-quality production lenses to shoot three-dimensional miniatures.

The process camera is designed to accept special lens mounts that can provide either an automatic or manual focus of the lens. The automatic focus feature is limited to optical printers and animation stands, where the camera support is fixed and camera movement is carefully calibrated on a metal track. Manual focus requires a method for seeing the image at the camera aperture opening. The process camera may either have a prism viewer that inserts into the aperture and deflects the lens light to a magnifier eyepiece, or use a direct view of the aperture by a *rackover* system. A rackover is a rack-and-pinion mechanism that can side shift the camera body and film gate a few inches to expose the aperture to a direct view by the camera operator. Again a magnifier eyepiece is used to enlarge the lens image on the magnifier ground glass screen.

Animation cameras, such as the one in figure 2-7, are very similar to process cameras in design and function. The camera shown is a Neilson-Hordell 16mm animation stand camera. The lens is a 28mm f/3.5 Nikkor automatic lens in a special mount that permits a lens change without altering the alignment of the optical centering of the image in the camera aperture. The 16mm magazine, with a standard 400-foot (120m) film load, is mounted opposite the lens. This arrangement is different from the Acme and Oxberry process cameras, in which the magazine is at right angles to the lens optical path. This animation camera permits two pieces of film to be run through the gate at the same time, a feature required for a special effects technique called *bipack* printing. Process cameras also permit two thicknesses or more to pass through the gate. This similarity, as well as the many manual and automatic controls, places animation cameras in the same category as process cameras.

Often a standard production camera can be reworked to perform

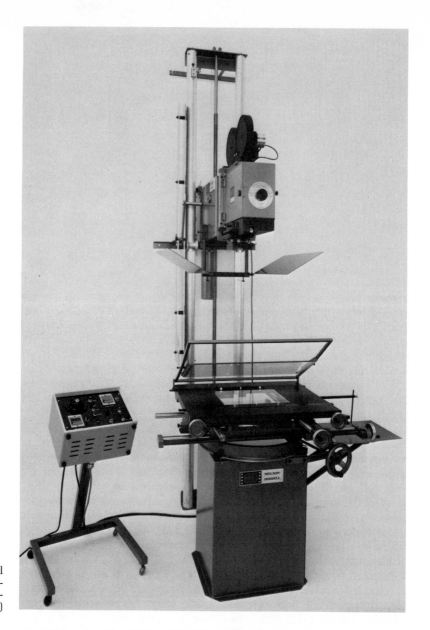

2-7 The Neilson-Hordell 16mm animation stand camera. (Courtesy of Neilson-Hordell, Ltd.)

as a process camera or precision animation camera. Two such cameras are shown in figures 2-8 and 2-9. The 16mm Bolex H16, modified by J-K Camera Engineering for use on their optical printers, is quite different from the camera seen in figure 2-1 (a Bolex H16 Reflex). A special printing motor has been added, as well as a track and lens bellows with a sharp El-Nikkor 50mm f/4 lens. Note the focusing tube directly above the left end of the lens bellows. The tube's 90-degree prism and internal ground glass permit a magnified view of the full gate aperture for critical focus and framing. The extension bellows produce copy ratios with the 50mm lens of 1:4 to 4:1 for, respectively, image reduction or enlargement.

2-8 The 16mm Bolex H16 modified for use on an optical printer. (Courtesy of J-K Camera Engineering, Inc.)

2-9 A Fries 35R. (Courtesy of Fries Engineering, Inc.)

Figure 2-9 is a Fries 35R, a Mitchell Standard/High Speed camera converted by Fries Engineering. This 35mm reflex (through-the-lens viewing) camera is designed specifically to meet the critical film tolerances required for special visual effects and animation. Although not a process camera, the Fries 35R is designed with the same precision for film handling and exposure controls. Interchangeable aperture masks, lens mounts, and lenses enable the 35R to shoot either the studio production footage, or footage to be used in background projection or optical printing. The modular design of the camera's internal components offers great flexibility in meeting special effects requirements. Two different motors can be used—a variable speed animation motor (12 to 120 frames per second and single frame), or a crystal controlled sound-sync motor (24 or 25 frames per second).

Basic Camera Components

Both production and process cameras have components that are very similar in purpose, although adapted to the specific type of camera. A brief description of the essential camera components follows.

LENS

The purpose of the lens is to focus light from the subject or scene onto the raw film stock held in the camera gate aperture. The lens controls the size of the image and provides a measure of control to the overall image sharpness and focus.

Photographic lenses contain a number of internal lenses, usually four or more pieces of rare-earth optical glass called the *lens elements*. Each lens element is designed to pass the light with no change in the light's intensity or color.

Aberrations are tiny defects in the lens elements that distort the passage of light to some degree. Although rare in high-quality lenses, the types of aberrations include: *chromatic aberration* (distortion of image color), *coma* (blurring of the image near the frame edge), *as-*

tigmatism (improper convergence of the light rays, which forms an unsharp image), and *spherical aberration* (curvature of straight lines that distort the image). These optical flaws, present in various degrees in cheap, simple lenses, cause defects in the film image that are difficult to repair. For this reason, special effects cameras use lenses of superior quality that correct any color or optical aberrations, called *apochromatic* lenses.

The two important factors of every lens that affect the film image are the *focal length* of the lens and the *diaphragm aperture* used to make the shot.

The lens focal length is the distance (measured in millimeters or inches) between the optical center of the lens and the focal plane when the lens focus is set at infinity. The lens infinity symbol is marked as ∞ and the focal plane (on the camera body) as ϕ. The lens focal length is inherent in the design of the lens and is determined by the lens manufacturer. A 75mm lens produces a sharply focused image at 75mm with any camera it is mounted on, regardless of the film size. For this reason such lenses are called *fixed focal length lenses* or *prime lens*. Special lenses with movable internal elements permit the elements to be positioned at various focal lengths. These are *variable focal length lenses* or *zoom lenses* and can be shifted through a range of settings during photography. As with prime lenses, the zoom lens focal length range is determined by the lens manufacturer. Zoom lenses tend to be slightly less sharp than prime lenses of equal focal length. This is because rigid fixed lens elements are more stable in position than movable track zoom elements. For this reason, zoom lenses are generally used for studio production work and prime lenses for special effects and opticals that require superior quality.

The lens focal length determines how large a portion of a scene in front of the camera will be exposed in the camera gate aperture. The lens *field of view* is the visual area defined by a lens of any focal length. The field of view varies with different focal lengths in both prime and zoom lenses. Each lens has a specific viewing angle, so the field of view is measured in how many degrees of coverage are provided by the focal length. The standard lens for any motion picture camera shoots about 23 degrees across the scene in front of the lens. This is approximately the field of view provided by a 25mm lens for 16mm cameras and a 50mm lens for standard 35mm cameras. Lenses of short focal length have a field of view broader than 23 degrees. A 28mm lens for a 35mm camera shoots an angle of nearly 43 degrees. This is a *wide angle lens*. The same camera fitted with a 150mm lens covers only a narrow 8.3 degrees. Lenses well above (by at least 50 percent) the standard focal length camera lens are called *telephoto* or *long lenses*. These lenses tend to compress the distance between the subject and camera and flatten the perspective in the finished shot.

The three types of prime lenses are shown in the photos that follow, along with a variable focal length zoom lens. Figure 2-10 is a Bausch & Lomb 50mm f/2 Super Baltar standard lens seated on a Mitchell R35 Mark II camera (35mm). Figure 2-11 is a super-wide (over 165 degrees) 2.5mm f/1.8 lens for a 16mm camera. At the other extreme is the large telephoto seen in figure 2-12. This lens for 16mm is a

2-10 Bausch & Lomb 50mm f/2 Super Baltar lens seated on a Mitchell R35 Mark II. (Courtesy of Mitchell Camera Corp.)

2-11 A super-wide 2.5mm f/1.8 lens. (Courtesy of Century Precision Optics, Inc.)

2-12 A 1,000mm f/5.6 Tele-Athenar lens. (Courtesy of Century Precision Optics, Inc.)

1000mm f/5.6 Tele-Athenar weighing over 14 pounds (6.46kg). Its field of view is only 1.3 degrees, with a minimum focus distance of 125 feet (38.1m). Both the telephoto and super wide lenses are manufactured by Century Precision Cine/Optics Company. The zoom lens in figure 2-13 is a Pan-Cinor Zoom for the 16mm camera. It features a variable focal length of 12 to 120mm and a self-contained reflex viewfinder system. The zoom action is controlled by the lever rod extending from the lens midsection.

The second major lens factor is that of the shooting aperture set by the lens diaphragm, also called *the iris*. The diaphragm, made up of interlocking thin metal blades, creates the opening within the lens to pass light on to the film. The size of the opening controls the

THE CAMERA   **35**

2-13 Note the magazine attachment shoe on top of the camera. (Courtesy of Bolex)

amount of light striking the film emulsion. The different diaphragm hole sizes are indicated by markings on the outside of the lens barrel, either in "f" or "T" stop numbers. A lens may have both f/stops (marked in white) and T stops (in color) on the diaphragm ring. The lens *f-number*, abbreviated as f/number, is the ratio of focal length to lens diameter. Each f/number step mark on the lens barrel represents a doubling or halving of the light striking the lens, depending on the direction of the f/number change. Each step mark is called the *f/stop* of the diaphragm opening.

The T stop is a calibration of the actual light leaving the lens. While the f/stop is a ratio and mathematical, the T *stop* (for "transmission") is actually measured on a light-reading meter device. Two lenses of the same focal length will have the same f/stop, but different T stop positions for the same number. This is because each lens is slightly different in construction, optical density, and number of lens elements and coated lens surfaces. Lenses marked in T numbers provide a more accurate exposure setting.

The lens shooting aperture and focal length determine the scene's depth of field, field of view, and the amount of light transmitted to the film emulsion. Because these factors are variable with the many different lens sizes, standard lens charts are recommended. Charts for both 16mm and 35mm film gauges can be found in the *American Cinematographer Manual,* published and regularly updated by the American Society of Cinematographers. Reference guides for all focal lengths and depth of field tables in the *Manual* and similar publications provide a handy aid for the cinematographer shooting a special effects setup.

MAGAZINES

Professional 16mm and 35mm cameras are generally designed to carry the unexposed or raw film stock under 100-foot (30.5m) lengths in attached supply cartridges called *magazines*. Made of metal or plastic, the magazine is easily unclipped from the camera body plate when the film is fully exposed and replaced with a fresh roll housed in an identical magazine. The film stock inside the magazine, which is hinged to open like a clam shell, is tightly wound on small plastic bobbins called cores that rotate freely. A small electric *film takeup* motor is often coupled to the magazine bobbin spindle that winds the film and helps prevent the magazine from jamming.

Magazines are divided into two circular chambers: the front chamber holds the raw film stock, and the rear holds the exposed footage. An exception is the coaxial magaine for Eclair 16mm and Arriflex 35BL cameras. This type of magazine houses the film feed and takeup side by side on a single motor-driven spindle.

Standard magazine sizes have a film capacity of 200 feet (61m), 400 feet (123m), 1,000 feet (300m) and 1,200 feet (361m). Magazines can be seen on the cameras in figures 2-1, 2-2, 2-3, 2-7, and 2-9. Figure 2-13 shows clearly the magazine attachment shoe at the top of the camera. In this photo the shoe opening is covered with a removable light-tight plate. This arrangement permits the camera to be used without a magazine for shooting short lengths of film, in the form of 100-foot (30m) rolls. These rolls are on metal-flanged spools called *daylight load* spools that fit inside the camera body side-by-side with a similar empty *take-up* spool to hold the exposed footage. If longer lengths of film are required, the daylight spools are removed and a film magazine containing the proper length is attached to the camera body to replace the light-tight plate in the attachment shoe. The special bipack magazine in figure 2-5 is actually two separate 400-foot (123m) magazines that feed into the camera together. The bipack magazine is limited to the 400-foot size for both 16mm and 35mm formats.

FOOTAGE AND FRAME COUNTERS

Magazines are sometimes equipped with builtin devices that display how much footage has been run through the camera. These *counters* use an internal roller and lever assembly to ride the outer edge of the film roll. This is linked to a pointer and footage scale on the outside magazine shell. The count, however, is only an approximate measure and not adequate for the accurate footage and frame counts required for special effects work. A more reliable counter is one linked to the camera's shutter drive mechanism. One turn of the drive shaft equals one frame of exposure. Linking a veeder-type digital counter or indexed gear disk counter to the turning drive shaft produces an exact foot or shot frame length measurement. These accurate counters are usually located at the side or rear of the camera. Each shot is recorded by the number of frames exposed. The counters can be used continuously on a number of shots in a single roll or be manually reset to zero when a new magazine load starts.

MOVEMENT MECHANISMS

Film stock is advanced through the camera by a drive and exposure assembly called the *movement* or the *intermittent*. The movement is the core of all motion picture cameras. It consists of an assembly of pin-edged wheels, called *sprocket gears,* that engage the film sprocket perforations, and a moving *pull-down* claw that pulls successive frames into position for exposure. The actual exposure is by the *shutter* mechanism, which passes light to the film emulsion at a precise rate of separate exposures. The movement assembly also includes a device to hold the film stationary in the camera gate aperture. This is to ensure accurate film *registration,* which is the precise superimposition of two film frames of the same size. The device keeps the film area flat and assures that the image will be in the same place on every frame exposure. In the simplest production camera, a polished metal plate called a *pressure plate* serves as a relatively stable registration device. However, the pressure plate alone is inadequate for a high degree of image registration. In higher-quality cameras, and especially cameras used for process and special effects photography, a system of stubby pegs called *registration pins* is also used to engage the film's sprocket holes and keep the frame steady during exposure.

Figure 2-14 shows a Bolex camera interior with the movement assembly at the left of the photo. The white arrows indicate the direction of film through the camera. The sprocket gears are the two white chrome disks. Above and below the gears are shaped plates to bend the film properly, creating a *film loop,* for travel through the aperture gate. A spring-loaded polished plate presses the film firmly against the aperture plate for exposure by the shutter and lens, which is located but not shown at the far left. Although the Bolex camera is an excellent 16mm camera for general photography, the use of a simple pressure plate for registration is not suitable for special effects work requiring highly accurate optical registration. However, the Bolex is often used for low-budget animation effects when precise frame registration is not critical. Compare the sophisticated 35mm Mitchell camera movement and registration system seen in figure 2-15. This movement uses a dual pull-down claw unlike the single Bolex claw method. In addition the film is held in place by the pressure plate and four registration pins.

Accurate registration requires that every frame in a film strip be exposed in exactly the same position as the previous frame. A loss of registration is a common problem in special effects photography. It is marked by uneven shifts or jiggle in the shot subject from frame to frame. Accurate registration is critical to the most important technique in special effects visuals: *composites.* A composite is the combining of individual subjects (elements) shot separately into a single scene. Loss of registration of any one element causes a poorly positioned composite. The problem is compounded by the common practice of shooting individual elements with different cameras. All cameras used in special effects work must provide a high degree of optical registration in the picture frame.

REGISTRATION SYSTEMS

To assure a proper registration of the film frame, special effects cameras for production, animation, or process work use a pin registration system. The pins, also known as *pilot pins,* anchor each frame at the camera aperture plate during actual exposure. Two or

2-14 Bolex camera interior, movement assembly at the left. (Courtesy of Bolex)

2-15 The interior of a 35mm Mitchell, showing camera movement and registration system. (Courtesy Mitchell Camera Corp.)

2-16 Acme film movement, Bell and Howell type. (Courtesy of Photo-Sonics, Inc.)

four pins are used, flanking the vertical sides of the aperture. They fit into the film sprocket holes and prevent any slippage of the frame as it is being exposed by the shutter.

Two basic pin systems are applied to special effects camera movements: the Mitchell system, used in production cameras, and the Bell & Howell, used in animation and process cameras. Most high-quality cameras (and likewise pin-registered projectors) use one of these two designs.

The Mitchell movement, developed primarily for Mitchell cameras, has a pair of pilot pins that move into the film sprocket holes as the double-pronged pull-down claw disengages. After exposure, the pins withdraw and the film can be advanced to the next frame.

The Bell & Howell movement uses a pair of nonmoving fixed pins.

THE CAMERA

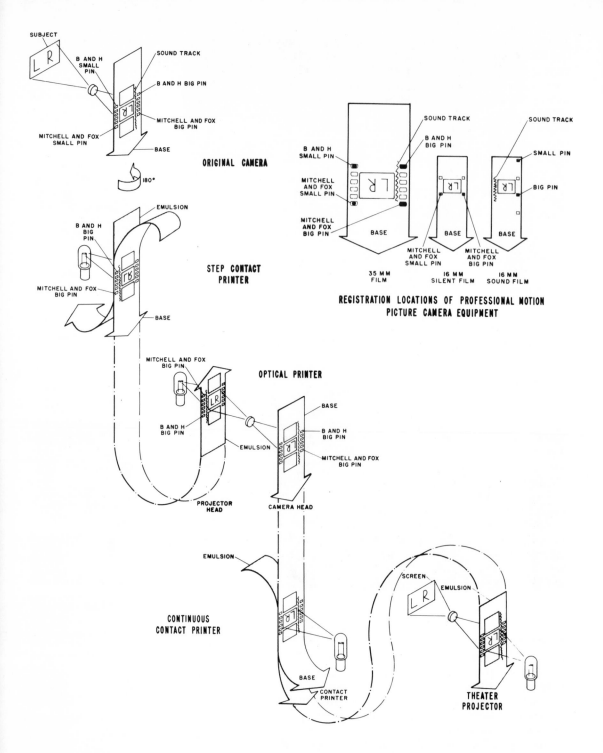

2-17 Registration systems used in professional motion picture cameras and process equipment.

(Courtesy of Photo-Sonics, Inc.)

These pins, located on the aperture plate, remain stationary during the entire movement cycle. The film is pushed onto the pins, which engage the sprocket holes and keep the frame steady during exposure. The film advance mechanism then lifts the exposed frame off the pins, pulls a new frame into position, and pushes the sprocket holes onto the pins. Although the system sounds mechanically difficult, it actually has fewer moving parts than the Mitchell system. Fewer parts mean less adjusting to maintain accurate registration. Both the Oxberry and Acme process cameras use Bell & Howell–type movements.

SHUTTER

The basic shutter is the device that permits the light from the lens to strike the film emulsion. The most common camera shutter is the rotating disk type. A wedge-shaped opening passes in front of the raw film stock in the aperture and allows the full passage of the lens image light. Since the disk rotates at a constant predetermined speed, the actual degree of exposure is based on the size of the wedge opening. A large wedge-shaped angle—the opening is measured in degrees of arc—lets more light pass on to the film emulsion than a small wedge-shaped angle. For this reason a camera rotary disk shutter is rated by degrees. At a shooting speed of 24 frames per second, a 160-degree shutter produces a film exposure of 1/54 second. A 90-degree shutter at the same frame rate produces an exposure of 1/96 second. The camera frame rate is an important exposure factor. At 48 frames per second, the same 160-degree shutter now provides an exposure of 1/108 second. Tables of exposure times at various camera speeds and shutter angles can be found in the *American Cinematographer Manual*. Such reference tables are very useful to the special effects cinematographer, who must often work with unusual camera speeds and predetermined exposure values.

A *variable shutter* is a special disk shutter that permits the wedge angle to be changed from fully closed (dark) to maximum size (full exposure). The variable shutter can change the exposure in situations in which both the camera speed and lens aperture size are fixed. Figure 2-18 shows four different positions of a variable shutter, ranging from a fully closed to a maximum angle opening. The rotation of the shutter is across a camera aperture. The shutter itself is made of two disks, one movable relative to the other to form the wedge opening angle.

On most production and process cameras, the variable shutter angle is adjusted by a lever or rotary dial mechanism. Figure 2-19 shows a Bolex 16mm camera variable shutter lever. The lever can be moved to any fractional interval of the guide, which is marked to indicate positions of closed, 1/4 open, 1/2 open, 3/4 open, and full open.

A rotary dial type of variable shutter control is shown on the Neilson-Hordell animation camera in figure 2-20. The knob plate to the right is marked in degrees as well as 24- and 32-segment calibrations for in-the-camera fade and dissolve effects. The shutter can be manually set from 0 to 170 degrees. The viewfinder on this camera is located directly below the shutter. The lens is at the bottom middle of the camera body. The Acme process camera in figure 2-5 is also equipped with a large dial variable shutter control.

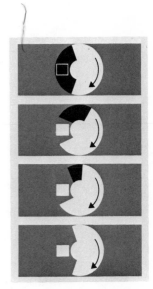

2-18 Four different variable shutter positions.

2-19 Bolex 16mm variable shutter lever. (Courtesy of Bolex)

2-20 Rotary dial type of variable shutter control. (Courtesy of Neilson-Hordell, Ltd.)

CAMERA MOTORS

Modern cameras use an electric motor to run film through the camera. However, special effects cinematographers still use the terminology of the pioneer camera crank for certain speed effects: *undercranking* for speeded-up action, *overcranking* for slow motion, both early mechanical methods for these effects. Although a few portable modern 16mm and 35mm cameras operate on springwound clockwork motors, all professional special effects cinematography is done with electrically powered motor drives.

These motors are specialized according to the particular purpose of the camera.

Wild or *variable speed motors* offer a range of speed settings, calibrated in frames per second. They are used primarily for shooting silent footage, miniatures, or speed-related visual effects.

Synchronous motors, often called *sync motors,* run at more precise speeds than wild motors. They are used for filming sound-recorded subjects. The sync motor uses a repeating electrical pulse as standard reference for a constant speed. The pulse can be generated by the 60-cycle alternating line current (AC power) or by an electrically vibrated unit called a piezocrystal oscillator. The latter system is called a *crystal-sync motor.*

Interlock motors keep a projector and camera shutter in step: when the projector flashes an image on a screen, the camera shutter is open. This coordinated action is essential to special effects projection techniques. Without an interlock motor, the camera would shoot at slightly different speeds from the projector, and the camera would shoot an occasional blank screen because the projector shutter was closed.

Stepper motors are unique precision motors that operate in a different manner from conventional electric motors. Ordinary motors use a continuous flow of current to produce a steady movement of the rotor, the turning part within an induction motor's nonmoving stator structure. A stepper motor, on the other hand, is driven by a stream of programmed electrical pulses provided by a microprocessor driver circuit. Each digital pulse advances the rotor a fraction of the full revolution, or a step increment. As long as the pulses continue, the rotor will turn, each pulse separately advancing the degree of rotation. If no pulse is supplied, the rotor stops turning at that point. The total number of steps required to complete a full rotor revolution is based on the step angle built into the different types of stepper motors. The smaller the degree of step, the more accurate and smoother the rotation.

Stepper motors are popular because of their high degree of positional accuracy, reliability, and consistency of operation. The pulse-controlled motor drive is easily interfaced to microprocessor and minicomputer control systems and peripherals such as printers, disk storage units, plotting tables, machine tool positioners, and other motion-related mechanical devices. Since the motor drive system can be programmed to repeat a mechanical motion with a high degree of accuracy, stepper motors are frequently encountered in motion-control camera systems, automated animation stands, automated optical printers, and special-purpose motion devices. Stepper motors are often used in motorized miniature craft to simulate the repeating action of radar scanners, searchlights, and gun turrets.

Animation motors are special-purpose motors usually limited to animation stand cameras or other cameras engaged in single-frame photography. Based on a stepper motor or an electromechanical solenoid mechanism, the animation motor is designed to provide an accurate frame exposure without fluctuation over the extended shooting periods required by animation cinematography. The heavy-duty animation motor is generally not a standard component of a camera and is purchased separately and mated to a specific camera model. Animation motors are not used on cameras intended for ordinary studio production work because such work is done at sound synchronization speeds of 24 frames/second and standard sync motors are more compact.

Animation motors may also offer a limited range of frame rates beyond the single-frame mode. This permits a number of shooting speeds, such as those for shooting titles, artwork, or miniatures. These motors are also essential in optical printer cameras to shoot duplicate films, in-camera special effects, and related frame rate film effects.

Figure 2-21 shows a Fries 120M2 animation motor connected to a Mitchell 35mm camera. This motor connects directly to the camera movement shaft. Powered by a 30 volt DC battery or transformer, the motor provides an accurate single-frame exposure of 1/8 second at a 170-degree shutter opening. Other speeds available with this versatile

2-21 A stepping motor, here connected directly to the drive shaft. (Courtesy of Fries Engineering, Inc.)

special effects motor include a crystal-controlled 24/25 frames per second and a variable selector range of 12 to 120 frames per second in both forward and reverse. A different animation motor design is on the modified Bolex camera shown earlier in figure 2-8. This stepping motor is manufactured by the Superior Electric Company. The motor, which connects directly to the drive shaft of the Bolex camera in this photo, is a standard type of stepper motor used in a great many special effects devices, miniatures, cameras and camera conversions.

VIEWFINDER SYSTEMS

The *viewfinder* is an optical system that enables the cinematographer to see what the camera lens is seeing at the aperture focal plane. It is an essential part of a special effects camera, since accurate frame focus and composition is required for placement of the shot subject elements.

The oldest form of camera viewfinder is the offset finder that attaches to the side or top of the camera body. This optical system approximates the field of view of the camera lens. When a different lens is put on the camera, the viewfinder must likewise be adjusted for the new field of view. If this is not done, the two different views of the scene will result in a faulty composition. It is called *parallax* error and occurs when the viewfinder's line of sight does not match the lens's optical path. In other words, the viewfinder is not aimed at what the lens is shooting. Parallax error is most frequent when shooting close to the subject.

A *rackover* viewing system is better than the offset type of viewfinder for shooting close objects and for critical focusing of the image. It allows the camera body to be shifted a few inches to one side of the lens. The lens remains in the original position anchored to a camera base plate. A magnifier inserted into the gate aperture gives the cinematographer a view of the scene exactly as it will appear on film. When satisfied with the compositional framing and focus, the cinematographer shifts the camera body back into place and exposes the shot. The rackover system is a slow method of viewfinding that is restricted to nonmoving camera setups often required by animation and optical printing work.

Reflex viewing systems use an arrangement of glass prisms and partially silvered glass or mirrors within the camera body to reflect the lens view to an eyepiece ground-glass screen. This gives the cinematographer an undistorted view of the scene shot. Another advantage of the reflex optical system is that the scene is visible in the eyepiece during actual photography. The cinematographer can easily follow the subject action and hold focus during any camera moves.

Two types of reflex viewing systems are most common: the *split beam* and the *mirrored shutter*.

The split-beam system places a semisilvered mirror or prism behind the lens, but in front of the shutter curtain, to deflect a portion of the lens light into the viewfinder optics. Figure 2-22 shows the prism-type beam splitter and associated optics for a Bolex H16 Reflex camera. Figure 2-23 traces the light of a subject through the reflex system to an eyepiece magnifier. The main advantage of this type of reflex system is that the image is seen independent of the shutter action.

2-22 Cutaway of Bolex H16 Reflex's prism-type beam splitter and associated optics. (Courtesy of Bolex)

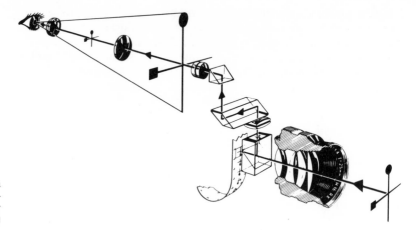

2-23 Path of light from subject through reflex system to eyepiece. (Courtesy of Bolex)

This results in a flicker-free view of the scene subject, although some light is lost in the exposure by use of the beam splitter.

The second type of reflex viewfinder replaces the prism beam splitter with a highly polished mirrored shutter. The mirror is on the lens side of the shutter and at a 45-degree angle to the optical axis. The incoming light is deflected at a right angle into the viewfinder optical system in a manner similar to the arrangement shown in figure 2-22. Except for the light that passes to the film through the shutter opening, all the light goes into the viewfinder. This results in a brilliant image on the viewfinder screen. A slight flicker effect is sometimes apparent because of the rotating shutter wedge intercepting the reflected beam. A variation of the system uses a mirrored shutter disk for the reflex image alone and a second nonmirrored shutter at the aperture for the actual exposure on the film stock.

The *video tap* or *assist* is a small television camera coupled to the reflex viewing system that sends a secondary image to a remotely positioned video monitor screen. This allows the scene being photographed to be seen by other production personnel and recorded on tape for instant evaluation. Figure 2-24 shows the video camera attached to the Fries 35R camera. The camera is a high-quality 2/3-inch (19mm) low light-level video camera. The video image is black and white. A 12-volt DC power supply is needed to operate the video camera.

Video assists are frequently used on studio production and animation cameras. The video tape playback of a scene rehearsal or miniature setup allows the progress of the photography or animation to be checked "on camera" and corrected or refined if required to yield a better result. Video-assisted camera viewing is also used in situations where the camera's physical placement makes direct viewing impractical, such as on high boom cranes, in confined spaces, or on aircraft nose or wing camera mounts.

The *reticle* is the ground-glass viewing screen in a viewfinder system. The glass is engraved, etched, or otherwise marked with lines to show important points and aperture boundaries. The *reticle lines* generally indicate the center of the aperture, any aspect ratio boundaries, and the clear or safe action areas to frame the shot for reproduction on television and other formats. Figure 2-25 is an example of a reticle

2-24 Video camera attached to Fries 35R. (Courtesy of Fries Engineering, Inc.)

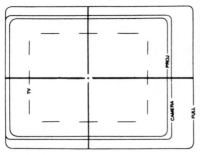

2-25 Oxberry type of animation camera viewfinder reticle showing cutoff areas.

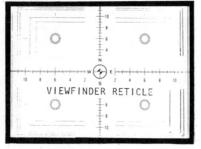

2-26 Twelve-field optical printer reticle for 16mm Bolex. (Courtesy of J-K Camera Engineering)

used on Oxberry-type animation cameras. The television frame boundary or TV cutoff is superimposed as a broken line over the viewfinder image. Other lines show the full camera aperture as well as the actual frame area that will be on screen when the film is later projected. Figure 2-26 is a viewfinder reticle for a process or animation camera. The fine-line interval markings in both horizontal and vertical directions enable the camera operator to place the subject elements precisely at any point in the field of view.

IN-CAMERA SPECIAL OPTICAL EFFECTS

A few optical effects can be produced by the cinematographer at the time of original photography. These effects, called *in-camera opticals*, are done by controlling the exposure of the film or the camera frame speed.

Production cinematographers rarely resort to the in-camera optical methods since lab printing of optical segments gives more control of the final effects. However, for some applications, such as multiple images or exposures, the in-camera exposure of the separate elements on the original negative film assures the best possible quality composite. For the student and low-budget filmmaker, the in-camera methods are an inexpensive alternative to printer-generated effects.

The main disadvantages of in-camera work include the following:

1. the risk of a mistake that would require reshooting the original scene;
2. the extra cost of planning the shot and added rehearsal time;
3. the inability to redo because the effect is on the original footage;
4. the need for inflexible order of some effects, such as fades and dissolves.

In-camera opticals fall into two separate groups: *lens-based* effects, which are *fade, multiple exposure, lap dissolve,* and *split screen;* and motor-based effects, such as *fast motion, slow motion, pixilation* or *single frame, time lapse,* and *reverse* action.

Lens-based In-Camera Effects

The *fade* is a gradual darkening of the film image across a predetermined number of frames. A *fade-in* goes from full black to full scene brightness. A *fade-out* is the reverse, from bright to full black. Fades are commonly used to open or close a film or as a transition optical between shots. In-camera fades can be done several ways:

1. Use the variable shutter to reduce or increase exposure. Some production cameras and nearly all process and animation cameras have devices for automatic fades of the variable shutter across a precise number of frames. Other cameras use an accessory fade device, such as the RX-Fader attachment for the 16mm Bolex H16 REX camera.
2. Change the lens aperture diaphragm size. Called closing or opening up the lens, this action requires an accurate frame counter to insure that the fade is timed correctly. Changing the aperture also causes a noticeable change in the depth of field.

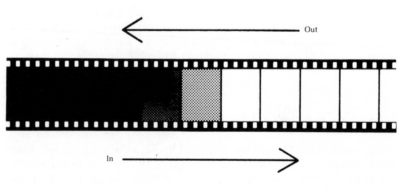

2-27 Fade-in and fade-out.

Fade

THE BASICS

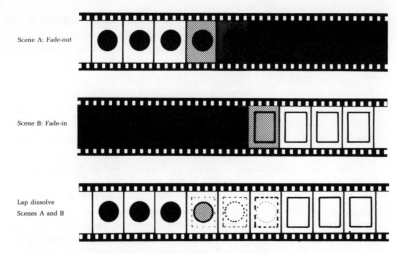

Scene A: Fade-out

Scene B: Fade-in

Lap dissolve
Scenes A and B

2-28 Lap dissolve.

3. Slowly turn a pair of polarized filters to right angles of each other. The reduction of light simulates a true fade, although in bright scenes some highlights may penetrate the full black position. Polarized filter fades are not as reliable as the diaphragm or variable shutter fades.

The *lap dissolve* is an optical transition containing a fade-out superimposed over a fade-in on the same number of frames. It is also called simply a *dissolve, cross dissolve,* or, in animation, *X dissolve.* The result is a gradual loss of the first shot as the new shot builds in intensity. The transition has no black frames in the segment on screen, as in the fades'.

The in-camera lap dissolve requires three steps:

1. Photographing the first scene and a timed fade-out by frame count.
2. Closing the shutter to black and rewinding the exposed footage to the first frame of the fade-out.
3. Photographing a new shot starting with a fade-in. The fade-in stop frame is matched to the original fade-out stop frame across the same number of frames.

A *multiple exposure,* also called a *double exposure* or *superimposition,* is less complicated than a fade or dissolve. A number of exposures, usually two to four, are placed on the same frame area by repeatedly using the same original negative for the new shot. After the initial shot, the lens is covered or the shutter fully closed and the film rewound to the starting frame of the shot. A new shot or double film run is made, called a *pass* of the original negative.

Double exposures are often used to create "ghosts" (semitransparent images) in a scene. For example, the interior of a room is photographed and the film is rewound. A new shot is then made over the first of a costumed actor standing in front of a black curtain. The resulting footage is of the actor superimposed on the room. Set details and furniture are partially visible through the actor's ghostlike body. The effect can be made even more ghostly by reducing the exposure of the actor, so that only the highlighted areas appear with nothing at all in the shadow areas.

IN-CAMERA SPECIAL OPTICAL EFFECTS **49**

2-29 Two-pass composite: A. Fire wizard in original scene.

2-30 B. Live action fire element shot against black wall.

2-31 Final Composite: C. Fire element added by double exposure.

Care must be taken to avoid a general overexposure caused by the overlay of two fully lit scenes. Each shot should be made at less than the normal exposure meter reading. One to one and a half stops below normal is enough to give a good shadow density and still retain bright highlights in the composite shot.

The multiple exposure technique is not limited to ghost shots or title superimpositions. The camera aperture can be selectively masked by opaque pieces of paper called *mattes* to reserve portions of the frame for certain elements. By careful composition of the scene and mattes, new subject elements can be added to the original shot.

Figures 2-29 through 2-31 show a simple double exposure shot. An actor (a wizard in this case) is photographed in the scene. The script calls for his body to burst into magical fire. For an in-camera optical, the original scene is rewound and a new shot made of a miniature blaze of fire against a black fireproof backdrop. The two separate images of actor and fire are combined in the single scene. The use of a storyboard panel and careful camera placement aid in positioning the two elements one over the other.

The *split screen* is a variation of the simple double exposure. The scene is filmed twice, but only half of the scene is exposed in each camera pass of the negative. Black paper mattes block off half of the frame in each exposure. The processed footage shows the entire scene, each half seamlessly combined. If the matte is not exactly placed to cover the entire previous exposure, a thin visible seam called a *matte line* will separate the two halves of the shot. Matte lines are flaws, and the shots should be scrapped and new footage made of the original scene. The split screen technique is often used to let an actor play a twin in the same scene. The shot must be rehearsed several times to make sure that the imaginary dividing line between the two shots is not crossed. If they are crossed, the actor will seem to disappear into thin air when he is blocked from the shot by the obstructing matte. If desired, this disappearance can be used as a special visual effect in some types of scenes that require a subject to suddenly appear in or vanish from the scene.

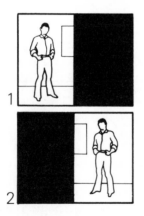

2-32 Split screen.

1: 1st pass
2: 2nd pass
1 + 2: split screen composite

THE BASICS

Motor-based In-Camera Effects

The standard film camera and projection frame rate is 24 frames per second. Any deviation from this rate causes a visible shift in the moving elements of a shot subject or scene. In most production situations the standard film speed is the only one required for the bulk of the shooting. However, special effects cinematography relies on flexible camera motor speeds to permit various motion and animated effects.

Slow motion (often called *Slo-Mo*) is the term for an image photographed at speeds above 24 frames per second. For example, a speed of 48 frames per second halves the subject's apparent speed. *High-speed cameras* are designed for frame rates well above normal, to about 400 frames per second. For the super-slow motion needed to photograph exploding miniatures and the like, special high-speed cameras, such as the 3M Wollensak Fastax WF2, have a rotating prism instead of the standard disk shutter movement assembly and offer frame rates from 700 to 18,000 per second. Speed and frame rate tables for many camera makes can be found in the *American Cinematographer Manual*. The cinematographer must also compensate the lens aperture for high-speed frame exposures. A 150-degree shutter produces an exposure of 1/58 second at 24 frames per second. The same shutter at 128 frames per second reduces the exposure to only 1/307 second. This means that the original setting of, for example, f/8 must be opened to f/3.6 in order to keep the exposure level the same. If a small shooting aperture is needed to keep the depth of field for a miniature setup, then the lighting level of the shot must be boosted five-fold to keep the same exposure. Conversion factor tables also can be found in the *Manual* for camera speed aperture compensation for speeds above and below the normal 24 frames per second.

When the camera is run at slower than normal speed, the subject appears to move faster than normal. This effect is called *fast motion*. It is just the opposite of the slow motion effect. The relationship of the light intensity, lens shooting aperture, and frame rates is similar to the factors required for slow motion shooting. Charts in the *Manual* help in calculating the proper exposure of the subject scene.

Two motor effects, *pixilation* and *time-lapse* photography, are both based on the single frame rate of exposure. In most cameras a special animation motor is needed to provide accurate single frame exposures over an extended shooting session.

Pixilation is a simple trick shot that animates living subjects instead of shooting the subject at a normal 24 frames per second. A frame is exposed, the subject moves forward and poses in a still position, and the next frame is exposed. When the processed film is projected the effect is of a peculiar jittery movement in the subject's actions. If the frame exposures are shot at the apex of a subject's repeated leaps, the result on film is one of a flying subject. The times when the subject is on the ground are not photographed, leaving only the leap positions on the film.

Time-lapse is similar to pixilation except that the exposures are made over a much longer period. Time periods of minutes, hours, days and even months lapse between successive frame exposures.

When the film is projected, the subject appears to move quickly and the slow action over long periods is compressed visually in the rapid projection of the film frames. The result is quite dramatic as an optical effect.

Effects Quality

Each pass of the original footage through the camera gate increases the chance for scratches, worn sprocket holes, and film jams. Despite these dangers, the in-camera multiple pass techniques are still used occasionally in contemporary special effects. In-camera composite photography produces sharper and less grainy images than the usual optical printing duplicates. The in-camera method offers the maximum quality in a composite image because all the separate shot elements are exposed on the original negative. This produces a fine-grained *first generation* composite instead of the contrasty and grainy *second generation* composites common in optical printing methods.

Examples of high-quality in-camera composites can be seen in *2001: A Space Odyssey*. In this film many of the spaceship-and-background shots were made by separately exposing each miniature on a single negative, the individual exposures done sometimes months apart. Care was taken to assure that the separate spaceships and planet backgrounds did not overlap and produce a double-exposure ghost effect. The movement of each spaceship was carefully planned by preparing story boards and marking the camera viewfinder with action boundaries. The finished composite shot was built up from many separate in-camera exposures on the original master negative. The first-generation quality of the finished composite added greatly to the sense of realism in the final film print.

In-camera effects can be useful for many types of shots but tend to be less flexible than traditional optical printing methods are. Shots that involve many overlapping elements and separate backgrounds cannot be adequately done by simple in-camera exposures on the original negative. For complex effects work, other methods such as process photography and matte techniques must be used.

Special Effects Filters and Other Lens Attachments

3

THE FILTERS

A *lens filter* is the easiest and most frequently used method for creating a visual effect in an ordinary straight shot. Filters and filterlike lens attachments offer the cinematographer a wide range of image modifiers that change the mood or character of a scene subject. The selection of a proper filter for any shot is based on the individual experience and aesthetic preference of a cinematographer. Dozens of filter manufacturers offer special effects filters in all styles, sizes, and degrees of effect.

Filters should be handled with care and their surfaces protected from dirt, fingerprints, oil, and scratches. Any of these defects degrade the image light as the rays pass through the filter material. Figure 3-1 is a Tiffen soft-jacket pouch for safely storing four filters. Figure 3-2 is a Tiffen filter case for holding seven round (series 9) or square (3 × 3-inch) filters. The case has a tough, ribbed plastic exterior shell and an interior of high-density foam that absorbs shock vibrations that can crack a filter. Before a filter is mounted on the lens, it should be carefully inspected for any surface abrasions and cleaned for both use and storage.

In general production work a lens filter is used to achieve the proper scene and lighting color, to control contrast, or to adjust the overall exposure level. Common camera filters include the neutral density (ND), color conversion, and polarizing filters. Basic cinematography filters are grouped in several categories.

Color-Compensating (CC) filters: Adjust the blue, green, or red colors of a shot's white light illumination. Also used in process cameras or printers to compensate for color shifts from shot to shot.

Contrast filters: Enhance or reduce the contrast (bright-to-dark value ratio) among elements of a scene.

Conversion filters: Match the color balance of the film emulsion to the daylight or artificial lighting source.

Light balancing filters: Adjust for small differences in the color (color temperature) of the light source.

Polarizing filters: Reduce or eliminate glare and reflections; also, darken a blue sky for image contrast.

3-1 Soft-jacket filter pouch. (Courtesy of Tiffen)

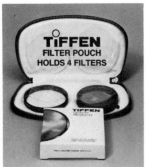

3-2 Padded filter case. (Courtesy of Tiffen)

Reciprocity filters: Compensate for odd color shifts due to extreme exposure times or *reciprocity failure,* in high speed frame rates or long time exposures (extremely long shutter open time).

The neutral density, polarizing, and color-compensating filters can be considered simple special effect filters because they permit the cinematographer to alter the film image selectively. Filters intended for visual effects are designed to produce more specific and dramatic alteration of the subject or scene than can be achieved with the filters listed above. Figure 3-3 shows a set of general photography filters made by Tiffen, a major manufacturer of film, television, and still camera lens filters. A cinematographer usually has a similar variety of filters on hand to meet the needs of a camera shot.

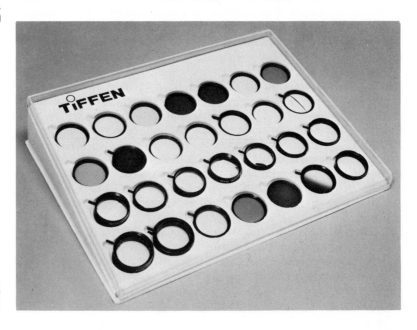

3-3 Set of general photography filters. (Courtesy of Tiffen)

Filter Materials and Types of Special Effects Filters

Filters are composed of various types and grades of optical materials. These are the most common.

1. Gelatin sheets (called *gels*) dyed with color metal oxides
2. Gelatin laminated to a sheet of optically flat glass
3. Optical glass alone dyed with colored metal oxides
4. Plastic resin cast in optically flat sheets

Filters are either round, square, or rectangular. Round glass filters are commonly sized, in millimeters, to fit a number of standard lens diameters. They have a threaded collar that allows the filter to be screwed directly to the lens front. Adapter rings, called *stepup* or *stepdown rings*, permit a single filter to be threaded onto different-sized lenses. Figure 3-4 shows three such stepping rings.

3-4 Three stepping rings. (Courtesy of Tiffen)

Round glass filters without threaded collars are usually designated by the *Series* system. The diameters range from Series IV (20.8 mm) to Series IX (82.4 mm). The filter glass fits inside the lens hood on the lens front rim and is locked in place with a screw-type retaining ring.

Round filters are also offered in slip-on and bayonet mounting collars.

Square filters, such as those in figure 3-1, are intended for mounting in front of the lens, but in a special filter-holding frame called a *matte box*. A slot or movable filter holder allows the filter to be readily inserted or replaced. A matte box with a round sunshade is shown in figure 3-5. This unit is made by the Arriflex Corporation. The lightweight matte box is shown from the rear, and reveals the two 3 × 3 inch (76mm) filter frames and Angeniuex zoom lens adapter.

Some cameras also permit a small gelatin filter to be inserted in front of the aperture plate, within the camera body.

Color Shift Filters

Single color filters add emotional impact to any ordinary shot. A special fantasy or mood effect is easily produced by shifting the entire color balance of a shot toward the yellow-red (*warm*) or blue-green (*cool*) hues. Single color filters are made in a range of both vivid and pastel colors. Strong color overlays shift the normal color scale to an unnatural overall cast. Paler color filters impart more subtle

3-5 Combination lens hood and filter drawer rack. (Courtesy of Arriflex Corporation)

3-6 Single color shift filter.

3-7 Graduated color filter.

3-8 Dual color filter.

3-9 Tricolor parallel filter.

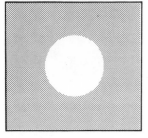

3-10 Color spot filter.

coloring by tipping the color balance toward a single dominant color.

The cinematographer should always clearly label the color effect on the shot information board, or *slate,* and on all data sheets sent to the processing lab. This will prevent the lab from attempting to correct the "odd" color cast to a more normal color balance.

Single color filters (and other color shift filters) slightly reduce the amount of light reaching the film emulsion. This is because the filter glass passes only a selective portion of the color spectrum and absorbs the rest. The loss of light must be compensated for by an increase in the lens aperture or shutter angle if the filtered footage is to match a nonfiltered shot on the same roll. The degree of exposure increase is called the *filter factor.* Exposure increases one full stop opening each time the filter factor doubles. If two filters are combined the filter factors are multiplied for the correct exposure factor.

A *graduated single color* filter has color extending only midway across the filter. The filter color is strongest at the filter edge and fades gradually toward the midline. The remaining area is clear glass.

This filter corrects weak or poorly saturated scenic colors, such as a flat contrast scene on an overcast day. It permits manipulation of any natural coloring to create a mood or variety in the scene.

Dual and *tricolor* filters have two and three contrasting color segments within the same filter frame. Dual filters are commonly used to add color intensity to sky and ground for special visual impact. Tricolor filters do the same, except the horizon midline to bottom area is broken into a background color and a foreground contrasting color.

Dual and tricolor filters are used to add color contrast to large areas of the scene during location photography. The color segments of the filter are usually placed parallel to the horizon to coincide with naturally occurring scene boundaries. In some cases a vertical arrangement of the segments may be used to alter the colors of corridors, channels, and similar upright compositions. The selection of the segment colors can also provide a method of highlighting a specific area or level of a scene. Care must be taken not to have any object or actors cross two or more segments, as this will betray the use of the filter and distort the color effect as the subject passes from one color segment area to the next. The camera usually cannot be panned or tilted when dual or tricolor filters are used.

A *color spot* filter is a single color filter with a clear center area. The center spot serves to retain the subject's natural coloring in the surrounding single color field. This frame effect of pure color helps to accentuate whatever subject is focused on in the clear center. The filter is most often used for romantic mood or dreamlike fantasy effects.

Diffusion Filters

A *diffusion* filter softens the overall sharpness of the lens and, consequently, the clarity of the film image. The filter reduces the contrast and surface details of the subject being filmed. It is commonly used to smooth fine wrinkles, hard lines, and facial blemishes of an actor in a glamour shot. The filter is also useful for adding a sense of depth or atmospheric perspective to a studio scene or miniature. (Depth in a normal shot is enhanced by increased perspective. *Linear perspective* provides depth by causing forms to appear smaller as distance increases from the camera viewpoint. *Atmospheric perspective* makes the forms appear dimmer and more out of focus as they grow more distant.)

A diffusion filter is made from a piece of flat optical glass cut into a round or square shape. The outside surface is finely etched or lacquered to scatter a portion of the light. This light scattering is *diffusion* and is sometimes referred to as *soft focus*.

Diffusion filters are graded to provide various amounts of diffusion, the range determined by the manufacturer. Tiffen's line of Softnet diffusion filters are in densities of 1 (least diffusion) to 4 (most diffusion). Harrison & Harrison, another major filter supplier, offers diffusion filters rated from 1 (least) to 5 (most), with each step double the previous grade. The cinematographer chooses the correct grade for the desired diffusion or can gang filters together in the filter holder and increase the diffusion beyond the normal range.

Figure 3-12 shows the effect of a diffusion filter (grade 5—heavy diffusion) on the subject in figure 3-13 (no filter).

Diffusion filters are used in special effects cinematography to impart a softer look to the scene. When combined with single colors and other effects filters, the diffusion filter can lend a fantasy or romantic spirit to the shot.

A *center spot diffusion* filter is a standard diffusion filter with a clear center. An example of this filter is the Tiffen filter in figure 3-15, which shows the filter in a series No. 9 mounting ring. The filter keeps the center area sharply focused on the subject, free of any diffusion; the surrounding area is diffused and less sharp. The effect is to isolate or *vignette* the main subject from the rest of the scene. The filter is similar in purpose to the color spot filter because it focuses the audience's attention on the central subject.

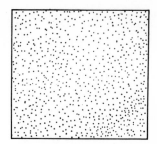

3-11 Diffusion filter.

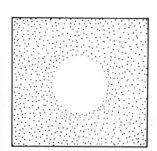

3-14 Spot diffusion filter.

3-12 Effect of a grade 5 diffusion filter.

3-13 Same subject, no filter.

3-15 Center spot diffusion filter. (Courtesy of Tiffen)

THE FILTERS

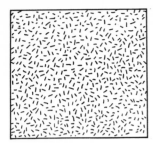

3-16 Fog filter.

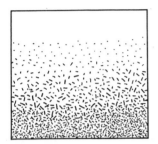

3-17 Graduated fog filter.

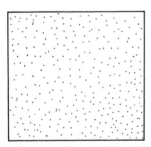

3-20 Low contrast filter.

3-21 Sky control filter.

Fog Filters

A *fog filter* produces a mistlike veil over the entire scene. It is similar to a diffusion filter. The filter is a piece of optical glass with a finely ground surface designed to scatter the light. It simulates the way real fog diffuses light and reduces contrast. Real fog has a luminous quality; the fog filter approximates the same effect by spreading the light into the shadow areas of the scene. A grayish veil appears to overlay the entire image area. As with diffusion filters, fog filters are graded in various densities. The Harrison & Harrison regular fog filters are offered in ten equally spaced steps to simulate all natural fog conditions. Tiffen has filters in grades 1 to 5.

Normally a fog filter does not require any additional exposure increase, unless so specified by the manufacturer. Tiffen, for example, recommends about a half-stop increase in the exposure for the first four grades and a full stop for No. 5 to prevent a loss of image contrast.

Natural fog appears to increase in density as the subject moves further from the camera position. A fog filter, however, produces a uniform diffusion over the entire image at any position relative to the camera. The cinematographer must compensate for this uniform fog veil and not position finely detailed objects close to the camera position. The filter will cloud the small details of the foreground in exactly the same degree of fog as the more distant background. In real fog the foreground objects are more distinct than objects located in the background. A *graduated fog* filter simulates natural fog in this respect. This filter, like the graduated color filter, extends the fog effect only partly across the filter glass. The cinematographer retains as many foreground elements as possible in the clear or nearly clear area at the bottom of the filter, with the background elements reserved for the heaviest diffusion in the top part of the filter. This graduated effect can be seen in figures 3-18 and 3-19.

Double-fog filters are designed to overlay even heavier fog effects than regular fog filters, reducing the image contrast even more drastically. These filters are also available in a range of densities; the higher grades require substantial lighting contrast to keep shadow and highlights from disappearing.

Low Contrast Filters

A *low contrast* filter reduces the image contrast without diffusing the highlights. This filter is often referred to as a *low con*. Like fog and diffusion filters, it is available in a numbered range of contrast steps.

Sky Control Filter

A *sky control* filter is designed to solve exposure problems in scenes containing a bright sky and dark foreground. In these scenes the proper exposure for the ground area produces a harshly overexposed sky area. The sky filter compensates for this with a neutral density filter in half of a clear filter sheet. The ND portion of the glass reduces the light intensity of the sky area so the exposure ratio is more evenly balanced.

3-18 Shot with no filter.

3-19 Same subject with graduated fog filter.

Diffraction Filter

A *diffraction* filter is a special color effects filter that creates a number of rainbow streaks extending outward from the bright highlights of a subject. It is made of optical glass or clear plastic that has been etched with thousands of microscopic lines. These lines form ridges that act as tiny prisms and break up or diffract the light passing through the filter. Ordinary white light is split into color spectrum ribbons. The effect appears as color rays ranging from violet to yellow to red along each ribbon or ray. Since most of the light passes directly through the filter with little diffraction, the overall scene is not deformed and does not require exposure compensation.

The diffraction effect produced by two different ridge patterns can be seen in figures 3-23 and 3-24.

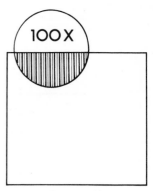

3-22 Diffraction filter.

3-23 One example of a diffraction filter effect.

3-24 Second example of the same filter effect.

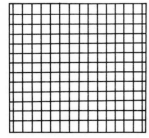

3-25 Star pattern filter.

The diffraction filter is frequently used on the lens of the animation camera to add sparkle to backlit art titles or line work. In other situations the filter can be used to add color effects to fantasy, dream, or romantic mood photography.

Star Cross Filter

A *star cross* filter generates starlike streaks of light that extend from every major highlight in a night shot or shot involving highly reflective objects such as glass and polished metal. The filter is also called a *starburst* or *cross screen*.

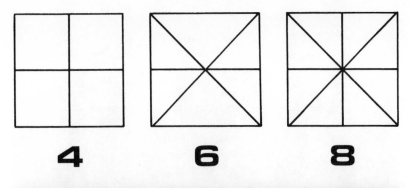

3-27 Four-point star filter shot.

The filter is made of optical glass engraved with tiny but not microscopic lines that form a grid across the entire filter area. The spacing and angle of the grid lines determine the star patterns. The standard grid patterns are four, six, or eight star lines, as in figure 3-26.

The grid line spacing is used to grade the width of the star rays. Tiffen, for example, offers four-point stars in 1mm, 2mm, and 3mm grids, and eight-point stars in 2mm and 3mm grids. The smaller the grid spacing, the sharper the star point line around a highlight.

Figure 3-27 shows a four-point star filter shot taken of pinholed backlighted title art. Some filter mount frames permit the entire filter to be rotated, which adds a spin to the star points.

Star filters do not require any exposure compensation, but the grid lines act as a partial diffuser and degrade the shot a bit. The finer the grid pattern, the softer the details in the subject image. The use of a coarse grid reduces this problem but still gives a striking star effect to the scene.

THE FILTERS   **61**

3-28 3P prism (triple image) attachment shot.

OTHER LENS ATTACHMENTS

Multiple Image Prisms

Effects attachments for the camera lens also include a number of nonfilter devices called *prisms*. These attachments mount directly to the first element of the lens. Unlike regular filters, prisms cannot be used in the matte box filter drawer because of their thicker glass and close optical relationship to the camera lens.

The prisms are designed to bend or refract the light rays passing through the glass. This results in a distorted subject image. The usual prism fragments the image to create a series of repeat images in the same shot. Figure 3-28 shows subject photographed through a 3P (three parallel repeats) prism attachment.

The prism is made of clear optical glass, and its surface is covered with a series of faceted segments that determine the arrangement and

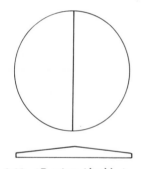

3-29 2P prism (double image) with cross-section.

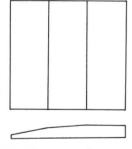

3-30 3P prism with cross-section.

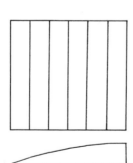

3-31 6P prism with cross-section.

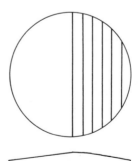

3-32 6P with half plain prism (half plain, six repeat images) with cross-section.

3-33 3R prism (three radial images).

number of repeated images. Depending on the facet design, the prism repeats may be linear, radial, or concentric to the main subject. A number of standard prism designs are shown in figures 3-29 through 3-35. Each creates a distinct arrangement of the repeat images. The cross-sectional view shows how the surface is shaped to create the particular arrangement.

The multiple-image patterns are also affected by the camera lens focal length. Wide angle, short focal length lenses produce repeat patterns clustered in the central area of the frame. Telephoto, long focal length lenses tend to spread the patterns toward the frame edges. Almost all prism attachments are designed for use with a wide angle prime lens. Stopping down the lens aperture from a wide open setting greatly improves the sharpness of the secondary or repeated images. These images are often less sharp than the main or central subject, with a slight lack of contrast and color saturation. For this reason some experimentation must be done to determine the correct aperture setting and focal length when a specific repeat pattern of images is desired.

Round prisms in graduated ring sizes are commonly in rotating ring frames so that the repeats can be arranged at any angle relative to the main subject. Continuous movement of the ring during the exposure results in a carousel effect of repeats orbiting the main subject image.

A *double* or *compound prism* consists of two separate prism pieces within a single double ring mount. The arrangement of the rings permits the prisms to be moved relative to each other. Rotating the top prism with its position rod aligns the prisms to form two or four repeats of the main subject. This prism is shown in figures 3-36 (two-image setting) and 3-37 (four-image setting).

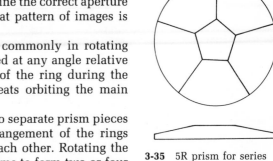

3-34 4R prism with cross-section.

3-35 5R prism for series #9 mounting ring.

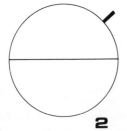

3-36 Compound prism: two-repeat position.

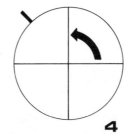

3-37 Compound prism: four-repeat position.

Split Field

The *split field* attachment is a special purpose attachment that is half of a close-up supplementary lens in a ring mount. As with standard close-up supplementary lens attachments, the split field is mated to a particular sized lens. Figure 3-38 shows the standard split field design: the lens in half of the ring, nothing in the other half.

The two different sections of the attachment are known as *split field* because they create two distinct fields of focus in the same scene shot. The upper, empty half is focused at a far-distance subject,

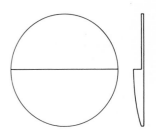

3-38 Split field with cross-section.

the half lens on a closer subject usually within inches of the lens. Both will appear to be in focus. This effect creates the illusion of an enormous depth of field *(deep focus)* in the shot. Care must be taken to limit the two subjects to their respective lens areas. Any crossing of the unseen midline division will result in the part extended being far out of focus.

As with standard close-up supplementary lenses, the split field is graded in magnifying strengths of $+\frac{1}{2}$, $+1$, $+3$, and $+4$ diopters.

Matte Box

A *matte box* is a combination filter rack and lens hood assembly that attaches directly to the front of a camera lens. In addition to holding standard filters, the matte box can be fitted with cutout mattes, opaque masks of black paper or painted glass. Mattes are needed for various kinds of special visual in-camera effects.

The matte box is considered a standard lens accessory for all production cameras. They are not, however, found on process cameras or animation stand cameras. Figure 3-39 shows a standard matte box design. Made by Arriflex Corporation, it is shown with two filter holders at the rear of the box, lightweight support rods, and a mating ring for the prime lens of an Arriflex 16SR-II camera.

The basic matte box consists of a pair of rectangular metal frames connected by a black rubberized accordion *bellows*. The frames can be positioned along a single rail to accommodate different lens focal lengths and fields of view. The front frame can be moved forward or backward relative to the back frame, which attaches directly to the lens front via a suitable *adapter* or *mating ring*.

The front frame position relative to the lens is an important factor if a cutout matte is in the frame. The closer the matte is to the lens,

3-39 A standard 16SR bellows matte box design, with filter holders, lightweight support, and 16SR II camera. (Courtesy of Arriflex Corporation)

the less sharp it will be along the cutout edges. If the matte is too close to the lens, it will be too unfocused to properly mask the intended scene area or subject. Other factors that affect the front frame matte sharpness are lens focal length, shooting aperture, and focus setting.

Matte box effects work best with wide angle and standard lenses of about 55mm and under. These lenses give a sufficient angle of view and depth of field to keep both a cutout matte and the background subject in focus. The box frame must be adjusted so as not to be included accidentally in the image itself. A poorly positioned front frame cuts off or darkens the edges of the scene when photographed. Figure 3-40 shows this unintentional border or vignette effect.

3-40 Matte box edge vignette.

Each lens must be checked by a reflex view of the scene with the matte box in place. The cinematographer can quickly see any problems by closing the lens to the smallest f/stop position. Wide apertures have a shallow depth of field and a slight matte box vignette may not be visible until the lens is set to the shooting aperture.

There are usually upper and lower grooves in the front frame of the matte box to allow for the insertion of a special effects screen or matte card. On-location effects require a mask size of about 4 × 5.5 inches (102 × 140mm) with a standard lens. A glass or acetate clear sheet may also be inserted into the matte box frame to superimpose captions, arrows, circles, or other painted symbols over the scene. Title captions require that the lens be focused on the lettering rather than the background scene for maximum legibility.

The simple cutout matte, made of flat black presspan or bristol board 1/40 inch (0.6mm) thick, is a visual effects device with a long history. Early silent films are peppered with shots that use a cutout matte as a storytelling device: a spy's keyhole view, a soldier's binocular view of a battlefield, a heart around two young lovers. Although dated, the cutout matte effect is still an easy-to-do and attention-getting visual effect. Figure 3-41 is an illustration of three matte cards, two on black pressboard and one on clear glass with dry transfer letters.

The cinematographer determines the proper exposure of a shot with a cutout matte by meter-reading the scene without the card. Automatic in-camera exposure meters must be manually adjusted or the dark card will be wrongly read and produce a badly overexposed shot.

The split screen special effect described earlier with figure 2-32 is easily done in the camera by using black matte cards to cover half the matte box frame.

Subject viewed through binoculars

Keyhole

piece of celluloid or sheet of glass

Titles on a fixed or moving backround

3-41 Matte box front frame inserts.

4 Animation I:
Two-Dimensional Effects

The word *animation* describes a wide range of photographic techniques that create the illusion of movement in drawings and in real objects. Fantasy and science-fiction films often rely on animation methods for achieving various visual effects. A basic knowledge of animation is fundamental to understanding how these magical images are created.

Animation can be divided roughly into two categories: *two-dimensional (2-D)* and *three-dimensional (3-D)*.

Two-dimensional animation involves flat artwork for cartoons and title graphics. It is known as 2-D because of the artwork's flat dimensions and animation method. Three-dimensional animation involves real objects, primarily puppets and miniatures. The term *3-D* is not to be confused with the 3-D effect of stereo photography that provides an illusion of depth in a projected film scene. Here, the 3-D refers to the puppet itself, a three-dimensional solid object.

The methods of 2-D animation will be discussed in this chapter; 3-D puppet animation, in the next. Although considered separately here, the two animation methods are sometimes combined to achieve various composite effects.

THE ANIMATION PRINCIPLE

By definition, animation is motion. All films involve some kind of movement, but in traditional live-action films, the subject motions are natural and often spontaneous. In animated films the reverse is the rule: all motion is artificial and planned ahead of time by *an animator* or *animation artist*, a human being who creates motion effects.

Animation techniques require a clear grasp of how natural live-action movements are recorded on film. The subject movements are photographed by the motion picture camera. The camera shoots a precise number of individual frame exposures for a span of time, usually 24 frames per second. Each frame is a snapshot that breaks down the subject's continuous movement into a series of separate exposures. Each snapshot frame is a unique picture, with no two exactly alike although all are similar. When the filmstrip is processed and projected at the standard frame rate of 24 per second, each frame is flashed onto a screen in the same order as photographed. The viewer sees only a split-second glimpse of the scene frame before it is replaced with the next frame. Instead of seeing the filmstrip frames as individual pictures, the eye blends them into a continuous movement that reproduces the original subject movement in the scene. This illusion of movement is created in the viewer's mind by an optical phenomenon called *persistence of vision*. An image focused on the viewer's retina stays for a fraction of second after the actual image is no longer visible. The successive frame images on the movie screen overlay one over the next to produce the illusion of movement by the slight differences in the subject's position in the frame.

Animated films capitalize on persistence of vision by photographing a series of still or motionless images that are changed slightly in each advancing frame. When projected, these images appear to move in the frame. The animator or animation artist who makes each still drawing or photograph can control any motion in the finished film by arranging the still frame subject positions. The amount of shift or differences in the subject's placement from frame to frame affects the type of motion seen in the projected film. Large differences in the subject frame positions result in the appearance of fast motion; small differences result in slow action.

The fact that the illusion of motion can be controlled by slight changes in successive frame exposures is the fundamental working principle of all animation techniques. From simple paper flipbooks to elaborate feature-length animated film productions costing millions of dollars, all animation stems from the simple principle of changes in the subject's position from one image to the next.

The film animation techniques described below follow this basic principle. Each method is presented separately, but techniques can be creatively combined for any unusual visual image. Professional filmmakers often expand some simple animation to fit a given situation involving animation scenes. Animated segments may also be presented as part of a live action film or contribute to the special visual effects within a composite shot.

CAMERALESS FILMS

Animation effects can be generated at a basic level without using a camera. These *cameraless films* are created directly on the film stock without resorting to photography. Images are drawn, dyed, engraved, or painted on 16mm or 35mm film stock or on clear leader film. Color and black-and-white emulsions are easily scraped onto the film with a blade or needle to develop patterns of unique character. Waterproof felt tip pens or laundry markers used as drawing tools permit the animation artist an unlimited creative freedom. Waterproof inks adhere to the acetate film base without crawling or cracking as they dry. Cameraless films have two basic visual forms: the *frameless freeform image* and the *registered frame*.

Frameless Freeform Image

The frameless freeform image is the easier of the two cameraless films. Figure 4-1 is an example in two film sizes, 16mm and 35mm.

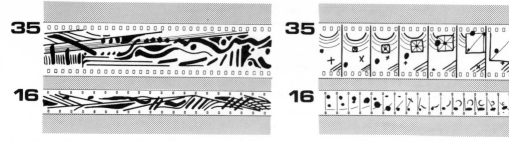

4-1 Frameless image: Freeform film.

4-2 Frameless image: Animation film.

The freeform drawings on the film are made without regard for any registration or frame lines. The artwork often appears as broad colorful strokes and loops that extend over the film length. A rough rule of thumb is that the more parallel the stroke is to the film edge, the less weave in the line on screen when projected. If the lines are drawn across the filmstrip at a 45-degree angle relative to the film edge, they will appear to cross the screen swiftly as the filmstrip runs through the projector gate. The general result of a freeform film is a frantic display of vividly colored and randomly abstract images.

If the original film is used as a master image for optical printing or contact printing even more complexity can be achieved in the moving images. Each run or *pass* of the original through the printer can be separately filtered to control the color changes in the printed duplicate film. By shifting the printer lens slightly out of focus, a softer, glowlike pattern is superimposed or replaces the hard edge of the original lines. Such techniques enable the original hand-drawn film image to be made more dramatic through the interplay of subtle and dominant motion patterns.

Commercial applications of freeform animated films include their use as relatively inexpensive backgrounds for titles and for unusual-looking transition passages, for example with fantasy or rock music scenes.

Registered Frame

The second basic cameraless technique is the registered frame approach, illustrated in figure 4-2.

This method calls for the animation artist to draw individual images for each frame of a filmstrip. The small frame-by-frame variations produce the animated movement effects. The method requires considerable concentration since hundreds of drawings are needed even for a short film. A film lasting only one minute would need over a thousand separate images (60 seconds × 24 frames per second = 1,440 frame drawings). For this reason, and to save time, the frame art is often simplified enormously, sometimes reduced to just stick-figure drawings.

A simple frame registration method is essential if the individual picture elements are to be drawn accurately in the same relative position from frame to frame. Without accurate registration of the successive drawings, the finished image jumps erratically when projected.

The easiest registration method is to use an outline frame drawn on grid graph paper. With, for example, clear leader film, the film stock is placed over the guide frame with the sprocket holes centered on the upper and lower frame lines. The horizontal lines visible through the film base permit the animation artist to place the different elements for each frame. The grid within the frame boundary helps to determine how much space is needed for each movement change.

An easy way to create frame registration lines is to draw directly on film that has been previously exposed to a blank card and processed. This is best for reversal stock or duplicates. The result is a series of blank frames along the length of film.

A more precise method of registering an image on film is to use a device similar to a pin-register camera movement. A lamp and a beam splitter within the unit superimpose the previous frame drawing onto the new area in the aperture of the device. This allows the animation artist to see exactly how much spacing is required for every change of the action drawing.

ANIMATED DRAWINGS

The most common method for producing animated films is the photography of sequential drawings. Each drawing displays a slight change in the subject's position. When photographed in the proper order, the drawings produce the illusion of movement.

Figure 4-3 shows a simple walking subject. Each step position imitates that of a real walk sequence. Only the right leg movement is shown here, made of eight interval drawings. A full walk movement would require sixteen or more drawings.

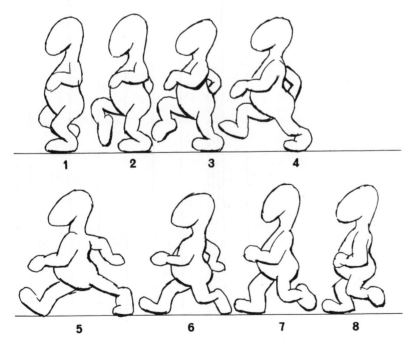

4-3 Half walk cycle—right leg (8 or 16).

Cartoons are a familiar form of drawn animation. The format encompasses a diversity of styles. Cartoons range from the slapstick Saturday morning three-minute comedies to the expensive feature length 90-minute productions by Walt Disney Studios, Ralph Bakshi, Don Bluth, and other animation studios.

A simple cartoon is relatively easy to make. All that is needed is a supply of paper, pencils, pen and ink, and a securely positioned motion picture camera. The artist draws an image on the first sheet, places it in front of the camera lens, and makes a single frame exposure. The drawing is then traced onto a second sheet and slight changes are made in the action character. The new drawing is placed in front of the camera in the same registered position as the first drawing. An exposure is made, the drawing removed, and a new drawing is made. The procedure is repeated until the film is totally exposed.

An alternate and more efficient method is to prepare all the drawings first and then shoot them in a separate photography session. The artist

PROD NO.	SCENE NO.	ANIMATOR		BG NO.		FOOTG	sheet

ACTION				4	3	2	1	BG	CAMERA	
		1								
		2								
		3								
		4								
		5								
		6								
		7								
		8								
		9								
		10								
		11								
		12								
		13								
		14								
		15								
		16								
		17								
		18								
		19								
		20								
		21								
		22								
		23								
		24								
		25								
		26								
		27								
		28								
		29								
		30								
		31								
		32								
		33								
		34								
		35								
		36								
		37								
		38								
		39								

4-4 Exposure sheet.

must use some numbering system for each drawing or risk mixing up the shooting order. The record-keeping for this simple cartoon points out a fundamental practice in all animated film productions: each piece of art requires careful identification in order to maintain the proper shooting order and to keep track of the photography.

To create a simple identification system, merely number the drawings on the backside or at the edge out of the camera shot. A camera equipped with a frame counter will indicate the exposure numbers for easy reference. If the artist-animator wishes to move or pan the camera across the drawing a more detailed instruction sheet is needed.

4-5 Registration holes in cel.

Figure 4-4 is an *exposure sheet* of the type used for animated films. The ruled columns and block areas permit specific camera and action instructions to be indicated for every frame. The exposure sheet can be used by someone other than the artist-animator as a guide to the proper shooting of the animation drawings. In professional studio productions, the animation artist is not responsible for the camera photography. The actual shooting is done by a camera operator who follows detailed written instructions on an exposure sheet for every scene in the film.

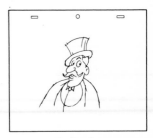

4-6 Pencil sketch on paper.

CEL ANIMATION

Almost all modern cartoons are made using artwork painted on *cels*. A cel is a clear plastic sheet punched with three registration holes along one edge. Figure 4-5 is a basic cel. The word derives from "celluloid," an early and highly flammable plastic used by pioneer film animators. Modern cels are made of less flammable material, usually cellulose acetate, diacetate, or triacetate. The cel's purpose is to support a drawing or portion of a drawing over a separate background sheet. This saves the animator from having constantly to redraw nonmotion parts of the scene.

4-7 Inking: Outline in ink (on top of cel).

In practice the cel method is simple: a preliminary sketch is made on paper, traced with ink onto a cel, and the backside painted with opaque colors that adhere well to the plastic material. These three steps are illustrated in figures 4-6, 4-7, and 4-8.

Each cel is placed over a painted background and photographed by a camera attached to a vertical assembly called the *animation stand*. Figure 4-9 shows a professional stand, with both the camera and the adjustable *compound table* below the lens for the cels and background art.

4-8 Opaquing: Finished cel (painted on back).

The standard animation cel measures 10¼ × 12½ inches. Holes punched along the top or bottom fit registration pegs on the compound table of the animation stand. A precision punch, similar to a large paper punch, is shown in figure 4-10. The three-hole pattern conforms to spacing standards of the *Oxberry* or *Acme* registration pegs, the two major registration systems.[1] Although the cel is so thin (.005 inches) that it appears transparent, the plastic's optical density slightly darkens the background sheet. This requires slightly more exposure

---

[1]Acme standard has one 1/4-inch round hole in the cel edge center with one 1/8- × 5/8-inch slot hole in line on each side. Holes are 4 inches from center to center. Oxberry standard is identical except the round hole is 7/32 inch and in-line slot holes are 1/4 × 1/2 inch.

4-9 Animation stand and compound table.

4-10 J-K animation cel punch.

compensation than when shooting the background without the cel in place. When four cels are overlayed in register, the overall effect is to darken the shot substantially. Each cel slightly darkens the values of color in the cel below. Special paints are available that are graded to the standard four levels of cel positions on the compound table.[2] A single color is separated into four different shades, one shade for each cel level.

[2]See Appendix for paint suppliers.

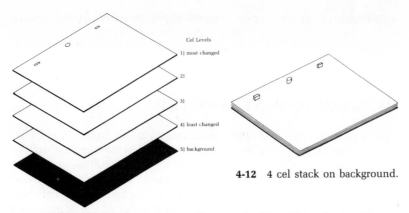

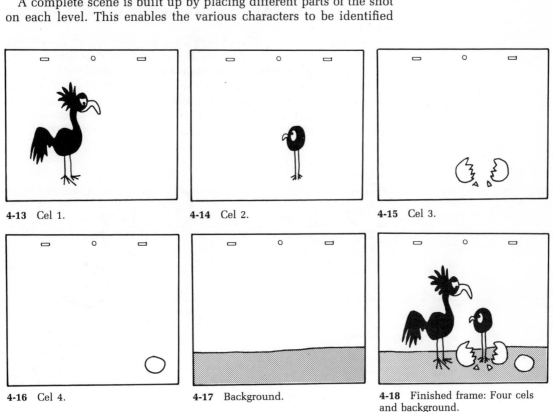

4-12 4 cel stack on background.

4-11 Cel levels.

The number of cel levels on the registration peg bars of the compound table remains constant, usually at four levels and a background sheet. Each cell at each level contains only a single character or portion of a character. The cels are layered to form a whole character scene. Figure 4-11 shows how the cels are arranged. The frequently changed cels are on the top level; the background sheet is on the bottom. If fewer than four painted cels are needed, a clear empty is added to keep the same optical density of the shot exposure.

A complete scene is built up by placing different parts of the shot on each level. This enables the various characters to be identified

4-13 Cel 1.   **4-14** Cel 2.   **4-15** Cel 3.

4-16 Cel 4.   **4-17** Background.   **4-18** Finished frame: Four cels and background.

by a reference cel level number on the exposure sheet like that shown earlier in figure 4-4. A simple scene using separate cel levels is demonstrated in figures 4-13 through 4-17; the assembled scene is shown in figure 4-18.

DRAWING ANIMATED MOTION

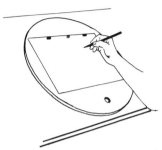

4-19 Twelve-field animation disc.

The animation artist first draws the character action in pencil sketches on thin translucent paper. The paper is punched in the same registration system, Acme or Oxberry, that is used on the animation stand that will photograph the final cel artwork. The artist uses a special drawing support called an *animation disk*, illustrated in figure 4-19. This thin aluminum disk has a standard peg bar for registering the paper sheet, and a square frosted glass insert sheet. The frosted glass permits the artist to see several sheets of paper drawings stacked together when a special *backlighting lamp box* is attached to the back of the disk.

The first step in the drawing of an animation character movement sequence is to establish the extreme start and stop positions of the action. Usually the professional animation artist draws only the *key extremes* of the action. Assistant artists then sketch all of the intermediate drawings, or *in-betweens*, that link the two key extremes. Working this way frees the animation artist to plan the essential movements of the scene quickly without getting bogged down in the many routine interval in-between drawings.

The falling ball in figure 4-20 is an example of a basic set of key extremes.

The same action is displayed with all of the intermediate in-between positions in figure 4-21. Each of the in-between drawings is later transferred to a separate cel for animation photography.

Once the individual paper sketches are approved by the chief animator, a test film is made of the pencil drawings on the animation stand. The pencil test is shot on cheap black-and-white negative film to keep the costs low. It produces a white line on black that allows

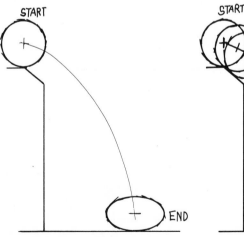

4-20 Key extremes.

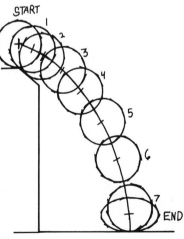

4-21 Seven in-betweens.

ANIMATION I

an animator to check the flow of the scene action. This is especially valuable in complicated scenes with several animated characters. The test allows changes to be made before the art is transferred to expensive acetate cels. Since painted cel preparation is both costly and time consuming, a pencil test is a good investment and a way to avoid wasted effort.

SPECIAL PURPOSE CELS AND DRAWINGS

Cycle and Hold

Special purpose cels help keep production costs down by allowing the efficient breakdown of moving and nonmoving parts within a single character. These cel drawings are based on the repeating or cyclical movement patterns of the subject, and are called movement *cycle drawings*. Walking, running, and flying all involve repeated leg, arm, or wing actions that continue as long as the action is maintained.

Figure 4-22 is representative of a flapping wing cycle. The downward stroke of the bird's wing flap is made up of four cel drawings. These same four cels are reused in reverse order for the upstroke of the wing. The complete wing flap action consists of seven steps that require only four cels to produce.

The entire figure of the flying bird was redrawn for each cel drawing in this example. The technique is called *full animation*. A more economical method that saves drawing production time is known as *limited animation*. Only the action part of the subject, e.g., the bird's wing, is drawn on a cel. The body, which has no motion itself, is put on a single cel and used with all the wing portion cels. The body cel is called a *hold* cel, because it is held in the scene longer than the individual wing cels. Figure 4-23 is the hold cel of the bird's body. Figures 4-24 through 4-27 show the partial wing action cels for the flap cycle. Figure 4-28 shows the combined hold cel and first

4-22 Initial sketch of wing positions (for complete flap cycle up and down).

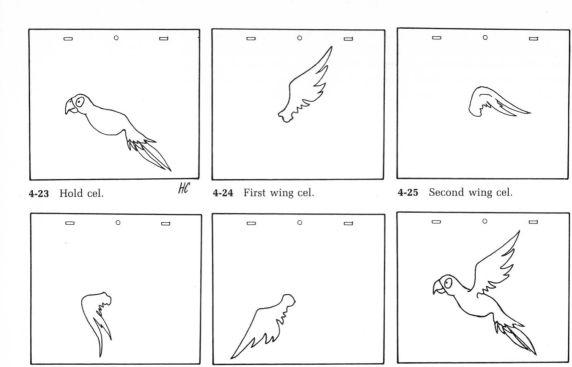

4-23 Hold cel.   *HC*   **4-24** First wing cel.   **4-25** Second wing cel.

4-26 Third wing cel.   **4-27** Fourth wing cel.   **4-28** Hold cel and first cel of flap cycle.

wing cycle cel to make a complete bird for the frame exposure. After the exposure, the wing cycle cel is replaced with the next wing cel in the cycle and a new exposure made. This procedure continues through an entire flapping sequence for as many frames as needed to complete the flying shot.

Because of the repeated use of cycle cels as well as for any changes made in a hold cel, the use of an exposure sheet is essential. The notes on the exposure sheet synchronize the cel replacements in the proper order to any changes made in the background and any camera movements such as pans or zooms.

The saving of time and money provided by using cycle cels is considerable. Each character does not have to be drawn in complete form on each individual cel, thus the total number of cels is reduced, as are the costs of production. The technique of limited animation via hold and cycle cels is frequently used for low-budget animated cartoons, commericals, technical or industrial films, and simple character animation. Most feature length animated films, however, use the more expensive *full animation* technique, which calls for each movement and gesture to be completely drawn on a separate cel and results in a more fluid and lifelike movement than limited animation. Such films often call for greater complexity and subtlety per frame exposure than can be produced by the hold and cycle cel technique.

Rotoscope

A special form of animated drawing is the *rotoscope action* character. In ordinary animation the animation artist imagines the character and draws the intended movements with some exaggeration to enhance the motion effect. Such stylized drawings are marked by the squeeze and stretch extremes of character movement that often border on the comical, almost as if the character had a rubber body. Rotoscope animation attempts to re-create lifelike motion by adhering to the natural look of a moving character without any exaggeration. The cel drawing is traced from the frames of actual film strips of live action subjects. Instead of imaginatively interpreting a movement, the rotoscope animator uses the outline tracing of the character movements to imitate the look of reality in a moving subject.

The finished cels, known as *rotoscope action act,* mimic nature by copying the action exactly as it appears on the film. This is quite different from the style of traditional animation, which often exaggerates the extremes of action for comedy effects.

The rotoscope art is prepared by first shooting a cheap black-and-white film of the subject. The processed film is inserted frame by frame into the special projector assembly, the *rotoscope,* of an animation stand camera. This device contains a pin-registered movement and a projection lamp. The single frame registered in the gate aperture is focused onto a sheet of paper on the animation stand drawing table. The paper is also punched with registration holes in the Acme or Oxberry system to assure accuracy in the position of later drawings. The animation artist then traces the outline of the needed subject action seen on the sheet. When the drawing is finished it is removed, a new sheet placed on the registration pegs, and the film advanced to the next frame. This procedure is repeated for every frame of the action of the character subject in the scene. Later the drawings are traced onto animation cels, *inked,* and painted, or *opaqued.* The background is provided by a separate piece of painted artwork under the rotoscope cel.

Figure 4-29 shows an action subject frame, a dog rolling a ball. Figure 4-30 is a rotoscope tracing of the same subject. The outline drawing is punched with registration holes to keep a proper placement of the subject in the sheet during photography and on all subsequent drawings.

Another major use of rotoscope art is to generate *holdout mattes* used in optical printing. The holdout matte is an esential part of the *traveling matte process* for composite shots, to permit live action subject footage to be combined optically with a separately filmed background scene. Rotoscope holdout mattes are made in the same

4-29 Action subject frame.

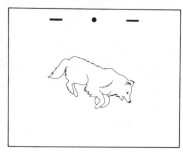

4-30 Rotoscope outline cel.

4-31 Rotoscope holdout matte cel.

SPECIAL PURPOSE CELS AND DRAWINGS

way as rotoscope animation outline cel drawings. For the matte the outline area is filled in with opaque black paint. The individual matte cels are then photographed frame by frame on the animation stand with a high-contrast black-and-white film stock in the camera. The animation camera lens field of view is adjusted to cover exactly the same area as the original master film frame of the live action footage. This will prevent any matte line misregistration shadows from fringing the subject in the later composite shot. Figure 4-31 is a holdout matte rotoscoped from the live action dog frame of figure 4-29.

MOVING BACKGROUNDS

In cycle cel movements the subject appears to walk, run, or fly, but does not move from the center of the cel. A pan action that simulates the movement across the camera's field of view can be achieved with the movement controls of the animation stand compound table. These controls are gear- and screw-driven mechanisms that physically move the artwork positioned on the tabletop. The cel can be moved or the background sheet advanced a frame at a time between camera exposures. The background sheet is punched with a series of registration holes to fit the movable peg bars of the compound tabletop. Since the background is usually several times longer than any one cel width, a number of repeat registration holes extend along the entire sheet. The background can then be moved to the extreme range of the compound peg bar movement limits, lifted, and a new background segment registered into position under the character subject cel. The different areas of the background edge are numbered for easy identification on the exposure sheet to guide the animation stand camera operator. Figure 4-32 shows a simple background arranged to simulate a moving landscape beneath a flying bird cel (a hold and single cycle cel combination).

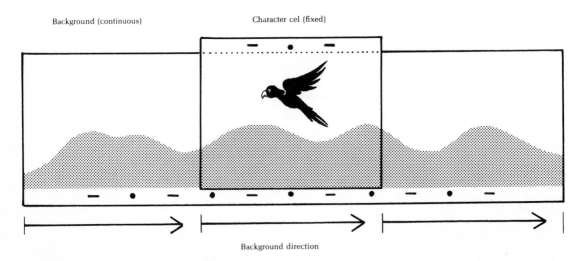

4-32 Fixed cel with single sheet background.

CUTOUT ANIMATION

The traditional cel method of animation is not the only method for animating flat art or characters. Instead of drawing the individual characters on cels, separate *cutout paper figures* can be placed over a background sheet. Cutouts are simple cycle illustrations or cutout actual photographs. A stiff paper is recommended for the cutout artwork, such as two-ply Bristol board. The cutout can be filmed directly on the background sheet positioned on the animation stand compound table. A better method is to glue the cutout figure lightly to a standard animation cel, which will keep it in place and flat on the background sheet. This is especially useful when figures cut from antique engravings or woodcuts clipped from art books are to be animated.

A flexible, jointed cutout can be made by using pins at the limb joints or thread taped onto the back of the paper. The animator can then easily shift the figure into new positions. To facilitate the placement of the limbs, a cel overlay marked with the intended in-betweens and key extremes of each action can be used as a guide between exposures. This overlay method is useful in technical animation, which is the animation of such things as machines illustrated by cutouts of gears, pistons, levers, and moving valves. Several moving cutouts can be properly positioned in the same shot with the correct speed interval for the animated machine operation.

The cutout whole-piece figures should be numbered according to cycle position. This ensures that the correct cutout will be used according to the written camera instructions.

Cutout animation can often be quite comical, since the figure movements can be broadly exaggerated. Automobiles, famous statues, ships, and graffiti are all grist for the animator's whimsy. One of the masters of cutout animation is Terry Gilliam of the *Monty Python* films. His short cutout cartoons are masterpieces of lunacy and satire. Similar effects are available even to the beginning animation filmmaker.

KINESTASIS

Kinestasis is a form of animation in which a nonmoving subject, such as a still photographic print, can be broken down into individual shots that when combined simulate movement. The term derives from *kine* (moving) and *stasis* (still). The technique is popular in television commercials and human interest news segments that use many still photographs to tell a story.

Kinestatic animation generally combines two types of visual movement:

1. Pans or zooms to create the illusion of subject movement
2. The various reframings of the same image in sequential order to simulate or reinforce action compositions

Dramatic still photographs can be animated into a film presentation with kinestatic techniques. Combined with a suitable soundtrack, much of the impact of the original still photo can be preserved and still be motion-oriented as film.

Kinestasis can also be used to shoot an animated story board to help visualize the scripted action. This use, often termed *animatic* presentations, relies on camera movement, zooms, quick cuts, and dissolves of individual story board panels to approximate the appearance of the finished film. In addition, the animatic presentation may use sequential artwork or story board panels to mimic cel-type animation, without the usual in-between drawings to smooth the action. The technique helps overcome the static quality of the standard storyboard, especially in commercials where motion graphics are stressed. Animatic artwork is occasionally used in feature films to plan a complex special effect action. A notable example of the animatic story board was used to plan the battle scene in *The Empire Strikes Back* between the rebel snow-speeder craft and the imperial giant "walker" mobile tanks. The final film matches the animated story board to a remarkable degree.

UNUSUAL ANIMATION MATERIALS

Flat animation is not limited to the photography of drawings, cels, and cutouts. A diverse number of materials are suitable for animation by direct manipulation under the camera lens.

Sand

Fine-grain sand is placed on a glass sheet. The sheet can then be either toplighted for normal effects or backlighted for high contrast effects. Free-flowing sand can be easily transformed from one figure to another distinctly different figure between frame exposures.

Clay

Ordinary modeling clay on glass or opaque background sheets is easily shaped. It is more solid than loose sand, thus permitting a more modeled surface and the addition of greater detail to the character being animated. Clay is available in a wide range of vivid colors.

Paint

Colorful, fluid drawings can be painted directly onto a backlighted translucent glass sheet with watercolors, oil paints, or tempera. When warmed and softened slightly by the heat of a lamp, wax crayons also provide a paintlike medium.

The potential number of unusual media is left to the reader's imagination. By constantly exploring the possibilities of nontraditional animation materials, the animator considerably extends the visual language of the art.

COMPUTER-BASED ANIMATION

The high cost and labor-intensive activity of traditional cel animation for professional films have severely limited the number of feature-length productions. In recent years attempts have been made to apply the expanding technology of computers to the generation of animation effects. A number of companies now use the computer to create short animated sequences for films, television station logos, and limited special effects for feature films. At present *computer animation* has not taken over in animated film, but many studios have expressed a strong interest in developing their own in-house computer animation departments, most notably Lucasfilm, Ltd., the creators of *Star Wars* and other blockbusters.

The most extensive use of computer graphics in a feature film is the Walt Disney Studios production *TRON*. About half of the film is computer-generated imagery. Other feature films that incorporate computer animated effects include *Westworld*, *Looker*, *Star Trek II*, and *Videodrome*. The trend toward high-quality computer animation effects will no doubt continue as new techniques and equipment develop.

Computer Systems

Two basic types of computer systems are used for animation: the *analog* and the *digital* image system. Both systems permit images to be processed and displayed on a high-resolution color video screen. The video images are then photographed by a motion picture camera and transferred onto film stock.

ANALOG SYSTEMS

Analog systems produce an animated image by processing the video signal from a television camera. A normal video signal is translated by the computer as a continuously variable electronic response, or analog, to the light striking the camera pickup image tube. The computer alters the video signal as it is displayed on the monitor screen. The displayed image can be compressed, stretched, or distorted in any direction by controlling the timing of the television screen scan lines. Other special effects can be achieved simply by altering the frequency or amplitude of the analog signal from the camera. These effects are generated by adjusting the computer knob control dials to create blurs, spins, ripples, color shifts, and total negative reversals of the image. Since analog systems process the television signal as it comes in, the system operates in normal time, or real time.

DIGITAL SYSTEMS

Digital computer systems create an image by generating thousands of dots that form the picture. These dots, called *pixels* for *picture elements*, are processed from mathematically based visual information instead of real images as in the analog systems. Digital animation is the most versatile form of computer animation. It gives the animator maximum control of the video image's form and color.

The pixels form a complete picture in a mosaiclike form. Figure 4-33 represents a magnified view of the pixels that form the number eight. Thousands of pixels are needed to form a complete computer image frame. Each pixel point is assigned a location and intensity by the computer memory. The pixel can be changed to any desired intensity, called *shading*, or the color altered throughout the entire image merely by changing the instruction code assigned to each pixel location.

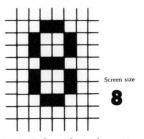

Screen size

8

4-33 Enlarged pixel matrix.

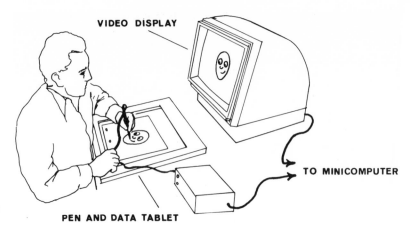

VIDEO DISPLAY

TO MINICOMPUTER

PEN AND DATA TABLET

4-34 Computer animation
video station.

How Computer Animation Works

The computer animator works at a special input device known as a *digitizing tablet.* Figure 4-34 shows an animator working at a *tablet animation station.*

A square surface area on the digitizing tablet corresponds to the computer display screen. Any specific position on the tablet can be recorded or mapped in the computer's memory. The animator "draws" with a hand-held electronic pen directly onto the tablet surface. Instead of making visible lines on the tablet, the electronic pen transfers the digital location code of each point in the line to the computer. The image drawn by the animator is then displayed on the computer screen in front of the tablet. Another part of the computer memory, called the *frame buffer,* stores the digital outline image for further refinement or additions.

A different data tablet, the *video color palette,* can be used to paint in the outline image stored in the frame buffer.

Using the tablet and palette devices, the animator can electronically create a single frame or *video cel* of an animation scene.

The computer animator must follow several basic procedures to generate a motion sequence of a computer-generated character or object:

1. Develop a story board to plan the action. This is the traditional method of planning visual effects for both film and video.
2. Determine the *data base.* In computer animation, the data base is a mathematical description of what the character or object's physical dimensions are to be. The computer can then generate an outline model of the data base from any perspective. The model is in the form of an outline or *wire-frame* rendition. Figure 4-35 is a computer-generated wire-frame image of a Subaru automobile by Digital Effects, Inc. The inside skeletal view of all important features will be removed later so that a fully modeled and shaded image is formed on the screen that simulates a three-dimensional effect. The computer's data base can generate a view of the automobile from any perspective possible from the lens angle of an imaginary camera.

4-35 Computer-generated wire-frame image of a Subaru. (Courtesy of DEI/Dana Cairns Prod., "Subaru" 1980)

3. Define the key extreme frames of the action. The computer animator shifts the wire-frame image to simulate the key extreme frame positions of traditional animation movement analysis. The computer animator also determines the modeling of the wire-frame object: outline or solid surface, translucent or transparent, and chooses colors and textures as well. Figure 4-36 displays two versions of an object, one as a wire frame and the other as modeled according to an imaginary light source. A similar treatment is given to every object in the key frames.

4. Calculate and program the object's speed, direction, and rotation in the scene. The object can fly, unrestricted by the laws of gravity, or accelerate and decelerate. The animator can also plot any camera actions, such as pans, zooms, or tilts, to coincide with the object's movements. The computer automatically calculates the frames required for any specific position between the animator's camera movement key extreme indications. The computer also draws all the required in-betweens by using the object's data base information.

4-36 Wire-frame object. Modeled object over wire frame.

5. Prepare a "pencil test" of the video image and complete the full modeling animation. After the computer has generated every cel of an action sequence, the frames are stored in the computer memory. Each frame can then be played back at the normal 24 frames per second to create a preview "pencil test" before the images are committed to film. The video images can then be taped or transferred to 35mm color film with a special motion picture camera, such as the Dicomed D48 film recorder.

What would have taken months to animate by traditional cel methods can be accomplished in a few weeks by high-speed computer technology and the resulting computer-generated animation.

Figures 4-37 through 4-39 show the complex and realistic details offered by computer-generated images. All of these frames were excerpted from productions by Digital Effects, Inc.

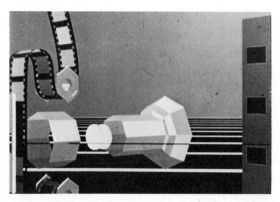 

4-37 (Courtesy of DEI/Marstellar, G. Parker, "Scientific-American-Crichton" 1980)

4-38 (Courtesy of DEI/Aoi Prod., "Kitazawa Valve" 1980)

4-39 (Courtesy of DEI/Kleiser, Rosebush, Leich, Cox, Loew, Prins, Deas, Cohen, "Times Square" 1979)

ANIMATION I

Animation II:
Three-Dimensional Effects

5

Three-dimensional animation is a special form of single-frame cinematography that involves puppets or jointed models. The technique is called *stop-motion* or *dimensional animation*. Whichever term is used (they are interchangeable), the basic idea is simple: an adjustable puppet or model is shot a frame at a time for an entire action sequence. The puppet's pose or features are changed slightly between each successive frame exposure. When the footage is projected, the puppet appears to move unaided and continuously within the physical space of what was a miniature set or scene. The puppet footage can be designed as a self-contained film or selectively combined with live action footage using process photographic methods.

USING PUPPETS

A character puppet can be based on a living subject or totally imaginary ones. Most animation puppets are based on imaginary subjects. Living subjects can be filmed live with less expense, and there is little reason to waste time and labor duplicating them as puppets.

The script usually supplies the inspiration for the puppet character. It gives a brief word-picture of the puppet's type, size, and action. The physical appearance is fleshed out in the key drawings created by the art director or production artist. The detailed drawings attempt to capture the dramatic action or look of the script shot description.

The next step is to prepare *model sheets* that show the important features of the puppet-to-be. Figure 5-1 is a model sheet, one of several, that details various textures and movement parts of a prehistoric-type imaginary creature.

The various model-sheet views of the imaginary puppet guide the animator in sculpting a nonmoving preliminary *clay model*. The art and verbal descriptions provided by the model sheet help the animator work out the "body language" requirements of the puppet's physical movements.

After the final appearance of the puppet has been approved for production, the story script action is illustrated in a series of story boards or continuity sketches. These drawings clearly indicate what is to be filmed by the animation camera, what by the production live action camera, and what parts of the shot will involve optical process

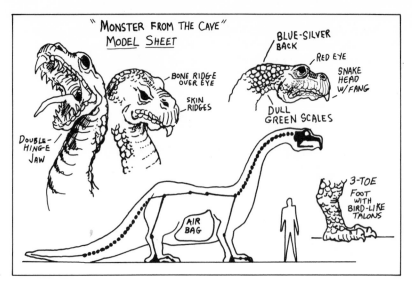

5-1 Model sheet.

photography. This layout of the shot in visual form shows specifically what part of the final composite frame will be live action and what areas are reserved for the animated puppet or miniatures. The pre-production planning enables the animation and live action cinematography teams to coordinate their separate activities.

Clay Puppets

The puppet is first sculpted in a hard clay such as Roma Plastelina #4 (Extra Hard). (Plastelina is a common choice for animation prototypes and is available in four grades of hardness.) The clay version has all the fine surface details that are to be reproduced in the final puppet. Once the model is approved by the key production members, the prototype is readied for casting in plaster or epoxy molds.

Clay is also a favorite medium for character puppets in animated films. The all clay-puppet film *Closed Mondays* won an Academy Award for its vivid and colorful animation. The flexibility of ordinary nonhardening modeling clay allows early access to the dimensional puppet format for student filmmakers.

For all-clay animated films, the figure puppets are usually limited to small sizes because of the soft nature of the clay. Puppets generally range from three to eight inches (76mm to 203mm) in height. Larger sizes require an inner support frame called an armature to support the heavy weight of the clay. A simple armature of aluminum alloy wire will serve if the puppet action is not complicated and the movements are limited so that a break in the wire at the bend points is prevented. Clay puppets lend themselves to metamorphic animation, in which the puppet is transformed between exposures into a quite different shape. This comical style is easily accomplished because of the easy modeling of the armature support.

Professional Feature Film Puppets

The simple clay puppet is not durable enough to meet the demands of complex stop-motion animation in feature-length films. The puppet's clay surface is too easily deformed by the animator's constant handling in the course of a scene's action. Even clay puppets with wire armatures must constantly be repaired as clay limbs sag, split, or slip free from the wire. Although clay puppets are often excellent for simple film characters, short films, or experimental use of the clay medium, most professional feature puppet animation is based on a different type of puppet. These professional puppets are made of latex rubber. The puppet's skin is tough but flexible, and it retains the original surface details after handling. Unlike the one-of-a-kind clay puppet, the professional puppet is cast from a master mold. This permits any number of identical copies to be made from an original design and thus reduces the need for constant repairs to a single puppet. When damaged, the puppet is merely replaced with a new puppet replica.

The professional puppet, usually ranging in size from 8 to 20 inches (7.6 to 50.8cm), also contains a more complex armature than the simple wire armature used in a clay puppet. The armature for rubber latex puppets is a jointed metal skeleton that can rigidly support the puppet's soft rubber body in any posed position. Early animation armatures were made of hard wood, but that soon gave way to the use of more durable metal armatures.

BALL-AND-SOCKET ARMATURE

The articulated armatures needed for professional animation puppets are made from hard metal materials such as stainless steel rods, ball bearings, and flat stock. The cost of the precision-made armature is determined by the number and type of joints needed for movement. Just as the human skeleton is made up of various kinds of ball-and-socket joints, the animation armature similarly uses the fully directional ball-and-socket arrangement for the metal limbs. Figures 5-2 and 5-

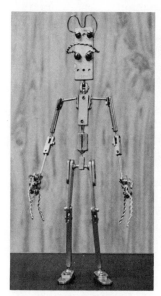

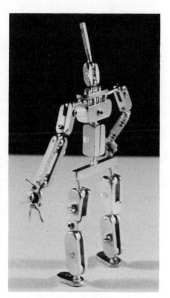

5-2 Armature for a two-legged puppet. (Courtesy of Rick Catizone/Anivision Ltd.)

5-3 Another example of an armature for a two-legged puppet. (Courtesy of Rick Catizone/Anivision Ltd.)

5-4 A flexible armature with ball-and-socket segments. (Model by Paul Mejias/ © Albert Mejias 1982)

3 show two armatures for a two-legged puppet model. Figure 5-4 is a flexible armature using ball-and-socket segments to provide a snake-like body for the puppet creature. This puppet also has a ball-and-socket arrangement for the head and pincer mouthpieces.

The armature joints are made as tight as possible to prevent slippage in the puppet's pose during the stop-motion photography. If any joint weakens, the center binding screws can be tightened by inserting a small screwdriver or hex wrench (Allen wrench), whichever is appropriate, through a tiny slit cut into the puppet's body material. The slit can then be sealed with a drop of liquid latex.

A note about the armature within the latex. Latex contains chemicals that work corrosively on a metal armature and cause rust. Such rust eventually stains the latex and corrodes the ball socket joints. To prevent this, the armature is usually protected by a coating such as chrome-plating or by wrapping the armature completely in thin plastic sheeting material such as common household plastic wrap.

Because the armature is relatively expensive, as a practical matter it can be stripped out of the puppet's body and reused or incorporated into another design when the original puppet is retired from production.

Building Puppet Bodies

There are two basic ways of making a puppet body for animation: the *buildup* method and the *foam latex casting* method. Each method produces a high-quality model, but the chief difference is in the time required to make the original puppet, and then multiple copies when needed.

THE BUILDUP METHOD

The buildup method is the older of the two, used to create the creatures of the early *King Kong* (1933). The puppet is made of layers of wax, cotton, and sheet latex modeled directly over the metal armature. Liquid latex rubber and flexible adhesives bond the various materials together. Large body sections can be blocked out with chunks of foam rubber glued directly to the armature.

The intricate arrangement of sheeting and rubber pieces can accurately simulate the way real musculature flexes and contracts. The strips of rubber imitate muscle and sinews beneath the thin layer of liquid latex skin. Wax and rabbit fur glued to the rubber skin mimic the appearance of natural skin and pelt.

The buildup method is usually reserved for one-of-a-kind custom-made puppets since the labor required is time-consuming and costly. Modern animators seldom use this slow process when several identical puppets are required over the course of a lengthy animated feature. Instead, they resort to an alternative bodymaking method that uses exact plaster or epoxy molds to cast a rubber puppet body from a clay prototype. This latter method is known as *foam latex casting* of the puppet.

FOAM CASTING: THE MOLD

Figures 5-5 to 5-19 illustrate the steps and materials used in the foam casting process.

A pair of negative half-mold pieces are made from the clay prototype. A hard plaster is used, such as the Hydrocal or Ultracal produced by U.S. Gypsum Company. Both are extremely accurate and slow-setting plasters. "Accurate" here means that the plaster neither expands nor distorts as it hardens or sets. The copy mold is much more faithful to the original than would be the case if an expanding soft plaster was used, such as ordinary plaster of paris or other common plasters.

Each half-mold piece is made separately by casting one side of the puppet at a time. The clay subject is divided with thin soft-metal shims or a builtup clay retaining wall. This wall extends completely around the clay figure and prevents the plaster from reaching the other side. Small clay marbles are pressed into the retaining wall that, when cast, will serve as impression keys to make sure the two mold pieces are registered together properly when casting of the puppet is done later.

After the first half of the puppet is completely hard, the retaining wall is stripped away. A release agent is then painted onto the exposed plaster seam. The release agent prevents permanent joining of the two plaster halves and permits their later separation. Suitable release or parting agents include diluted liquid soap, thin oil, shellac, melted wax, or a polyvinyl release agent made for the purpose.

The second half mold is then made by repeating the process on the clay puppet's other side. The plaster is built up to the same depth as the first mold piece. It should extend along the entire area formerly occupied by the retaining wall and fill the key impressions.

Once the plaster has set, the two pieces are carefully separated along the seam. The finished molds are then cleared of any remaining clay. Although the original clay prototype is eventually destroyed in the piece-mold process, the mold cavity retains every detail in negative form.

FOAM LATEX CASTING: THE PUPPET BODY

The mold pieces are then prepared for final latex casting of the puppet. A number of vents must be cut in the plaster mold to permit air to escape when the liquid latex is later poured into the closed mold. Trapped air, especially in the puppet's extremities, prevents the latex from contacting the mold at that spot and thus forms an unfinished or partial casting. Such defects spoil the details of the puppet surface and must be avoided. It is better to have too many air escape vents than not enough. The vents will fill with latex in the casting process as air is forced out of the mold by the pressure of the liquid latex. A large vent will serve as an entry hole for injecting liquid latex into the closed mold.

A mold release agent is applied in a thin coat to both halves of the mold. Various release agents can be used, such as lacquer, stearic acid, or a formula of zinc stearate mixed with castor oil. The latex supplier usually recommends a specific release agent for a particular latex. The release agent will prevent the finished latex casting from sticking to the plaster mold as it is removed. Both the mold and the applied release agent should be completely dry before the latex is poured into the mold.

The armature is positioned in one of the mold half-pieces. Thin wires can be used to brace a heavy metal armature in place in the cavity to keep it from slipping when the mold is closed. The wires can later be pulled free or snipped from the finished casting.

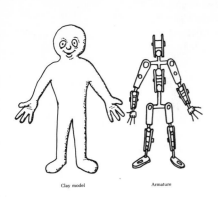

Clay model   Armature

5-5 Step 1: Casting.

5-6 Step 2: Clay wall with keys.

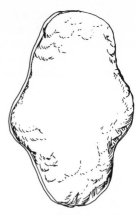

5-7 Step 3: Plaster buildup.

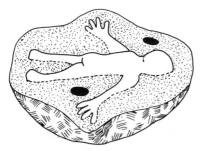

5-8 Step 4: Clay walls and keys removed. Mold-release agent applied to plaster upper surface.

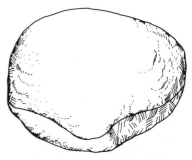

5-9 Step 5: Plaster applied to form second half.

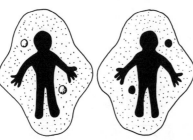

5-10 Step 6: Mold cavity coated with mold-release agent. (Note: Positive and negative key to align molds A and B.) Mold separated, clay model removed.

5-11 Step 7: Vents cut into plaster.

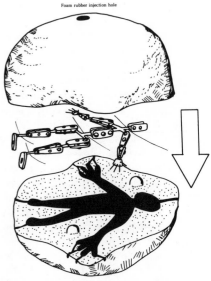

Foam rubber injection hole

5-12 Step 8: Mold assembly with armature. (Note: Armature on thin support wires.)

ANIMATION II

The mold pieces are fitted together and registered by the seam mold keys. The closed mold is held together by a thin wire band or, more simply, a heavyweight anchor such as a brick that firmly presses the two mold sections together.

The choice of casting material is based on several factors, such as cost, size, and puppet requirements. But almost all foam rubber puppets are of one of two types: cold foam latex and the heat-cured foam latex.

Cold Foam Latex. The cold foam is easier to work with than the heat-cured foam, but it is expensive if large or several puppets are to be cast. Two popular foams are Kryolan foam latex and the extremely soft Schram latex. Both are prepared in a similar fashion. Both also cure at room temperature without additional heating, thus the term "cold cure."

Manufacturers of cold foam latex often use different formulations of the basic material. In most cases the latex base compound requires special additives, two, three or even four separate chemical agents depending on the particular formula provided. For this reason the manufacturer's instructions sheet must be closely followed both for measuring the materials and for the proper mixing sequence of compounds. Any deviation can result in total failure of the latex to solidify and cure.

In general the latex base compound is mixed with separate gelling, foaming, and curing agents at the time the foam latex is to be used. Mixing is done in a small metal bowl; the latex is then frothed to a whipped cream–like texture with an electric kitchen mixer or similar table mixer. The mixing disperses the gelling and curing agents evenly to solidify the latex properly after it is in the mold.

The latex is placed into the mold cavity in either of two ways. It can be poured into each half of the open mold; the mold is then closed tightly to allow the latex to cure. This method is good for small molds. The other method is to inject the latex under pressure into a closed mold. This *injection molding* of latex is done with a piston-type cylinder device that forces the latex material into the mold through an injection hole cut vertically into the plaster top mold half. An ordinary caulk or manual grease gun with a bulk dispenser works well to pressure the foamed latex into every mold crevice. As the foam latex cures it becomes a porous, resilient mass of rubber in the shape of the original clay sculpture. After about twenty-four hours, which allows complete curing, the mold can be

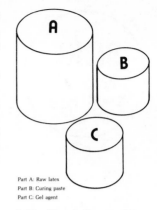

Part A: Raw latex
Part B: Curing paste
Part C: Gel agent

5-13 Step 9: Foam-rubber preparation.

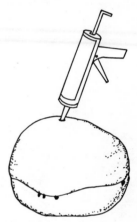

5-14 Step 9A: Method one: Injecting foam rubber into mold.

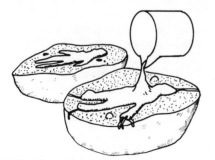

5-15 Step 9B: Method two: Pouring foam mix into each half, then assembling mold and weight.

5-16 Step 10: Heat cure foam rubber in air-circulating oven.

parted and the latex casting removed. The mold can then be cleaned, dried, and if necessary, prepared for a new latex casting.

Heat-Cured Latex. The other basic latex rubber casting material is heat-cured foam latex. The mold containing the cast material must be exposed to a low radiant heat (such as in a 200–300°F oven) in order to cure or vulcanize properly.

A suitable heat-cured foam rubber is the three-part RD 318C Foam Latex Kit supplied by the R & D Latex Corporation of Commerce, California. This kit consists of three components that must be measured and mixed: the raw latex, a curing paste, and a gel agent. The manufacturer's instructions should be followed exactly.

As with cold foam, the heat-cured liquid rubber is injected or poured into the mold. After a few moments, it solidifies partially and fills the mold. The closed mold is then placed into an air-circulating kitchen oven (not a microwave) and baked at a low temperature of 200–300 degrees F for three to five hours.

After the rubber is fully cured, the mold is separated and the cast rubber puppet removed. Any excess rubber fringes or flash are trimmed away with a razor knife. Incomplete areas, such as fingers or toes that did not fill with the thick casting liquid, are then individually constructed with liquid rubber buildup methods.

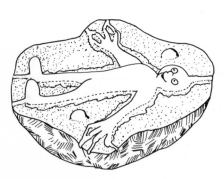

5-17 Step 11: When mold cools, separate halves and remove foam rubber casting.

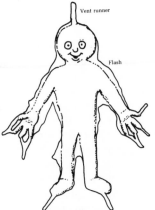

5-18 Step 12: Use razor knife to remove any excess foam or flash seepage from model.

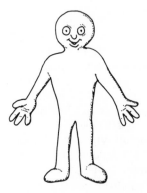

5-19 Step 13: Finished foam casting with interior armature ready for painting.

Any additional puppet features, such as teeth and fangs, horns and claws, are fabricated separately from hard rubber, ceramics, hardwood, or cast acrylic resin. Hard materials can be carved or filed into the required features and attached to the latex casting with a few drops of liquid adhesive. If a plastic or acrylic resin is used to make a casting of a feature originally sculpted in some other material, then molds of the original feature are made in plaster using the same procedures in casting the puppet body.

If the puppet needs hair, beard, or fur, a suitably colored section of crepe hair from a theatrical makeup supplier can be used. The crepe can be sewn to the latex skin or applied using a contact cement

ANIMATION II

adhesive. Actual animal fur can also be used if a pelt is available, such as a fine-texture rabbit fur. However, any fur intended for the puppet must be extremely fine-haired and trimmed to be in correct scale to the puppet's small body and look natural.

Color is then applied to the cast rubber puppet body based on model sheet specifications. Dyes or airbrushed paints are used. Coloring with a regular brush is not recommended because the relatively thicker paint fills in the fine surface details of the puppet skin.

Figure 5-20 shows a completed foam rubber dinosaur puppet containing a fully articulated ball-and-socket armature. The dinosaur is fitted with plastic teeth and lifelike glass eyes, and entirely painted in a natural lizard skin color.

5-20 Foam rubber dinosaur with ball-and-socket armature. (Model by Paul Mejias/ © Albert Mejias 1982)

5-21 Wing nut **T** tiedown.

SOME USEFUL TOOLS

Tiedowns

A *tiedown* is a small device for anchoring a free-standing puppet to the animation stage platform. Without a proper tiedown system, the puppet is unsteady and subject to sudden toppling. This would instantly ruin any stop-motion footage in progress, forcing the entire sequence to be reshot from the beginning.

A simple tiedown in a wire loop that holds the puppet securely by one foot to the stage board. A pair of holes is drilled in the stage board through which one end of the loop is inserted and fitted over the puppet's foot. The other end of the wire is pulled through the second hole and wrapped around a short dowel beneath the platform board. A twist of the dowel forms a tight braid against the board and keeps the puppet in place.

A more professional system is the T slot-and-wing-nut system used by the tiedown of figure 5-21.

The tiedown inserts into a hole drilled through the stage board and into a slotted hole in the armature foot pad plate. In practice the foot plate is hidden by the foam rubber body, but a small hidden slit cut into the foot bottom admits the narrow head of the tiedown T. The procedure is shown in figure 5-22.

The animator places the puppet's foot over a hole previously drilled in the stage board. The long screw of the tiedown is pushed through the hole, through the body slit in the sole of the foot, and twisted over the slot in the foot plate to prevent the tiedown from dropping back through the slot. A wide wing nut on the tiedown shaft is then tightened against the underside of the stage board and anchors the puppet in place. After the frame exposure, the wing nut is loosened, the tiedown is twisted back and slips easily out of the foot, and is removed from the hole. The routine is redone for every footstep of the action flow path.

The tiedown method requires that the puppet stride be plotted in advance. Alternating left and right foot holes are drilled in the line

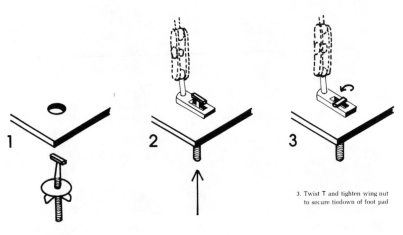

5-22   Tiedown of foot pad.

1. Hole for tiedown

2. Insert T into slot of foot

3. Twist T and tighten wing nut to secure tiedown of foot pad

of the action, with the correct spacing for the speed of the puppet's walk or run. The many holes are masked in the camera shot by using wooden plugs or removable putty painted to match the scenic ground color.

Figure 5-23 shows a variation of the tiedown that uses a threaded hole in the foot plate to accept a screw shaft. The tiedown shaft is adjustable to accommodate any given stage platform board thickness.

Aerial Braces

Flying puppets, such as birds, dragons, harpies, and other winged creatures, need a different mounting method from the tiedown system of ground-level puppets. This "flying rig" keeps the puppet in the air above the stage board and also permits it to be animated in flight across the camera's field of view. The special flying rig is commonly known as an *aerial brace*. One such brace is shown in figure 5-24. The aerial brace is usually custom-made by an animator to meet the production requirements of a specific shot or sequence.

5-23 Tiedown with threaded hole in foot plate.

Aerial braces have several other uses. They aid in stop-motion falling pieces, such as the collapse of a building or tree fall. Aerial braces are essential for the realistic running of ground puppets. In a real run, the legs are off the ground in midstride. The aerial brace supports the puppet body for the number of frames the puppet's feet are not in contact with the stage platform board.

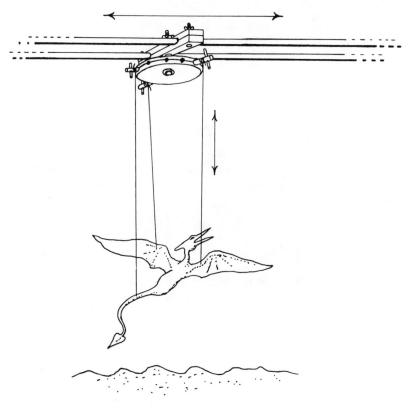

5-24 Aerial brace.

The height of the puppet from the stage is controlled by thumbscrew pegs, similar to those on a guitar, that wind the monofilament line or piano wire at a fractional interval. The crosspiece itself can travel along the support rails, the length of one rail marked in inches or centimeters to give a proper spacing for the animated forward or backward direction.

Wires can also be used not only to support a flying model, but to determine the "flight path" of any model along a particular direction. This *flying by wire* is one of the earliest methods used to simulate an airplane or spaceship in flight. The basic method uses a single long wire or pair of parallel wires stretched along an inclined angle across the stage. The model, such as an airplane, is attached to the wires either by small pulley wheels or by holes through each wing. The model can, on cue, slide forward down the inclined wires powered by the force of gravity.

The two-wire arrangement permits the plane's flying position to be stable, and if required, to be angled during flight by raising one wire higher than the other. In situations where the wires are parallel to the floor, the model is anchored to the wires. The wires, in turn, are either pulled by a technician using a spool-and-crank device, or for high speed action, a guillotine-style drop-weight at one end. In both cases the other ends of the wires are wound onto a tight-tension supply spool similar to a large fishing reel. The illusion of self-propelled flight can be enhanced by equipping the model with moving features, such as battery-powered propellers, rotors, exterior flashing or running lights. Flying by wire methods offer an advantage since the models can be filmed in actual "flight" rather than using the more time-consuming stop-motion animation.

Although the flying by wire method dates from the earliest special effects "tricks," the quality results can be seen in modern films,

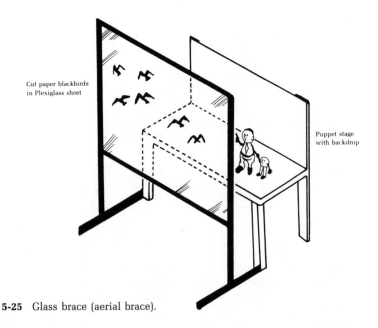

Cut paper blackbirds in Plexiglass sheet

Puppet stage with backdrop

5-25 Glass brace (aerial brace).

notably the fighter plane antics in *1941* and the rocket planes in *The Right Stuff*.

A variation of the wire aerial brace is the glass brace shown in figure 5-25. The glass brace is ideal for suspending several tiny puppets or airbrushed clouds in the shot. The glass sheet is also suitable for superimposing cutout figures of drawn characters in a realistic three-dimensional setting.

Surface Gauge

The *surface gauge*, also called a *center finder* or *head gauge*, is an industrial machinist's tool adapted to animation purposes. The standard device is shown in figure 5-26.

The surface gauge provides the animator with a fixed reference position through the tip of the long pointer arm. The arm is moved to make contact with the puppet. The puppet is then advanced a fraction of an inch from its original position. The surface gauge tip is then moved to the new reference position. For the actual camera exposure, the surface gauge arm is pivoted out of the shot frame. After the exposure is made, the pointer arm is pivoted back to the puppet to provide the reference point for the next change of the puppet's pose.

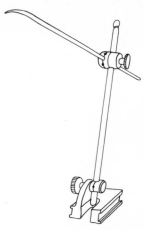

5-26 Surface gauge.

The pivoting action of the surface gauge is illustrated in figure 5-27 with a dinosaur puppet for the contact point. In this shot setup only the puppet's head would be animated with the gauge. Several gauges are needed if several parts of the model, such as arms and tail, are all in motion during the shot.

Figure 5-28 illustrates a professional gauge and puppet setup. The animator is Rick Catizone at work on a television film commerical in his Anivision Ltd. studio in Pittsburgh.

5-27 Surface gauge action.

5-28 A professional gauge and puppet setup. (Courtesy of Rick Catizone/Anivision Ltd.)

Replacement Part Animation

Even a simple puppet presents the animator with a challenge of keeping track of several adjustments to the puppet's head and limbs. The problems of movement escalate when the puppet's facial expressions and mouth opening must previsely match a previously recorded vocal soundtrack. In order to save production time required for the time-consuming and exacting effort of synchronization or *lip-sync* work in animation, animators often resort to an alternative method of puppet animation. Instead of posing the individual puppet features, the animator uses a set of previously prepared rigid pieces that duplicate the frame-by-frame movement adjustments. These individual pieces are called *replacement parts* for the puppet. Unlike the soft flexible puppet body, the replacement parts are solid separate pieces made from wood, wax, or plastic.

Replacement part animation is so called because one piece replaces another in the animated series. Replacements can be simply a mouth or eye piece, a whole head, or an entire body section. Replacement animation is often used with hands because of the fine detail it makes possible in each separate hand position. Small replacement parts can be attached to the blank area of a puppet face or body by small tabs inserted into slots cut into the latex body material. If larger body sections are to be replaced, then large pegs that fit more deeply into the latex body slots are used. The armatured puppet can be designed to accommodate the slot positions when the armature is made. In this way the armature will not interfere with insertion of the replacement parts.

The replacement parts are positioned in the same way as regular armature puppets, by use of a surface gauge to locate frame-by-frame reference points between camera exposures. If the replacement parts involve leg and foot positions, the use of the ordinary tiedowns will keep the puppet in position and the surface gauge will mark the upper torso of the puppet as leg replacements are changed between camera exposures.

Figure 5-29 shows a series of whole-face replacements for a character puppet. The mouth is formed into a different speaking position in each piece.

Partial mouth replacement pieces are shown in figure 5-30. The lower jaw of the froglike character puppet is detachable, the piece held in place by a pair of short pegs. Each syllable of a soundtrack is matched by a particular replacement piece. At the proper timing interval of frames of the narrative or dialogue track, an appropriate (and coded) replacement jaw piece is inserted into the puppet's mouth area and then photographed for the required number of frames of dialogue.

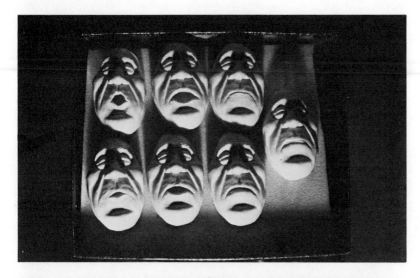

5-29 Whole-face replacements for a character puppet. (Courtesy of Rick Catizone/Anivision Ltd.)

5-30 Partial mouth replacements. (Courtesy of Rick Catizone/Anivision Ltd.)

Bar Sheets

To make the timing of the jaw replacement mouth pieces match the recorded dialogue of a soundtrack, a layout planning sheet is frequently used. This is called a *bar sheet*. It has a separate line for all the required components of the animation scene, such as camera frames, action, sound effects, music, and dialogue. A portion of a bar sheet is shown in figure 5-31. Each line of the labeled parts of the shot is normally extended, with several pages required for every speaking scene. The bar sheet allows each syllable of the recorded and timed dialogue to be marked and the required number of frames indicated. The animator, using a bar sheet, can then select the correct replacement piece for the syllable sound and photograph the piece for the correct number of frames to cover the spoken sound.

5-31 Bar sheet.

CAMERA MOVEMENT

Stop-motion cinematography utilizes many of the same camera pan, tilt, and dolly moves in live action footage. Such moves, however, are performed at a single-frame interval in exact synchronization with the puppet being photographed. The camera body position is changed in small intervals of one-eighth to one-quarter inches (2.5 to 6mm) over the course of the camera move. A geared camera support head with degree markings is best for the smooth swing and pivot actions produced by a narrow spacing between separate frame exposures. For lateral shifts of the camera, called a *truck* or *tracking shot*, the entire camera support is slid along a pair of securely anchored rails. A simple *animation dolly* is shown in figure 5-32. A pair of reinforced metal tubes attached to the surface of this wooden platform permits a stable and smooth slide for the camera support unit. The tripod head, fastened securely to the dolly board, is marked in degrees for the measurable pan action of the lightweight animation camera, such as a modified Bolex H16. The track rails themselves are evenly marked with fractions of an inch or a centimeter scale to make possible a precise record of the camera platform shift along the track between exposures. Any puppet centered in the camera viewfinder is kept centered in the tracking shot by inching the dolly platform along the track rails at a proper spacing for the puppet's speed of walk or run.

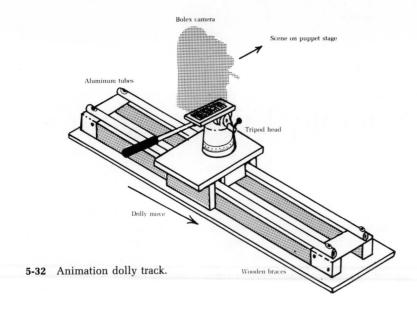

5-32 Animation dolly track.

FORCED PERSPECTIVE SETS

Forced perspective refers to a purposeful distortion of the set as viewed from an off-camera position. To the observer the set pieces seem oddly sized, with large pieces in the foreground and tiny pieces in a close background. However, when viewed from the camera's field of view, there appears to be an enormous depth between the various foreground and background pieces on the set. Figure 5-33 illustrates a representative forced perspective miniature set. Although the distance from the foreground and the background is only a few inches, the camera view of the distorted size relationship is just the reverse: the illusion of great distance.

Forced perspective sets are used to expand the scale of a miniature scene or model. The technique is often applied to sets with city backgrounds, mountainous landscapes, and forests. The main advantage of a forced perspective setup is that the camera lens' depth of field is tremendously exaggerated to create the appearance of a super-deep focus even though the model is being photographed close up. This distortion is undetected on screen and adds greater visual realism to the shot.

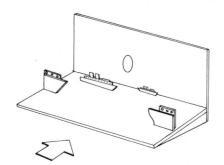

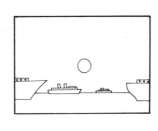

5-33 Forced perspective.

6 Special Effects Mattes

A *matte* is a mask that blocks or replaces a selected portion of a shot or film frame during photography. Matte work is a fundamental technique for many special visual effects that require two or more separate images to be blended or *composited* into a single composition. In the course of shooting a film, various types may be used in the production camera on location or later in the optical lab's process camera. Although the term "matte" often describes a number of related optical methods, there are only two basic kinds:

1. *In-front-of-the-lens mattes.* This type of matte is an opaque card, painting, or construction that is placed in front of the camera and photographed. This exposure is made either at the time of the original photography of a scene on the same film negative or later on a duplicate negative in the optical lab. (Some cameras permit a small mask to be placed *behind* the lens, just in front of the film emulsion. A metal shim is inserted into a slot in the camera aperture plate. The small mask is called a *focal plane matte* or *aperture matte* and works in the same way an in-front-of-the-lens matte does to mask selectively a portion of the emulsion from exposure. The aperture matte allows the picture frame to be *hard-matted* in various aspect ratios.)
2. *Optical printing film mattes.* This type of matte is made by photographic means on perforated film for use exclusively in the optical printer and process camera. The film matte enables actors and scenery to be separately photographed and later composited in the lab onto a single length of film.

IN-FRONT-OF-THE-LENS MATTES

Painted Glass Mattes

One of the oldest in-front-of-the-lens mattes is the *painted glass matte* or *glass shot*. It consists merely of a detailed painting done on a large sheet of plate glass positioned vertically at a given distance in front of the camera. The painted area replaces or embellishes any part of the set seen through the glass from the camera view.

A simple glass shot of a painted ship superimposed upon a more distant lake is seen in figure 6-1.

The large glass sheet is positioned upright in front of the camera

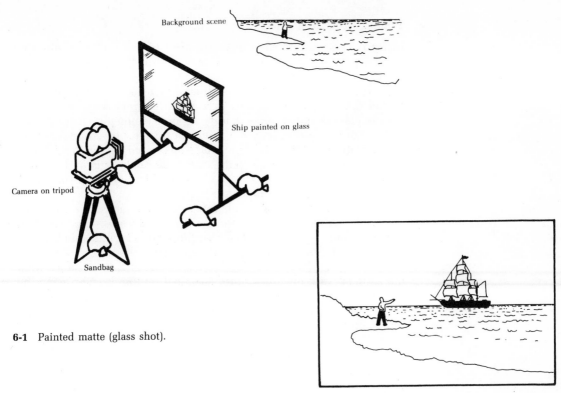

Background scene

Ship painted on glass

Camera on tripod

Sandbag

6-1 Painted matte (glass shot).

Finished composite

at a sufficient distance to keep focused both the glass painting and the live action subject beyond the glass. If the painting is done on location prior to photography, the artist must work quickly so as to anticipate the proper angle of light in the later shooting. The script may require that the artist paint a castle, a ship, a mountain range, or any number of scenery additions to the scene.

A replacement painting on glass extends parts of an unfinished set structure to complete a scene. Only a small portion of the set needs to be physically constructed since the artist can paint in the overall remainder. The artist constantly checks the progress of the painting by looking through the camera viewfinder. From the lens view the artwork can be positioned and blended to match any existing background scenery.

After the glass painting is completed, the scene composite is photographed. Both painting and real landscape scenery are optically combined in a single camera negative pass. Actors can be included in the shot, but they must be fully rehearsed to avoid crossing behind the painting matte area in the course of a dramatic action move across the lens field of view. This would result in the actor suddenly vanishing from the shot.

Glass paintings can also be used to provide foreground elements to an existing scene, such as adding a period 1890s locomotive to an empty train station set.

IN-FRONT-OF-THE-LENS MATTES   **103**

Foreground Miniature

Instead of painting on glass, an actual miniature of a set scene element can be positioned into the landscape within the camera's field of view.

A *foreground miniature* is a three-dimensional, highly detailed model that masks or replaces part of the original scene framed by the camera viewfinder. As with a glass shot, the miniature is positioned in front of the camera lens at a sufficient distance to assure that both the miniature and the live action and background will be in relatively sharp focus. A short focal length or wide angle lens and a small shooting aperture are usually the best combination for a successful foreground miniature composite shot.

Figure 6-2 illustrates a simple foreground miniature of a warlord's castle fortress positioned to occupy the horizon position. Note that the miniature also includes its own hilltop mound foundation blended into the shot. Such blending avoids an abrupt change in the scenery and makes the shot more convincing. Actors at a far distance from the camera walk toward a point specified by the director using the camera view as a reference for the castle's relative background position. In the finished composite shot, the actors appear to be heading toward the distant castle.

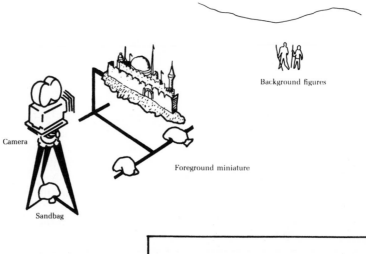

Background figures

Camera

Foreground miniature

Sandbag

Finished composite

6-2 Foreground miniature matte.

SCHÜFFTAN MIRROR

The *Schüfftan mirror* composite uses an angled mirror to put an actor into a painting or miniature placed opposite the camera lens. The mirror has the reflective coating on the upper surface of the glass instead of the more usual below-the-glass coating of household mirrors. Called a first surface mirror, the images reflected in the mirror are free of the faint double images that can be seen in ordinary mirrors, which are caused by light reflecting from both the upper (first) and lower (second) planes of the glass thickness. First surface mirrors are useful in many optical applications that require sharp-edge reflections. The first surface mirror is especially important to the Schüfftan shot because both the reflected image and miniature background must be seamless and free of tell-tale double images. Developed in the 1930s by Eugen Schüfftan, the technique has largely been superseded by modern optical printing methods. However, for low-budget and student film effects, the mirror process shot can produce composites of exceptionally high quality at a low cost.

Figures 6-3 and 6-4 illustrate the standard arrangement of the process. The setup shown is only approximate because the mirror framing of the miniature and actor is unique to any given production.

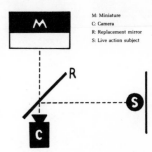

M: Miniature
C: Camera
R: Replacement mirror
S: Live action subject

6-3 Top view of Schüfftan matte.

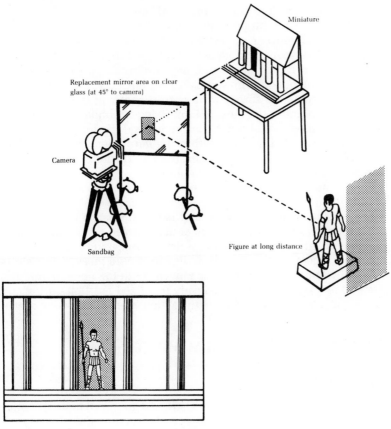

Miniature

Replacement mirror area on clear glass (at 45° to camera)

Camera

Sandbag

Figure at long distance

Finished composite

6-4 Standard Schüfftan matte arrangement.

A setup requires the camera, mirror, and background miniature to be securely anchored in position. The actor is likewise restricted to the area that will be composited into the miniature. Tape or chalk marks on the floor provide the stage area for the actor's movements during the shot.

Once the setup is arranged, the mirror is specially prepared for the shot. This is done by using a razor blade to carefully scrape the soft reflective coating from the glass surface. All coating except the area that reflects the live action actor and set pieces is removed. In this manner the mirror is transformed into a reflective stationary matte to superimpose the actor into the miniature seen in the now-cleared glass.

A reflex viewfinder on the camera helps the person scraping the glass to monitor the proper boundary of the matte as the mirror coating is scraped off.

Although using the Schüfftan mirror is time-consuming, the result is a perfectly matched mirror matte that fits into the appropriate area of the miniature in front of the camera.

Nodal Camera Mount

On-location glass shots and foreground miniatures are filmed with a fixed position or with the camera placed on a locked-down tripod. If any pan or tilt movements are required, the camera must be mounted on a special support head called a *nodal mount*.

In a standard camera pan head, the axes of the camera movement swing the camera body. In a nodal head, however, the pan and tilt axes of movement go through the optical center of the lens, which is the *nodal* point of the lens. All multielement photographic lenses have two or more nodal points, but in general the front nodal point of a camera lens is the point within the lens where the image light rays first converge. This nodal point is approximately where the lens axes pass through the aperture diaphragm.

The normal pan head is shown in figure 6-5 and the nodal pan head in figure 6-6.

The advantage of the nodal mount is that the camera can be tilted and panned without any apparent shifts between a close foreground painting or miniature and a more distant background landscape. If a regular camera pan head is used, the foreground piece visibly shifts out of alignment as the camera is moved. With the nodal mount the foreground piece remains rock-steady in a fixed position during any pan or tilt camera move to follow the action in the background scene.

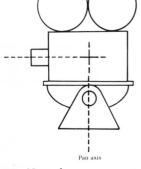

6-5 Normal camera mount.

Pan axis

6-6 Pan nodal mount.

Pan axis

OPTICAL PRINTING FILM MATTES

Process Matte Painting

The glass shot matte painting is also used in a strikingly different way for compositing painted images to live action after the original live action footage has been shot. This composite technique, simply called a *matte shot*, is performed in an effects studio or optical printing department using a process camera to photograph the painting.

6-7 and **6-8** Bipack magazine on Acme process camera (magazine cover removed to display film loaded on cores in upper and lower chambers). (6-7: Courtesy of Fries Engineering, Inc. 6-8: Courtesy of Photo-Sonics, Inc.)

The process camera used to photograph the matte painting on its easel frame uses the double-chambered bipack magazine. The magazine contains two separate film strips: one chamber pair for color-negative raw emulsion film stock, the lower chamber for a positive print struck or printed from the original live action color negative. Figures 6-7 and 6-8 show a rear view of the 35mm process camera with a bipack magazine, takeup motors, film counters, animation single frame motor, and video tap. Figure 6-9 is a simplified view of how the two separate films in the bipack magazine travel together through the camera gate. At the gate aperture the two films are pressed tightly together to form an emulsion-to-emulsion contact print of the live action footage onto the duplicating negative film stock.

The basic bipack matte shot is illustrated in figures 6-10 and 6-11, representing two separate passes of the duplicate negative film stock through the camera gate.

The live action positive is footage specially shot for use with a matte painting. A pin-registered camera is used to shoot the live action negative (which is used to print a positive). A pin-registered camera is essential to provide the steadiest image since any slippage in the live action frames would misregister with the matte areas of the painting. Misregistration produces hairline overlap defects known as *matte lines* in the final composite image. In addition the original live action footage must be composed by the cinematographer so that the activity of the actors is limited to the clear area of the painted

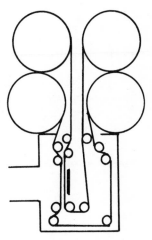

6-9 Bipack film through the gate of a process camera.

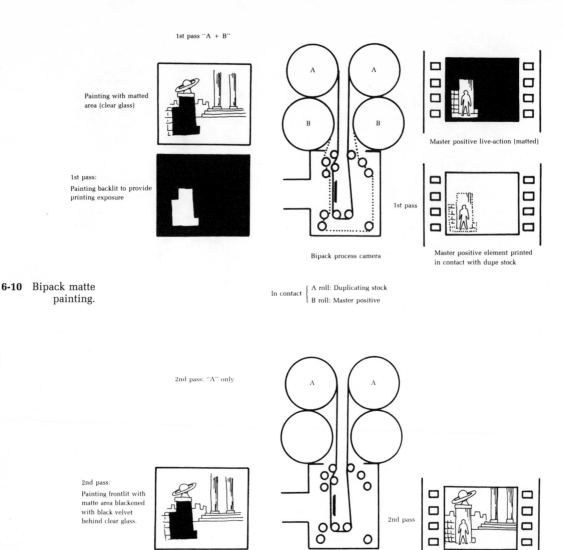

1st pass "A + B"

Painting with matted area (clear glass)

1st pass:
Painting backlit to provide printing exposure

A A

B B

Master positive live-action (matted)

1st pass

Master positive element printed in contact with dupe stock

6-10 Bipack matte painting.

In contact { A roll: Duplicating stock
B roll: Master positive }

Bipack process camera

2nd pass: "A" only

2nd pass:
Painting frontlit with matte area blackened with black velvet behind clear glass.

A A

2nd pass

Painting and master positive live-action composited on dupe stock

6-11 Bipack matte painting.

A roll: Duplicating raw stock

(A roll of clear dummy film is run in the B chamber of the magazine to keep the A roll at the previous focal plane in the camera gate).

matte. There can be no zooms or changes in tracking or focus in the live action footage intended for use as a plate.

The live action *master positive* used in the process camera bipack exposure is a fine grain/low contrast print. This minimizes any contrast and grain buildup in the copy that will be made from it. The positive is also timed, that is, uniformly exposed throughout to avoid any sudden bright or dark frames.

To prepare the matte painting, a single frame is clipped from a short length of developed negative or master positive. The frame clip, containing the live action and any surrounding set scenery, is put into the pin-registered aperture of the process camera. A lamp-equipped *rotoscope* device attached to the process camera projects the image of the frame to a large easel in front of the camera. Since the projected image is to be traced by hand, the glass sheet has been previously sprayed with a thin layer of paint. A flat white, gray, or black enamel will provide enough rough texture or tooth to accept both soft pencil and paints. The size of the glass sheet varies, but is generally in the area of 2 × 4 feet (.6m × 1.2m). Camera, easel, and glass sheet are anchored to prevent any slight movements once the matte painting procedure is started.

The matte artist sketches the outline of the enlarged live action projection. The live action area itself occupies only a portion of the whole glass. The artist fills out the rest of the glass by sketching directional guide lines that extend from any structural scenery in the live action plate, such as buildings, trees, roads, and columns. The artist uses these guide lines to create the proper continuity and perspective for the later painting. In this way the viewer will see painted areas matched perfectly to the live action area.

The painting is rendered in a range of low-contrast colors using opaque watercolor, acrylics, or oil paints. When the painting is finished the original area of the live action is carefully scraped down to clear glass. This becomes a "window" in the exact shape of the live action matte.

In the first camera run, illustrated in figure 6-10, the painting surface is not illuminated. Instead, a white card or frosted glass light box is placed behind the clear glass area. This card or light source acts as a contact printing light for the contact exposure of the master positive to the duplicate negative in the camera gate aperture. When the pass is completed the duplicate negative film stock will have only the required live action scene. The negative is rewound and readied for the second pass through the camera gate.

In the second pass the matte painting is lighted from the front, camera-side of the glass. This gives a full exposure for the painted details the artist has created. The white card or light source behind the matte window is replaced with a piece of jet-black velvet. The velvet is nonreflective and will prevent any further exposure in the live action matte area during a second pass.

After the second pass is complete, using only the color duplicate negative and a clear leader dummy film to maintain the camera focus on the two thicknesses of film, the duplicate negative will contain an exposure of both live action area and painting. The second pass exposures are shown in figure 6-11.

GLASS OVERLAYS

In some cases the realism of the matte painting can be enhanced by the addition of glass overlay sheets on the painting during the second camera pass of the negative. The overlay functions somewhat like an animation cel to superimpose moving elements over the painted areas of the matte shot. Examples of this kind of animated single-frame effects include airbrushed clouds, tiny automobiles moving on a roadway, or figures patrolling a fortress wall. In these examples the cityscape seen through the clouds, the roadway, and the fortress wall are all part of the matte painting. The moving elements are

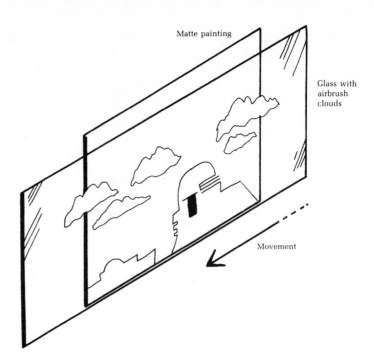

6-12 Moving elements animated over matte painting during photography.

separate paintings animated during the second pass. The overlay technique is shown in figure 6-12, clouds drifting around a futuristic penthouse on a tall building. The live action matte area is the dark rectangular window in the middle of the building.

MATTE LIGHTING EFFECTS

The matte painting is not restricted to full daylight shots. Night shots can be quite realistic if tiny lamps or spotlights are placed behind the glass to simulate natural or manmade lighting in the scene. The paint is selectively scraped to clear glass so that any pattern of lighting effects becomes possible. If a high intensity beam is directed toward the camera lens, a realistic camera lens flare can also be created. The use of a diffusion filter on the camera lens will further enhance the natural atmospheric quality of the painted scene's lighting.

All lighting effects are done as a separate pass of the duplicate negative to assure that important details of the painting will not be washed out by an overexposure caused by the lighting units.

Several representative lighting effects are illustrated in figure 6-13, along with a simple mounting arrangement for the lighting sources.

The Traveling Matte

A *traveling matte* moves or travels to match a subject's movements across the picture frame area. The traveling matte permits the subject to be superimposed onto a separately photographed background scene. Unlike the stationary matte, which limits the subject's action to only a portion of the background scene, the traveling matte allows unlimited subject freedom of movement. Such freedom is achieved by using

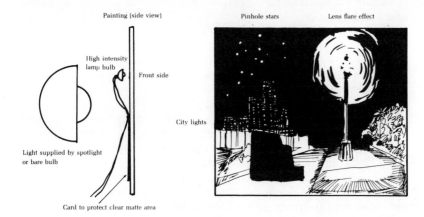

Painting (side view)

Pinhole stars

Lens flare effect

High intensity
lamp bulb

Front side

City lights

Light supplied by spotlight
or bare bulb

Card to protect clear matte area

6-13 Adding light elements by back lighting (exposed in separate pass in bipack camera).

the subject's photographic image to create a series of opaque masks for making a matching "hole" in the background scene. The hole conforms to the exact silhouette of the subject. The image of the subject is later used to fill the hole in the background scene by use of the optical printer.

THE BLUE SCREEN METHOD

The most popular form of traveling matte photography is known as the *blue screen* method. In most special effects films this method is used to composite live action or miniature footage into a separately photographed background scene. Both the live action elements or miniatures and background scenery can be in motion, an advantage over stationary mattes or various other process methods. The complete method involves several steps in studio cinematography and optical lab printing. Blue screen work uses high-contrast film mattes copied from live action or miniatures footage shot in a special studio setup.

The typical blue screen arrangement calls for an actor, miniature, or other subject to be photographed in front of a large backing screen of an intense blue color. The backing may be either a painted front-lighted screen or translucent dyed sheeting lighted from behind to produce a uniform intensity over the entire screen area. A common translucent blue screen is the Stewart T-Matte Blue Screen used in several major studios and effects facilities. A painted screen is most often used when the subject's shadow is to fall on elements of the background scene. A translucent screen produces a shadowless surround of the subject, a feature ideal for shooting flying miniatures, spacecraft, and live action subjects where a ground shadow is not essential.

The foreground subject—the subject in front of the blue screen—is lighted normally with white light. In blue screen work the important lighting factor is that both the blue screen intensity and color must produce an exposure density on the blue layer of the color negative

6-14 Blue screen traveling matte process. (1) Actor shot in front of blue screen in studio.

6-15 (2) High contrast negative of #1 with clear (blue) screen area and unwanted images of light stands and equipment.

6-16 (3) High contrast positive of #2.

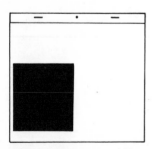

6-17 (4) Rotoscope of blue screen area only. Drawn on registered field cel and shot on animation camera on high contrast positive stock.

film greater than the white highlight of the live action foreground. Normally Eastman Color Negative 5247 or a similar color negative film stock is used.

After the live action subject is photographed, a pair of opaque black and white mattes is prepared in the optical lab from the processed color negative. These mattes, a matte and countermatte also called *male* and *female cover mattes*, are produced through a technique called *color separation*.

Color separation requires the color negative footage to be copied on *panchromatic* (equally sensitive to all colors) black-and-white positive film. Three copies are made, each positive printed through either a magenta, cyan, or yellow filter. These *separation positives* are a black and white record of the original scene's three primary colors—green, red, and blue. All natural colors are made up of these primary colors. The original scene's colors can be re-created by printing the separation positives in succession through the appropriate filter or filtered printing light.

Since the blue screen color is nearly equal to the maximum density of the color negative's blue emulsion layer, the screen area appears almost perfectly clear on the blue separation positive. The subject has a normal tonal range. However, the red separation positive renders the blue screen area as a black area surrounding the subject.

The red separation positive is then printed on a black-and-white *negative film stock*. This results in a film strip with a subject in negative tones surrounded by a clear blue screen area.

The blue separation positive and red separation negative are printed in bipack contact onto a high-contrast black and white film stock. The combined clear blue screen areas of the two films print as black. The combined negative and positive subject areas of the two films overlay to form a single image of sufficient density to prevent an exposure or print-through on the copy. This leaves a clear unexposed area on the processed high-contrast film conforming to the silhouette of the subject. The result is a film mask or *traveling matte*. A second matte, the countermatte, is contact-printed from this. Under ideal conditions these two mattes will exactly superimpose to produce a black frame. Slightly misregistered male and female mattes caused by imperfect exposures, overdevelopment (which alters the matte size as emulsion density changes), and disparate contrast produce imperfections that can be seen in the final composite as dark fringe or outlines on the matted-in subject.

The two mattes form a matte/countermatte combination to mask the original live action subject in precise registration with the subject's movements across the frame. In separate printing passes in the optical printer camera, the mattes permit the subject to be superimposed over a background scene on a single internegative. The basic procedure is as follows: the background footage and opaque subject matte (male) are printed in bipack contact exposure on an internegative film. The result is an unexposed area on the background exposure exactly matched to the shape of the subject. The internegative is rewound and readied for a second pass. This time the internegative is bipacked with the live action footage and the second matte (female). The second matte covers everything except the unexposed subject area on the internegative. In the second camera pass this unexposed area is filled in by the subject footage to produce a completely exposed composite image. When the background and subject footage are printed as separate color separation passes, the color values of the composite can be adjusted by filters for a balanced color rendition of both images.

Additional matte and countermatte pairs are commonly used for blue screen composite work. These mattes are called *supplementary* or *rotoscope holdout mattes*. Also known as "garbage mattes," they serve to mask unwanted studio equipment and lighting stands, reflections, and debris that may have been photographed with the blue screen element and transferred to the high-contrast mattes. The garbage mattes are hand-drawn tracings of the original footage frames, precisely photographed on an animation stand to register with the principal traveling mattes.

A simple blue screen setup and the various photographic and printing steps are illustrated in figures 6-14 through 6-24. This special effects shot is of an Ice Age hunter being attacked by a huge wooly mammoth on a frozen plain. Both man and beast (a stop-action puppet) are photographed separately and composited with blue screen traveling

6-18 (5) Processed rotoscope holdout "garbage matte" to remove light stands and debris from original blue screen shot.

6-19 (6) #2 and #5 run in bipack to make holdout matte on negative high-contrast film stock.

6-20 (7) Countermatte (burn-in matte) on high-contrast positive film stock.

6-21 (8) Puppet background scene filmed.

6-22 (9) Background and puppet plate.

6-23 (10) Holdout matte (#6) run in bipack with background shot (#8).

6-24 (11) Actor added by running #1 and #7 (burn-in matte) in bipack.

matte. The mammoth shot is a standard dimensional animation setup filmed as a background plate. The blue screen is used only for the single figure of the hunter. If the scene had several hunters, each would be separately blue-screened for compositing to the background plate scene.

REVERSE BLUE SCREEN

A variation of blue screen technique is the *reverse blue screen* method developed by John Dykstra's Apogee, Inc., effects facility. In this system the traveling matte results from a number of computer-controlled camera matte passes over a specially prepared miniature.

The first pass by the camera is the detail or *beauty pass* to record the naturally lighted surface features and motions of the miniature. In a second pass the miniature is illuminated by a bank of ultraviolet black lights only. The black lights cause a clear but light-reactive coating (the multiphosphor coating) painted over the miniature's body to fluoresce or glow at a sufficient level of intensity to make a negative film exposure. This negative is used as a printing master for generating all the required *holdout* and *burn-in* mattes and countermattes.

The Apogee reversal of the standard blue screen exposure method permits composites to be made without the troublesome holes in the miniature caused by reflections of the blue screen around the miniature.

The reverse blue screen process was extensively used in the film *Firefox* to produce the complex flight sequences. A single frame from *Firefox* is shown in figure 6-25, along with all the film matte steps required to produce the shot via the reverse blue screen multiphosphor coating technique.

INTERIOR BLUE SCREEN

The usual arrangement of a blue screen shot is to simply have the subject act in front of the screen. A different approach is to mount the blue screen outside a full-size mockup interior for inserting exterior miniature backgrounds beyond the windows or ports of the mockup. The mattes are generated by exactly the same method described earlier, except that instead of a silhouette of the action figure being formed, the entire window area is matted. Figure 6-26 demonstrates the blue screen arrangement and a finished composite of a planet and starfield beyond the spacecraft windows.

The Sodium Light (Yellow) Screen Method

Another traveling matte process screen method is the *sodium light* or *yellow screen* system. This system, developed by Rank Organisation and currently used by Disney Studios, uses a special camera equipped with a beam splitter prism to make two simultaneous exposures of a subject on normal color negative film stock and a black-and-white traveling matte.

In the yellow screen process, the studio foreground live action subject is lit normally, but the background screen is lit by a bank of sodium vapor lamps. This gives an intense yellow color to the screen behind the actor subject.

The camera used to photograph the screen subject uses the prism

A. Beauty pass (normal light)

B. Matte pass positive (ultraviolet light)

C. Matte pass negative

D. Background scene

E. Holdout matte

F. Bipacked background and holdout matte

G. Beauty pass negative

H. Burn-in matte

I. Color dupe negative

J. Final composite frame

6-25A–J Apogee reverse blue-screen traveling matte. (Firefox photos courtesy of Apogee, Inc.)

Finished composite with outer space
background visible in window areas

6-26 Blue screen with inte-
riors (windows or ports). Life-size mockup interior with blue screen backing open window areas

to send an image to each of two magazines set at right angles to the
prism. The prism splits the exposure beam very precisely: one image
is recorded on film normally toned and colored, the other image is
recorded on film sensitive only to the yellow screen and produces
a jet black screen with a clear subject matte area. A countermatte
can be struck from the yellow screen matte and make a matched set
for optical printing. The heart of the yellow screen system is the
special beam splitter prism that optically passes only the sodium
light wavelength portion of the light spectrum to the black-and-white
film.

Rotoscope Matte

Figure 6-27 shows one example of the standard rotoscope cel technique
applied to mattes. Such a hand-drawn matte is often used to create
raygun laser beams and rocket engine blast exhaust effects. A full
effects scene is staged on the studio set, with the proper timing
between the firing of the ray gun and any explosion impact or actor
collapse. The live action footage is rotoscoped with the animation
stand rotoscope projection unit and the registration field chart. The
required number of empty frames are projected down onto the table
and the ray beam drawn, using a straight-edge and pencil, across the
distance between the gun and the impact reference position. The
line is then transferred to cels and photographed at the identical
field setting to generate the mattes. The resulting ray could be printed
either as a hard-edged beam or a glowing soft-edged beam merely
by controlling the optical printer lens focus.

Frontlight/Backlight Traveling Matte

The frontlight/backlight traveling matte process is an economical way
to generate a holdout matte at the same time the normal tonal and
color exposure of the subject is being made. The traveling matte
method produces a filmstrip containing both the properly exposed
beauty frames and an alternating checkerboard of a high contrast
subject matte silhouette. Frontlight/backlight process photography is
best suited to miniatures and puppet stop-motion animation.

    The procedure for producing a frontlight/backlight matte is simple

116   SPECIAL EFFECTS MATTES

1) Original scene (hand with raygun)

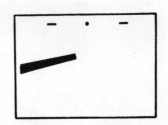

2) Rotoscope cel of ray beam

3) Holdout matte of ray beam

4) Burn-in matte (for color ray)

5) Final composite (beam from raygun)

6-27 Rotoscope matte.

6-28 In this frame from *Flash Gordon*, several rotoscope rays can be seen around the cluster of buildings. (The strange sky of the planet Mongo was created by water tank photography. See Chapter 11). (R/Greenberg Associates. *Flash Gordon*. Client: Famous Films/Universal Studios)

OPTICAL PRINTING FILM MATTES

6-29 Live action dancers are surrounded by rotoscope light outline in the film *Xanadu*. The individual dancers are traced for each frame of the sequence to permit the glowing outline to follow each movement the dancer makes. (Courtesy of R/Greenberg Associates. *Xanadu*. Client: Universal Studios)

Film background (plate)

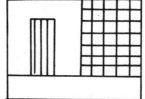

Reversal film—camera exposure

Shot "A" and "B" on alternate frames

A) Front light shot of stop-motion puppet on stage

B) Back light shot to silhouette puppet

Finished composite

6-30 Frontlight-backlight traveling matte process (part 1).

although relatively time-consuming. The subject miniature or puppet is positioned in front of a flat black screen. One frame of film is exposed at a single frame motor rate. The black backing screen is immediately replaced with a large fluorescent panel lightbox fitted with a translucent white cover plate to diffuse the light output evenly. The camera now sees only the silhouette of the puppet. A frame is exposed. Changes are then made to animate the next frame position of the puppet, a new beauty frame exposed and then the lightbox backlight exposure framed. The cycle continues for every frame of puppet action throughout the entire effects scene shot.

The entire checkerboard of beauty and matte frames is then processed and printed in an optical printer set to a *skip frame* printing rate. Every other frame is skipped and not printed on a particular length of film. The skipped frames are reserved for a second length of film. Thus the optical printer produces two separate film rolls from the original checkerboard frontlight/backlight film strip.

The two separate film strips are then used on the optical printer to generate the standard printing mattes in the manner of a blue screen composite shot procedure. Figure 6-30 shows the separate shot components of puppet and background plate scene and the finished composite. The drawing also shows a checkerboard exposure on a length of reversal film stock. Figure 6-31 shows the optical printing steps to print the two mattes and the color master for compositing with a background scene.

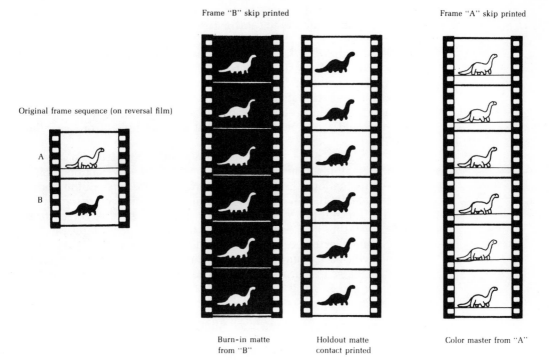

6-31 Frontlight-backlight traveling matte—skip printing.

7 Rear Screen Projection

Rear screen projection process photography, which is also known as back or rear projection process, combines live action subjects or puppets in a studio setting with a previously filmed background scene. The background scene is simply an image projected onto the back side—the rear—of a large translucent screen. The screen is located behind the actors or puppets. The camera shoots both the foreground subjects and the background screen image at the same time to form a single composite scene. Figure 7-1 shows the basic arrangement of screen and camera, with lighting and a central subject.

In recent years the rear screen process has largely been replaced by the traveling matte and front projection processes for general live action/background composite shots. These newer methods produce a brighter background image and better color rendition in the final composite than the rear screen methods. The traveling matte also offers greater flexibility in camera movement and angles when shooting live action or studio elements.

Despite the drawbacks, the rear screen process is still used for many kinds of special effects shots that involve a subject and a moving background. The most common are chase scene insert shots, automobile or aircraft window backgrounds, and studio simulations of exotic locations. The rear-projected background images provide scenery and movement in shots that are too difficult or hazardous to film live.

Rear screen projection is used frequently in composite shots of animated stop-action puppets interacting with a live action subject. In such situations the rear screen setup is the reverse of the normal arrangement: the live action footage is projected onto the screen behind the puppet foreground. This permits a smaller screen to be used than the life-sized screen normally needed for composite shots with human actors. Since the screen is scaled down to back the small puppet, the background is likewise reduced. This reduction is beneficial in that the screen projection is more concentrated, thus providing a brighter screen image for the composite shot.

The basic rear screen process shot is a simple arrangement:

1. A *camera* and *subject* to be photographed
2. A *translucent screen*
3. A *projector* behind the screen.

These essential elements are shown in figure 7-1.

120

THE SCREEN

The screen is made of a translucent gray-toned or white seamless plastic sheeting material with grommets spaced evenly along the edges. The sheet is stretched taut on an upright metal frame or wooden T support. It is held in the frame by a single cable line laced through the grommets that loop into eyelets attached to the frame along the screen perimeter. The frame must increase in size in direct and precise proportion to any increase of screen size in order to provide proper screen flatness and avoid warping.

Norman O. Dawn introduced the rear-projected composite in his 1913 film *The Drifter* with the use of a small, sand-blasted glass sheet to back his actor. Glass screens, fragile and expensive, were superseded by the flexible screen made of cellulose acetate, in the early 1930s. Developed primarily by Sidney Saunders, the large canvaslike screen measured 16 by 20 feet and was first used to provide the composite backgrounds in the 1933 film *King Kong*.

The Saunders screen was superseded by the seamless rear projection screen. Developed by Frank Vesley in the late 1930s, this screen enabled larger screen sizes to be used without visible seams, which flawed the projected image. These early screens were made of nitrocellulose and were extremely flammable. Vesley improved his screens, and in the early 1940s his company, the Flatlight Screen Company, was purchased by the Plastex Corporation. There Vesley taught a Plastex employee named Roy C. Stewart the special techniques to produce large and seamless plastic sheets for process screens. In 1946 Roy Stewart, along with Marshall and Clifford Stewart, purchased the screen department from Plastex and formed the Stewart Filmscreen Corporation. Today the company is the world's leading supplier of studio process screens for rear projection. The largest rear screen ever made by Stewart measured 46 × 84 feet (12.8m × 25.6m) for Paramount's *The Ten Commandments*. Popular selections of Stewart rear screens for special effects work are:

Filmscreen 200   A gray-toned flexible screen that soaks up ambient light to give a higher image contrast. This screen is common in TV studio set and stage productions for projected scenery.

Lumiflex 130   A low grain, neutral white screen recommended for the composite rephotography of projected images and miniature or puppets.

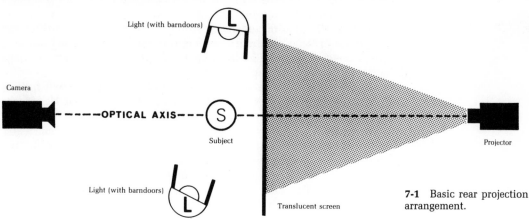

7-1   Basic rear projection arrangement.

Stewart Hi-Trans   A standard studio process screen specifically designed for large scenic backgrounds on a studio sound stage.

For low-budget and student filmmakers, an inexpensive rear projection screen material is available through Edmund Scientific Company. Marketed as *Lenscreen*, the flexible plastic sheeting is composed of microscopic light-spreading cells that act as tiny lenses to distribute the projected image evenly. Lenscreen material can be ordered in various sizes, although the roll stock is restricted to a 6-foot (1.8-m) width.

THE PROJECTOR

To project stationary backgrounds, a heavy-duty projector called a *stereopticon* is used. The projector is designed to handle color transparencies, termed *stereos*, in large-format sizes such as 4 × 5, 8 × 10, and larger. The larger the stereo, the more detailed and lifelike the background projection will appear when rephotographed by the studio camera. The projector has an increased cooling system to circulate air throughout the gate aperture. This cooling and additional glass heat absorbers keep the stereo flat in the aperture during projection by a high-intensity lamp. Any warping of the transparency by heat can create an obvious distortion on the huge rear screen image and ruin the shot. The projector lens also provides an extremely flat image across the entire area of the transparency. The projector is usually equipped with adjustment controls to permit the stereo to be shifted in the aperture so any selected portion of background can be centered on the screen.

Moving backgrounds, such as seen from a moving vehicle, are supplied by film footage expressly shot for the purpose of background projection. The footage, termed *a plate*, is projected by a high-intensity film projector equipped with a register-pin system in the frame advance assembly. The use of a register-pin keeps the film from slipping at the gate aperture between successive frames. Any slippage would be easily seen as a slight tremble or "jiggle" of the large projected background behind the stable objects and actors standing in front of the rear screen. For this reason, ordinary projectors without registration systems are unsuitable for large background projections. In addition, standard 16mm projectors do not produce lamp light that is powerful enough for a uniformly bright image across the screen if used for large background projection. Bigger format projectors, usually running 35mm or 65mm film, are more suitable. These projectors offer the advantage of large film frames with greater image detail. The projectors are also equipped with high-intensity lamps for a bright screen image suitable for rephotography by the studio camera.

Figure 7-2 is a large studio background projector. Shown here is a Mitchell 35mm projector with a McCauley (Peerless) HC-15 arc lamp.

In addition, the shutter of a motion picture projector is electrically interlocked to the shutter action of the camera. This permits the two shutters to synchronize so both will be open at the same time. An out-of-sync shutter on either the camera or the projector produces an intermittently dark or no-image screen and gives the projected background scene an obvious flicker.

7-2 A studio background projector. (Courtesy of Mitchell Camera Corporation)

The projector light source is designed to provide a high-intensity beam uniformly across the screen. The light source output must also match the color temperature of the lighting used to illuminate the foreground set in front of the screen. The standard projector light sources in professional films are carbon arc units, which balance with studio lighting.

Any visible color shift in the background plate scene can be compensated for by glass-mounted color-correction (CC) filters inserted into the beam. Filtration of the projected background is preferred over any post-production attempt at lab correction of false colors. Because the background is shot in the same frame as the foreground, any lab color corrections are intended for the overall color imbalances of the shot rather than for separate foreground and background imbalances.

The need for an evenly bright image over the camera's field of view is complicated by the spread of the projected beam. Both camera and projector are on the same optical axis. This arrangement causes the projected image to be brighter in the center of the screen with a gradual darkening toward the edges. The brighter center is called the hot spot of the projection.

The light falloff that creates the hot spot effect can be reduced with a long focal length lens on the projector. However, the use of a longer lens demands extra-long studio space to accommodate the increased distance required between projector and screen to fill the screen with a full background image. Increased distance requires in turn a more powerful projection light source.

THE BACKGROUND PLATE

The background plate is filmed prior to studio use. The plate cinematographer plans the background shot with the final composite shot fully in mind. Among factors to be considered are the shot's elevation or angle of camera, the perspective, and the lighting directions needed to match the later foreground studio subject.

The choice of lens for the background camera is important since both the focal length and the shooting aperture determine the depth of field and composition of the shot elements. Although a single camera angle may be suitable for a single angle composite shot, the single background may not provide enough variety for the subject if several composite shots are filmed at different angles. The cinematographer can give coverage of any anticipated camera angle by shooting the background footage at various matching angles. These are generally shots of both above and below the original shot horizon, with extra head room in both framings.

Since the background plate is usually shot on negative film stock, a positive print is used in the projector. The extra printing step, or *generation*, increases both grain and contrast of the original image.

Contrast and grain increase or build up in each subsequent generation print of the original negative. Figure 7-3 shows the generation steps in the rear projection process. At each step from the original negative the contrast and grain are more harsh and noticeable.

Because of the problem of grain and contrast buildup, the background negative is printed on a low-contrast fine-grain film stock. This choice is important to produce a quality result in the final composite. In practice the composite image is shot as a first generation foreground subject with a second generation background. The disparity can give an obviously faked look to the final composite unless every effort is made to minimize the differences in grain and contrast between the two.

One method of minimizing the optical problems of the background plate is to use the largest film stock gauge for the original plate negative. Generally 35mm plates are used. Large-budget films may use the more expensive 65mm and lateral 8-perf Vistavision for a detailed high-quality background image. Thirty-five millimeter plates are shot at full aperture instead of the smaller Academy aperture frame. The Academy aperture is a metal frame mask that is inserted into the camera gate's original aperture (or *full* aperture). The mask covers the portion of the negative that will later be occupied by the sound track strip in the finished print. The resulting picture area is an industry-wide standard for theatrical films established by the Academy of Motion Picture Arts and Sciences. However, since no sound track is needed on a background plate, the Academy mask is removed from the camera aperture to give an extra bit of negative for the picture exposure. This in turn provides a slightly larger plate frame, with increased image detail and reduced visual grain defects.

Another inherent problem in rear-projected backgrounds is the apparent grain or visual texture of a translucent screen material. When an image is projected onto the back side of the screen the diffusion effect of the plastic degrades the image a bit. On large screens the texture problem is less obvious except when the studio

1) Original background plate negative

2) Positive projection plate from negative

Rear projection screen image

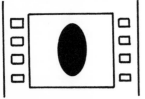
3) Camera negative

4) Camera projection positive

7-3 Generation.

camera shoots a medium or close shot of an actor standing near the screen surface. The usual remedy is to move the actor a bit further from the screen and shoot the scene with the screen slightly out of focus. The latter can be done either by adjusting the lens focus distance to the subject or by changing the shooting lens focal length or shooting aperture to reduce the depth of field focus. A more telephoto lens focal length provides a shallower depth of field to reduce the screen focus. Changing the lens shooting aperture to a wider setting to decrease the depth of field, however, must be compensated for with a matching change in the shutter exposure rate to keep the exposure level the same as in earlier camera shots, if any.

If a small rear screen is used to provide backgrounds to animation puppets, the problem of screen texture is more pronounced. In such arrangements the studio camera is quite close to both puppet and screen. Since the background projection will be matched to the small screen size, any defect or obvious texture in the screen itself will be significant during rephotography. To minimize the screen texture grain, animators sometime resort to a motion technique. The screen is physically shifted slightly between successive stop-motion frame exposures. No single point of the screen texture is in the same location for adjacent frames. Without this stationary reference, the screen is not obvious to an audience. This technique, however, does not reduce the actual grain of the projected scenery, only the screen texture.

REAR SCREEN AND PUPPET COMPOSITES

The rear screen technique is one of the basic and relatively inexpensive methods used to combine a stop-motion puppet and a human actor in the same frame.

The most obvious way is simply to place and film the puppet in front of a rear projected live action background shot. This frequently used method puts the puppet in the foreground of the scene, and all the human activity is restricted to the background plane.

Although placing the puppet in the foreground is adequate to blend the puppet and actors into a single composition in many simple composite shots, the method tends to become monotonous and artificial. To overcome this, the *stationary matte* or *static matte* process permits an exchange of the two activity planes of the screen composite: the actors are in the foreground and the puppet in the background.

The stationary matte method consists of a relatively simple arrangement of glass sheets painted with opaque black areas or mattes that selectively mask a portion of the projected background image.

Figure 7-4 illustrates a basic setup for the stationary matte. Prior to placing the puppet on the stage, a glass sheet is put between the camera and puppet stage. A matte is painted on the glass that masks an area of the projected background as seen on the rear screen from the camera position. The area to be matted is determined by the composition of the background scene. The easiest elements to utilize are any large shapes that form a backdrop to the live action actors, such as a wall, boulder, or vehicle. As with any background plate intended for process projection, the background's angle of view must coincide with that of the camera shooting the final composite image.

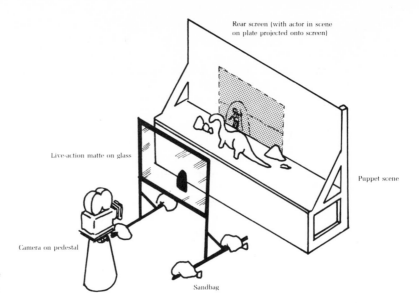

Rear screen (with actor in scene on plate projected onto screen)

Live-action matte on glass

Puppet scene

Camera on pedestal

Sandbag

7-4 Stationary matte arrangement.

STATIONARY MATTE

7-5 A. First pass: live action plate with countermatte.

7-6 B. Second pass: puppet scene with glass matte.

7-7 C. Final composite scene.

Likewise the background plate is originally shot so that any live action is composed in the foreground of the shot. This foreground activity becomes the area of the projected plate to be matted by the glass sheet's painted mattes. In figure 7-5 the projected image on the rear screen (projector not shown behind screen) contains both the live action and location scenery.

The matte is painted on the glass using the camera view of the background plate. This is to maintain a proper alignment between the boundaries of the screen image and the matte as seen from the camera. A tracing of the matte area on the glass made with a wax pencil permits the matte outline to be checked easily and any corrections made prior to painting. Once painted the matte cannot be moved without ruining the alignment between and among the camera, matte, and screen. This critical relationship means that the entire setup must be securely anchored for the duration of the matte shooting. The stationary matte process shot requires two separate passes of the camera negative: one pass for the live action image alone, and one for the puppet and projected scenery.

The matte shown on the glass sheet in figure 7-5 is only one of two mattes required for the composite. A second matte exactly complementary to it, the countermatte, is used to isolate only the live action elements in the first camera pass. This countermatte is a tracing of the initial matte and painted in reverse to it, i.e., the matte area is clear and the entire background is masked. The countermatte glass sheet fits into grooves on the glass support frame so as to be easily aligned with the original matte. In this manner the original matte glass can be removed, leaving the countermatte in perfect registration and aligned in the camera's optical path.

The shooting procedure is shown in the figures 7-5 through 7-7. The first pass is with the countermatte in place and no puppet on the stage. Only the live action element is exposed on the film; everything else in the background plate is masked by the countermatte. The

126

second pass, figure 7-6, uses the stationary matte to prevent any exposure of the live action area. The puppet is in place on the stage, and behind the puppet the location scenery is projected by the original plate. Portions of the puppet are masked by the stationary matte. These areas will not be exposed on the live action area already on the film. The result is an optical effect of the puppet appearing behind the live action, i.e., in the background plane of the composite shot. The finished composite is shown in figure 7-7. It represents one frame of film. The camera shoots the entire scene at single-frame speed to allow the animator to advance the puppet. Both the camera and process projector are electrically interlocked to synchronize each frame exposure. The camera lens is at a small shooting aperture to give the deep depth of field needed to hold both the puppet and screen image in sharp focus.

Depth Mattes for Rear Screen

One characteristic of simple rear screen and foreground puppet arrangements is that the puppet's feet are placed at the edge of the screen. The camera is usually at stage-ground level, so the lack of depth in the puppet's movement is not so obvious at first. However, a simple variation of the stationary matte process can place the puppet visually deeper into the background scene projected on the rear screen. The glass matte and countermatte arrangements are demonstrated in figures 7-8 through 7-15.

In this variation, the stationary glass mattes selectively mask the supporting puppet stage that positions the puppet at a higher and optically deeper plane within the background scene. The foreground area is replaced in a second camera pass. When done correctly the dividing boundary of the matted screen areas is invisible on film. The puppet appears to be at a point beyond the normal foreground plane and within the background.

Combined Depth and Shape Stationary Matte

A more complex variation of the stationary matte composite uses a matte shaped to match the outline of various structures in the projected background scene. Such structures are usually buildings, walls, or natural formations. The shaped matte masks out areas of the scene behind which the puppet is animated. The matted areas are filled in later with the full details by the second camera negative pass. When the shaped matte is combined with a depth placement of the puppet stage, the puppet can seem to move behind structures deep in the scene. The basic process is shown in figures 7-16 through 7-20.

The rear screen matte techniques for composite photography have been extensively used for fantasy, science-fiction, and prehistoric dinosaur films. The most masterful examples of mattes for rear screen and puppet composite shots are found in the Dynamation films by special effects animator Ray Harryhausen. His use of the matte process creates realistic interaction between puppets and live action projected actors. The illusion of both puppet and humans in the same scene is enhanced by the seeming physical contact between the projected image actor and the stop action puppet. This is done by the frame-

7-8 (1) Rear screen projected background.

7-9 (2) Usual position of puppet at bottom edge of screen.

7-10 (3) Raised platform places puppet position at "deeper" point in background shot.

7-11 (4) Painted matte to match "foreground" area to be in front of puppet position.

7-12 (5) Matte placed in front of puppet. Film is exposed in first pass through camera. Film is rewound for second pass.

7-13 (6) Painted countermatte to mask out background previously exposed.

7-14 (7) Countermatte in position. Puppet and stage have been moved away from screen. Film is exposed in second pass.

7-15 (8) Processed film shows finished composite. Puppet appears "deeper" in shot for more realistic effect.

by-frame replacement of a thrown or thrust object, such as a spear, in the projected scene with an exact duplicate miniature supported on an aerial brace. Figures 7-21 through 7-23 demonstrate how a spear can be superimposed into the shot composite. From the camera view the spear seems physically to make contact with the animated puppet. Such aerial brace shots must be carefully story boarded to plan both the original live action photography and the puppet composite angle of view.

Since the actors are required to play against a nonexistent adversary, a reference eye target is positioned out of the camera frame during the plate photography. This target, often a simple card at the correct height of the imaginary creature, gives a handy sight line for the live action actor to focus his attention and action.

LIVE ACTION AND PUPPET STATIONARY MATTE PROCESS

7-16 (1) Projected rear screen background with live action element in "foreground."

7-17 (2) Puppet placed in front of screen at proper height for shot.

7-18 (3) First camera pass: puppet and screen shot with glass matte in front of stage.

7-19 (4) Second camera pass: foreground exposed, background masked by painted glass counter-matte. Puppet stage removed for second camera pass.

7-20 (5) Finished composite as it appears on film. In "background" is the puppet, in the "foreground" is the live action element.

LIVE ACTION/MINIATURE INTERACTION

Rear projection of actor with short spear shaft

Puppet in front of screen

7-21 A. Puppet and rear projected scene.

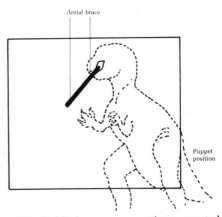

Aerial brace

Puppet position

7-22 B. Miniature spear section supported on wires and animated single-frame with puppet and plate background.

7-23 C. Finished composite: spear interacts with both puppet and man.

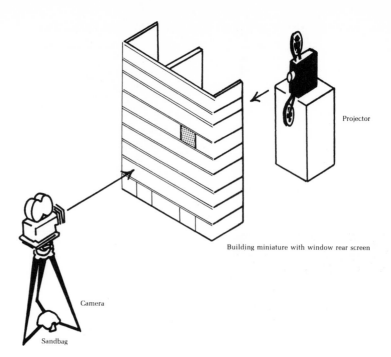

Projector

Building miniature with window rear screen

Camera

7-24 Miniature rear projection.

Sandbag

MINIATURE REAR SCREEN PROJECTION

The rear screen process is ideal for compositing previously filmed actors into a miniature building or vehicle. An example of a building window shot using a rear projected interior with moving actors is seen in figure 7-24.

The rear screen plate image in this example is supplied by footage shot of actors in a full-sized studio set. As with other plates, the shot is composed with the perspective correctly aligned to the process camera. The window of the miniature building is backed with a small piece of standard rear screen material, such as Lumiflex 130 cut to size. A projector, a high-quality 16mm, is placed behind the window. In some types of larger miniatures, such as a space station or moving vehicle, there may be enough room within the miniature to contain a small projector unit.

The use of a rear projected background adds to the realism of a miniature. Natural, nonanimated effects such as fire, smoke, or water can be used in the miniature scene and heighten the composite shot's reality.

REAR SCREEN PROJECTION

Front Screen Projection

8

Front *screen projection* process photography, which is also called *front projection,* is based on the projection of a background slide onto the front of a special reflective screen mounted behind the actor subject. Front projection systems can be devised with any conventional still, motion, or video camera. Because of the special reflective character of the screen sheeting material, front projected backgrounds are sharper and brighter than those of rear screen projections.

The front projection system has three basic components:

1. A *screen* of a highly reflective material
2. A *projector*
3. A *beam splitter* mirror

Figure 8-1 shows the arrangement of the projector and mirror before the camera on a *front projection platform rig.* Figure 8-2 illustrates the alignment of components and screen.

THE SCREEN

Front projection is made possible by the unique reflective characteristics of a particular kind of screen sheeting that produces an image bright enough for practical rephotography by a film camera. This material, a high gain sheeting called *Scotchlite,*[1] was developed in the 1940s by the Minnesota Mining and Manufacturing Company (3M) for use in highway markers and signs. A Scotchlite surface is uniformly covered with a layer of microscopic glass beads that act as tiny mirror lenses. Used as a screen, it reflects and concentrates the projected light far more efficiently than do ordinary white movie screens. This arrangement of micro-beads forms a special reflective layer called a *reflex surface,* the screen material a *reflex screen.* The major characteristic of the Scotchlite reflex surface is that nearly 100 percent of the light projected upon it is reflected back in a straight line toward the light source. The result is a screen image many hundred times brighter than that seen on standard white screens. The extremely bright screen image on the Scotchlite screen makes front projection

---

[1]Scotchlite is available in various grades. Sheeting 7610, 7615, and 7620 offer retroreflective images about 1,600 times brighter than those reflected from a white paper screen.

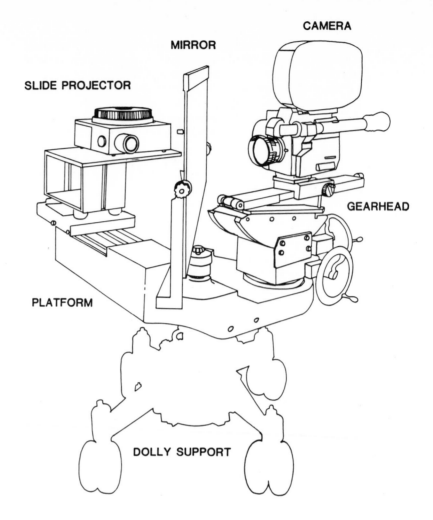

CAMERA

MIRROR

SLIDE PROJECTOR

GEARHEAD

PLATFORM

DOLLY SUPPORT

8-1 Front projection rig.

8-2 Basic front projection arrangement.

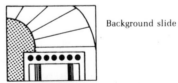

Background slide

Projector

Screen

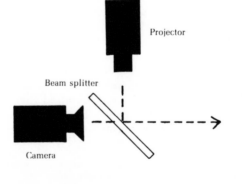

Beam splitter

Camera

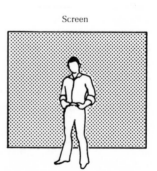

132

FRONT SCREEN PROJECTION

an improvement over the rear screen method of background scenery projection. However, the Scotchlite reflex screen is limited by certain optical characteristics. The Scotchlite image is reflected along a greatly narrowed field of view, at about 20 degrees away from the optical path of the projected beam. Beyond this narrow angle there is a dramatic fall off of screen image brightness.

The reflex surface of a single Scotchlite glass bead is illustrated in figure 8-3. The transmitted light beam is both refracted and reflected by the lens action of the microscopic bead. Millions of beads form a thin granular layer over the base sheeting material. The reflex image angle of the view for various Scotchlite sheeting grades is shown in figure 8-4. The different grades offer the cinematographer a choice in the reflected image brightness/contrast ratio.

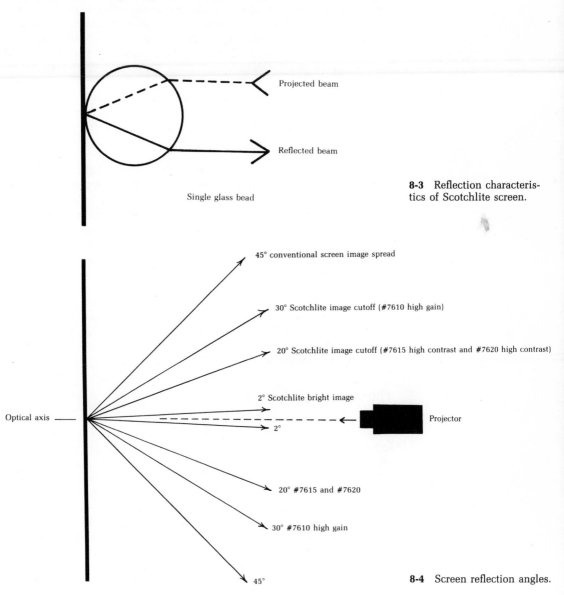

Projected beam

Reflected beam

Single glass bead

8-3 Reflection characteristics of Scotchlite screen.

45° conventional screen image spread

30° Scotchlite image cutoff (#7610 high gain)

20° Scotchlite image cutoff (#7615 high contrast and #7620 high contrast)

2° Scotchlite bright image

Optical axis

2°

Projector

20° #7615 and #7620

30° #7610 high gain

45°

8-4 Screen reflection angles.

THE PROJECTOR

A motion picture or slide projector is the device used for transmitting a background image to the reflex screen. The main requirement is that the projector produce a uniformly bright image across the entire background screen. Because the Scotchlite screen reflects the light so efficiently, the projector can be of a relatively low wattage rather than the high-intensity arc projectors needed for rear screen process photography.

An ordinary 35mm slide projector is sufficient as a systems projector if the reflex screen is small, as it would be for a miniature, and close-up shots are made only on the subject and screen composite. For large live action backgrounds, however, advanced design projectors are required. These projectors offer improved optics, precision adjustment slide and projector controls, and superefficient mechanisms for air-cooling the background slide over long periods of projection.

Some types of front projection systems use a specially modified studio camera as a projector mechanism. Equipped with a lamphouse and heat-absorbing condensers, the camera-based projector offers a precision dual pin-registered film advance movement often absent in standard motion picture projectors. One such setup is shown in figure 8-5, the Samcine front projection system. In this unit a 35mm Mitchell camera is engineered to project a high-quality background image onto the screen.

In front projection the quality of the projector's light output is an important factor in making a composite shot. Since the studio production camera is basically shooting the image formed by the projection lamp, the light source must have a *color temperature*, the Kelvin rating, that matches the filmstock emulsion in the camera. Any mismatch produces an obvious color difference between the background and forescreen subject that cannot be corrected when the film is printed. If black-and-white film stock is used in the camera, the problem of color shift is not as apparent in the composite image. Color process photography, however, demands a correct color balance among the film emulsion, background image, and forescreen subject lighting. Any projector light problems can be readily corrected by substituting the proper lamp or by inserting color-correction filter gels into the projector beam.

The Beam Splitter Mirror

The narrow reflection angle of the Scotchlite screen complicates the physical placement of the camera in relation to the projector and screen. Ideal screen brightness is achieved only when the camera is on the projector-screen optical path. However, if the camera is placed there, its body obstructs the projected lightbeam and renders composite photography impossible. The solution to this problem is to split the projected beam so that the projector itself can be moved to one side near the camera. The splitting of the light is done with a partially reflective mirror, a *beam splitter*, mounted at a 45-degree angle in front of the camera lens.

The projector, positioned at 90 degrees to the camera and screen, transmits its beam to the beam splitter that, in turn, deflects the beam

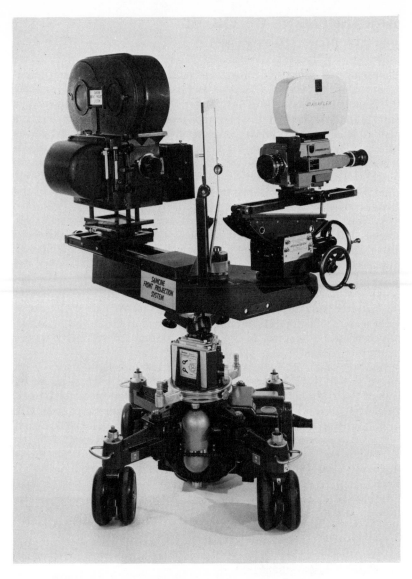

8-5 The Samcine front projection system. (Courtesy of Samuelson Group PLC, London)

toward the screen. The camera shoots through the partially transparent beam splitter to photograph the screen image. Since the camera and projector now share a common optical path, the image seen through the camera viewfinder is at maximum brightness. Some light is lost because of the filtering action of the beam splitter, but an exposure adjustment in the lens aperture or shutter can readily compensate for this minor light loss.

Beam splitters have the reflective oxide coating on the top of the glass sheet rather than underneath as with ordinary mirrors. This type of mirror is called a *first surface* mirror. It provides a high-quality reflection of the image free of the double image fringes that are common in household mirrors. The pristine qualities of first surface mirrors produce a crisp, bright background image regardless of magnification.

THE PROJECTOR   135

ARRANGEMENT OF FRONT PROJECTION SYSTEMS

The precise alignment of camera, projector, and screen is an important factor in the success of a front projection setup. When done properly the arrangement is self-matting during the actual photography. The actor's shadow, cast by the projector beam, will be hidden from the camera lens. His body will exactly mask (or matte) his shadow, which acts as a holdout matte in the background image. Since the camera is on the same optical path as the projector, the camera lens cannot detect the screen shadow directly behind the actor. Interestingly, the shadow can easily be seen from any position other than that of the camera view.

Any misalignment of the projector and camera will shift the actor's screen shadow into the shot and cause a dark fringe of matte lines along one side of the actor. Another cause of edge shadows is the nearness of the actor's body to the screen surface. If he is too far away, the actor will cast a larger shadow than his body can mask, causing a matte line shadow around the body. If the actor moves to the extreme sides of the screen, the body shadow cast will tend to slant away from the optical center of the screen. Both problems can be corrected by keeping all the subject action centered and near the Scotchlite screen.

Another factor in precise alignment is matching the background image size to the framing of the camera's lens. The actual projected size of the slide is based on the focal length of the projector lens. If the lenses on both the camera and projector match in focal length, then there will be no cutting or cropping of the slide. The background image seen in the camera viewfinder will correspond exactly to the total area being projected. On the other hand, if the projector is equipped with a shorter focal length lens than the camera, the result will be a larger image on the screen. A longer focal length lens produces a reduced image. The choice of the projector lens has an important two-fold effect:

1. the size of the screen image
2. the placement of the camera and the projector in distance from the screen and each other

LIGHTING THE SET AND SCREEN

Ordinary studio key and fill lighting units serve to illuminate the actors and set pieces in front of the Scotchlite screen. The reflected screen background is often bright enough to permit camera exposures of $f/16$ and higher, even on a medium speed film emulsion. Without supplementary lighting, the actors in front of the screen would appear (to the camera) as jet-black silhouettes. The bright background demands an equally high level of forescreen lighting. The appropriate balance of set lighting will prevent a harsh high contrast effect of the actor against the background and also will allow for full shadow detail exposures of the composite shot.

Excessive sidelighting of the screen, which is called *splash lighting,*

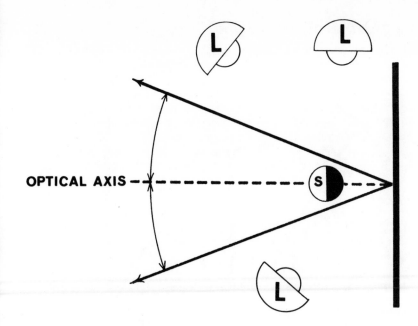

OPTICAL AXIS

8-6 Lighting arrangement (overhead view). Lights should be kept out of reflected image area to avoid reducing background color contrast.

is not as much of a problem as it is in the screen arrangement for rear projection process photography. Since the Scotchlight screen reflects light from a source lamp directly back along a narrow angle, splash light is bounced back to the lighting units, not toward the camera. The only real problem with splash lighting is that the fine granularity of the screen's beaded surface will be slightly accented.

The composition of the Scotchlite screen also plays a role in the lighting setup. Scotchlite screens are actually made up of two-foot (.6m) strips taken off a roll. The strips are adhesive-backed and applied permanently to a sturdy backing sheet. They must be placed horizontally with a generous overlap of at least one inch (25.4mm) to avoid an obvious seam between each strip. Strip application order is from bottom to top. Figure 8-7 shows the way a Scotchlite screen of strips is positioned relative to an actor.

8-7 Camera view of Scotchlite screen. The screen is made up of horizontal strips. Each strip is overlapped one or two inches to avoid a seam line. The adhesive-backed strips are applied bottom to top.

ADVANCED SYSTEMS FOR FRONT PROJECTION

The basic principle of front projection is at the heart of two new systems of process photography. Each system features a unique solution to a special effects problem that extends far beyond simple background scenery projection.

Zoptic

The *Zoptic* (zoom optic) *Front Projection System* solves one of the most vexing problems in special effects photography: How can an actor convincingly be shown to fly? The usual method is to tether the actor by thin piano wires a là Peter Pan, although this is a somewhat risky proposition for the actor dangling in the air. But the wire method limits movement and appears visually dull on film. The

8-8 Zoptic action. Figure moves from background to foreground. Plate image remains the same.

8-9 Camera fitted with Zoptic system. (Courtesy of Neilson-Hordell, Ltd.)

FRONT SCREEN PROJECTION

other route is to use the basic traveling matte process. But when this process is used with an actor positioned to "fly," it often entails frequent matte line defects and increased grain in the duplicate footage when matted to a background. The Zoptic system largely overcomes the drawbacks of both earlier methods. It also permits the actor to "fly" in an apparent depth within the background scene, while the actor's actual position relative to the camera remains unchanged.

Zoptic was invented by Zoran Perisic, who also helped earlier to create the special visual effects of Kubrick's *2001: A Space Odyssey.* Developed for *Superman, the Movie,* the Zoptic system made a spectacular debut in producing the realistic flying sequences.

Superman's magical power of flight is achieved by the special coordinated action of a pair of zoom lenses mounted on the front projection camera and projector. The lenses are linked by motorized devices that allow synchronized precision changes in the lenses' focal lengths during photography. The Zoptic-equipped front projection rig shown in figure 8-9 is a dual matte projector with Zoptic manufactured by Neilson-Hordell Company.

To appreciate the Zoptic system fully, an understanding of the Zoptic lenses is necessary. As the camera zoom lens increases in focal length, the projector zoom also increases in exactly the same increments. This causes the image on the Scotchlite screen to become smaller relative to the actor positioned in front. However, to the camera view, the effect is strikingly different. Because the camera zoom is synchronized to the projector, there is no apparent change in the background image size. The actor, framed by the camera zoom lens area alone, appears to shrink or grow in the stationary background. This illusion of movement in depth is further enhanced by the background structures that form a familiar scenery reference to the viewer.

The Zoptic action of projector, camera, and screen-image size changes is illustrated in figure 8-10. The *A* and *B* positions produce the images seen in figure 8-8 frames *A* and *B*. In a Zoptic shot, the action would be continuous throughout the zoom focal length range.

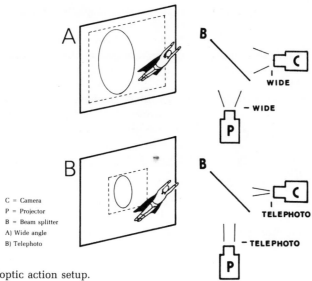

C = Camera
P = Projector
B = Beam splitter
A) Wide angle
B) Telephoto

8-10 Zoptic action setup.

Introvision

The *Introvision Front Projection System* is the ultimate in background scenery projection: an actor can move within a scene projection as if in an actual three-dimensional set construction. The Introvision-assisted actor can appear actually to move behind the set pieces as if they were existing solid objects rather than mere light images.

Invented by John Eppolito and his associates, the system was first used to produce a small amount of composite footage for the films *The Incredible Shrinking Woman* and *First Family*. Introvision made its real debut in producing the location backgrounds for the science-fiction film *Outland*. The system was used to render the gritty mining colony Con-Am 27 on the moon Io that orbits Jupiter. The colony was, in reality, only a superdetailed miniature. With seamless perfection, Introvision optically combined background shots taken of the miniature with shots of studio-bound actors. Many audiences were convinced that actual full-size sets surrounded the actors.

The Introvision process is based on a feature of the ordinary beam splitter that is usually considered a flaw: the *secondary image* on the camera side of the mirror.

Secondary images stem from the portion of the projector beam that passes through the partially reflective beam splitter and onto any convenient flat surface nearby. The light is then reflected back to the beam splitter and bounced into the camera lens. Often unfocused, the secondary image creates a soft glare that degrades the quality of the main screen image. In practice the secondary image is easily eliminated by a black curtain or a large black card called a *gobo* that is placed near the beam splitter and absorbs the projector's undeflected beam.

The Introvision concept exploits the secondary image projection to create a composite shot. The light-absorbing black gobo is replaced with a Scotchlite screen that intensifies the weak image. From a camera view, the enhanced secondary image is exactly superimposed over the main screen image. The combined situation of two identical but physically separate projections of a single slide image is the central principle in the Introvision setup.

The next step is to mask the separate slide projections to accommodate a foreground and a background plane. Only foreground elements will be contained in one projection and only background scenery in the other.

The two masks, the mattes painted on glass, are shown in the arrangement of figure 8-11. These masks work together like a static matte setup for rear screen process photography does. In this case the camera needs only a single pass to create the composite image, instead of two separate passes as in rear screen methods that use static mattes.

The dual matte arrangement serves two functions. It blocks out foreground elements of the main screen image in which the actor crosses in front during a move. It replaces the elements masked on one screen with the identical elements seen on the other screen.

From the camera view the separate screens are merged by the beam splitter into a seamless whole. All foreground elements, provided by the side screen, and all background elements, provided by the front

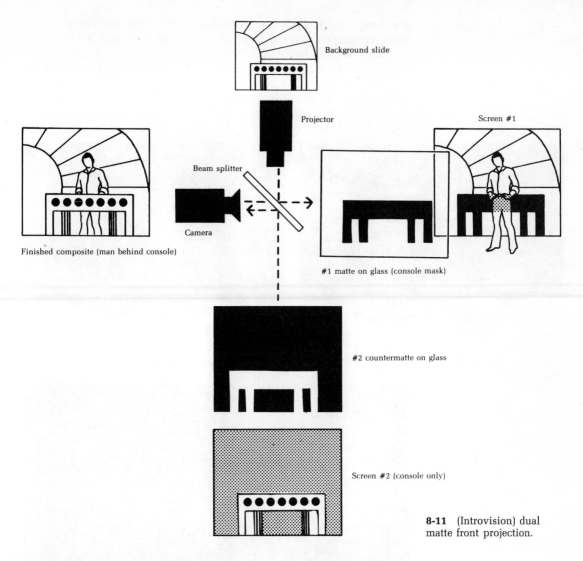

Background slide

Projector

Beam splitter

Camera

Screen #1

Finished composite (man behind console)

#1 matte on glass (console mask)

#2 countermatte on glass

Screen #2 (console only)

8-11 (Introvision) dual matte front projection.

screen, are superimposed without any matte line defects identifying the two different images. The actor, standing in front of the main front screen, is visually sandwiched between the two image planes. The result is that the foreground images appear to be actually in front of the actor since they block off the appropriate parts of his body from the camera view, and he appears to walk behind the foreground pieces as if they were real objects on the stage. The actual stage, however, is empty except for a few wooden platforms built to provide for the scene's different activity levels. The entire set consists of the huge Scotchlite screen behind the actor.

FRONT PROJECTED LIGHT EFFECTS

The basic front projection component arrangement can be modified to produce the effect of lighting in a miniature. The screen of Scotchlite sheeting is cut to form small windows, ports, running lights, or any required shape for a lighting effect. Figures 8-12 and 8-13 show a pair of Scotchlite headlights both before and after the projector light is switched on. Figure 8-14 is a miniature spacecraft with small chips of Scotchlite applied to the sides to simulate port windows. Imaginative applications of Scotchlite include projecting film scenes and special animated films onto the miniature set pieces.

8-12 Scotchlite headlights before projector light is turned on.

8-13 Headlights after light is turned on.

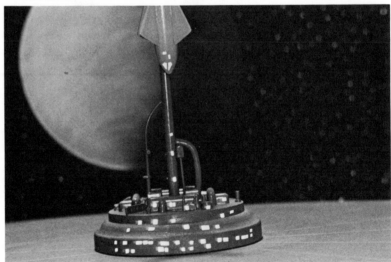

8-14 Miniature spacecraft with Scotchlite windows.

FRONT SCREEN PROJECTION

The Animation Stand

9

The *animation stand* is a basic studio machine used for the production of cartoons, to animate still photos, and to enhance film frames by the use of registered overlay cels. Standard studio animation stands are available from many suppliers to meet the production needs of both large and small film studios.

A typical animation stand consists of a *camera* that has been adapted for use with an animation motor, a support *column* and camera *carriage*, and a *table* parallel to the camera image plane. Lights are usually positioned at 45-degree angles on both sides of the table to create uniform illumination of the table artwork. The stand is equipped with a number of manual and motorized function controls that permit directional movements of both the table artwork and the camera height. A gauge or veeder counter indicates the exact position of the camera and table for easy reference to exposure sheet instructions. In addition, the animation camera is fully adjustable for in-camera effects such as fade, dissolve, and focus shifts.

Figure 9-1 shows a basic animation stand. This stand, a Fax Jr. manufactured by the Fax Company, displays all of the essential features of a quality professional stand.

BASIC STAND COMPONENTS

The Camera

The *animation camera* is mounted on the metal plate of the *camera carriage*, a counterweighted support that travels up and down the stand's steel column (or dual columns in many stands).

The camera is designed exclusively for animation or stand special effects photography. An example of a professional-grade animation camera is shown in figure 9-2. This camera is a Neilson-Hordell Special Effects Camera capable of accepting 16mm or 35mm film. It has a fixed pin registration movement. A builtin printed circuit motor permits single frame operation or continuous rates of 2, 3, 4, 8, 12, 24, or 25 frames per second. The shutter is a 170-degree fading shutter. Fades and dissolves can be programmed to any length from 4 to 999 frames up to a speed of 240 frames per second.

An ordinary production camera may be used on an animation stand

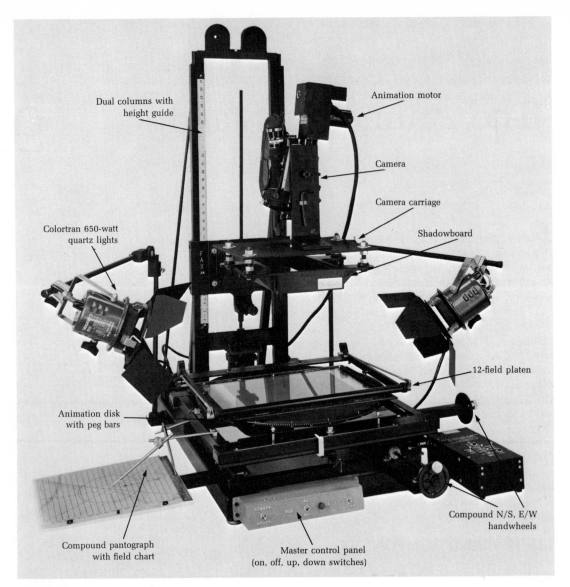

Dual columns with
height guide

Animation motor

Camera

Camera carriage

Colortran 650-watt
quartz lights

Shadowboard

12-field platen

Animation disk
with peg bars

Compound N/S, E/W
handwheels

Compound pantograph
with field chart

Master control panel
(on, off, up, down switches)

9-1 Basic animation stand.
(Courtesy of Fax Company)

but only if the live action speed motor is replaced with a special *animation motor.*

The standard unadapted camera motor is unsuitable for animation or single frame operation because the shutter drive movement is not designed for the prolonged subnormal running speeds common in animation photography. Any variation in frame exposures caused by an inconsistent shutter drive produces a noticeable flicker when the footage is projected. An animation motor delivers a consistent frame-to-frame exposure no matter what the frame rate speed setting.

The animation camera shutter is usually a variable or *fading shutter.* Since the frame exposure is dependent on the shutter angle, the variable fading shutter can be adjusted over a specified number of frames to produce fades, lap dissolves, and other exposure-based optical effects. The animation camera is often equipped with an additional shutter blade called a *capping shutter*. This shutter inserts a mask between the lens and the camera gate whenever the film is rewound or if a group of frames is to be skipped after exposure of an initial frame.

Raw film stock is supplied to the camera by the magazine. Most animation cameras accept seatings of magazines with standard 200-, 400-, and 1,000-foot capacity. The 400-foot magazine is the size commonly selected in both 16mm and 35mm formats both because of the magazine's light weight and because it is the average film length for a single shooting session. Four-chambered bipack magazines for special effects composite printing are also normally in 400-foot sizes.

The camera lens is automatically focused on the artwork by the

9-2 Studio animation camera. (Courtesy of Neilson-Hordell, Ltd.)

use of a linked cam-operated mechanism. The cam rides on the vertical rail column and adjusts the lens focus according to the rail column length interval. The cam is designed for a specific focal length lens. When the lens is replaced for one of a different focal length, the cam must also be exchanged in order to focus the new lens properly.

The Base

The animation camera is mounted on a rigid metal scaffold that keeps the camera securely positioned over the artwork to be photographed. The artwork is kept uniformly flat on the table surface by a sheet of plate glass in a hinged frame called the *platen* assembly.

Any reflections of the camera seen in the platen glass by the camera lens are reduced by a black board mounted just below the camera. The camera lens shoots through a lens-sized hole in the board, the remainder of the camera body being masked by the *shadowboard*.

The Compound

The large movable table that supports the platen and artwork is called the *compound*. Figure 9-1 shows the large compound frame beneath the platen assembly.

The compound is made up of a frame supported on two pairs of fixed rails. One set forms an East/West (E/W) travel and the other forms a North/South (N/S) travel. Hand wheels attached to screwthreads enable the compound frame to be moved either left or right, or toward or away from the stand's front operator position. Combination and diagonal moves are also possible by turning both sets of wheels simultaneously.

On large stands a gear-driven *turntable* is used between the compound frame and table support frame. The turntable allows the entire compound to be rotated 180 degrees. A simplified turntable without gear drive is the *compound angling ring*. This ring is used to angle the compound platen for a diagonal pan movement using only a single set of handwheels. Unlike the turntable, the compound angling ring is not used for animated rotation shots since it lacks both an accurate gear drive and position counters. Both turntable and angling ring are seen in the large stand compound table of figure 9-15.

The turntable is just below the platen and compound, and the angling ring is below it, supporting the entire compound.

Registration Bars

The artwork is accurately registered on the table-top compound by a system of pegs in thin metal plates, the *peg bars*, either Acme or Oxberry type.

Figure 9-3 shows two peg bars beneath the raised platen. These bars are arranged so that one bar holds the cel art and the other the separate background sheet. More sophisticated animation stands use as many as six parallel bars, each bar individually movable. In these larger stands, each bar, called a *traveling peg bar*, is positioned with a hand wheel crank that operates a rack and pinion movement assembly

9-3 Animation stand with platen raised and animation cel visible on the peg bars. (Courtesy of Fax Company)

connected to the bar. One full turn of the hand wheel moves a bar 0.1 inch (2.54mm) along its track. A lock on each hand wheel keeps the bar in place between moves. The position of each bar is read on a counter calibrated in intervals of 0.01 inch (0.254mm) to show any fractional turns of the hand wheel accurately.

Floating pegs are a set of peg bars that float independent of the compound assembly. These pegs, including a set of travel rails, leadscrews, hand wheel, and movement counter, are attached to the stand base or table support and extend over the compound. Any artwork registered on the floating peg assembly can be moved separately in any direction relative to the background artwork registered on the fixed or traveling peg bars of the compound disk.

The Field Chart

The *field chart* (also known as a *field guide*) is used by the camera operator to compose the artwork on the compound table and to plot pan and zoom movements. It is a plastic sheet engraved with a rectangular grid that represents the field of view covered by the camera lens. The field size changes as the camera is lowered or raised or if different lenses are used. The field size is indicated by a number which corresponds to the width of the area seen by a standard lens. A 1-field, noted as 1 F, identifies a shooting area exactly 1 inch (2.5cm) across. The normal range is 1 to 12 field, representing a width of 12 inches (30cm), although 18-field and larger are sometimes used for special shots. Since the field size depends greatly on the distance of the camera from the artwork for any given lens, each field photographed by the lens can be marked on the camera support column. These marks, called the *field position levels*, permit the camera to be placed above the artwork using the appropriate field number. The use of a field chart enables the camera operator to locate where artwork will be located in the field area being photographed at any field position level. Figure 9-4 illustrates a sample field chart (12-field size for a 16mm camera frame).

Punched with standard Acme or Oxberry peg holes, the field chart fits over the peg bars on the compound disk for camera lens framing and camera position.

The field chart uses the standard N/S and E/W marks and coordinate

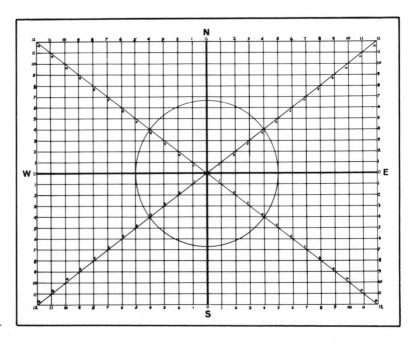

9-4 16mm field chart.

grid numbers to permit any camera framing of a table subject to be written on the exposure sheet. The rectangular division areas of the grid are of the same proportion ratio as the camera gate. Thus any size lens field can be specified by the chart's field numbers, as in a 4-field shot area, 8-field shot and the full 12-field view. The use of these different field numbers allows the camera zoom changes to be written as field numbers on the exposure sheet. A short zoom would go from a 10-field framing of the shot to a 5-field framing. All the camera operator needs to know is the start and stop field sizes and the timing of the zoom to animate the action using an exposure sheet as a guide.

The Pantograph

The *pantograph* is a pointer device that allows the stand operator to guide the table's lateral movements by following a reference line on a field chart. The field chart is attached to a small table fixed to one side of the table base. Pantograph bases can be seen in both figures 9-1 and 9-5.

Any move of the compound produces a similar directional movement of the pantograph pointer across a field chart. In practice the pantograph is used to guide the compound movement along a diagonal or complex curve instead of a simple lateral move. The pantograph relieves the operator of the need to compute mathematically the number of counter intervals in a combined N/S and E/W direction. Instead, a continuous line is drawn on the pantograph field chart that indicates the path the compound must follow. The pantograph pointer locates the exact placement of the compound at all intermediate positions on the pantograph field chart line.

9-5 Animation stand. Note Pantograph base. (Courtesy of Fax Company)

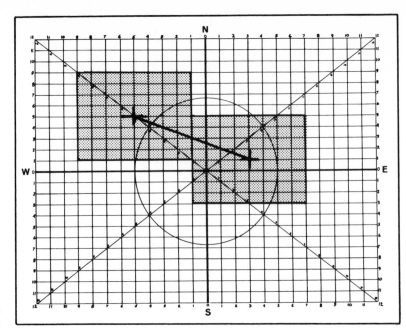

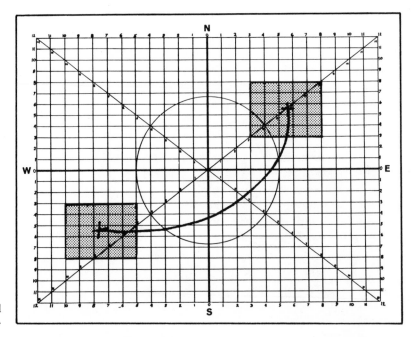

Two pantograph field chart movement guide lines are illustrated in figures 9-6 and 9-7. The first drawing shows a simple diagonal pan with the camera lens set at a 4-field framing within the full 12-field chart. The next drawing is a complex arc using a 2.5-field framing within a full 12-field chart.

As the pointer stops at each grid line coordinate, a small crosshatch mark can be made to show the completed frame exposure. This helps keep an accurate record of exactly how many exposures have been made in a single animation photography session. The crosshatch record avoids the accidental double shooting of any stop frame between sessions.

BASIC MOVEMENTS

The animation stand is capable of four basic kinds of mechanical movements. These can be used alone or in combination to create an illusion of motion in the artwork apart fom the animated action of the artwork cel changes.

The basic moves include the following:

1. *Tracking or zoom movement.* Tracking is the up or down slide of the camera along the support column. It permits a fast or slow change of the camera field of view during a shot, the final field being either larger or smaller than the starting field.
2. *Compound movements.* The compound allows the artwork field to be laterally shifted or panned East/West, North/South, or in any combination.
3. *Peg bar movements.* The traveling peg bars permit artwork painted on cels to be moved against a fixed background or vice versa, or a background moved in relation to a fixed cell on the fixed peg bars. Floating peg bars allow artwork such as a foreground cutout to be moved in any direction relative to the artwork registered to the fixed or traveling peg bars.
4. *Turntable rotation.* The turntable can spin the compound to provide rotational movement to the artwork. The compound angling ring can angle the compound relative to the normal field horizontal for easy diagonal moves using only the N/S or E/W hand wheel movement controls.

AERIAL IMAGE

An *aerial image* is a special artwork and background slide composite technique that employs a projector beneath the animation stand. Instead of a screen, two large plano-convex lenses are located in the glass insert area of the animation disk on the compound table. The lenses focus the image light provided by the projector and permit the image to fill the cel area of the animation disk. The resulting image is seen by the camera lens, although no screen is present to form the image. The projected image appears to be "in the air." (Since there is no actual screen as in rear-projected shots, the aerial image is not "washed out" by the stand lighting. Consequently the background image is photographed at the same time as the registered cel artwork is, rather than separately.)

An aerial image projector and animation stand are shown in figure 9-8.

This unit, manufactured by the J-K Camera Engineering Company, is arranged with the projector to one side of the stand. A first-surface mirror at a 45-degree angle to the projector deflects the optical path up into the camera lens. Such an arrangement of camera, mirror, and

9-8 Aerial image projector and animation stand. (Courtesy of J-K Engineering, Inc.)

projector is common to most aerial image systems. A different version of the system is shown in the Neilson-Hordell aerial image stand projector seen in figure 9-9.

This unit clearly shows the separate parts of the projector device. The high-quality flat-field process lens can be positioned anywhere along the twin track rails and increase or decrease the size of the aerial image seen by the camera. The middle component of the projector is the slide holder-compound unit. The slide can be moved up, down, or diagonally by adjusting the compound frame. Dials show the exact increments of any position change from a fully centered aperture position. This movement control is an important feature since the animation table compound cannot be moved once it is aligned with the projector's optical path. A move of the compound would cause

THE ANIMATION STAND

the aerial image lenses to be shifted out of the camera-projector optical path and destroy the aerial image seen beneath the transparent animation cel.

Aerial image techniques are frequently used to mix photographs of natural scenery with artwork painted on cels. A title or cartoon character can be visually added to any scene provided by a color transparency in the aerial image projector. The artwork is a painted cel placed over the lens mounted in the compound table. Since the camera lens sees both the artwork and the magnified background provided by the projector, a perfect mix is made without resorting to any mattes or other optical masks used to make composite shots. Likewise the projector can be fitted with a pin-registered motion picture projection unit to form aerial images of moving backgrounds containing live action elements. This permits a composite shot of the animated character with actors seemingly interacting with the cartoon figure.

COMPUTER-ASSISTED ANIMATION AND MOTION CONTROL

Ordinary animation stand movements require the camera operator to plot out and manually execute the compound pan moves and any programmed in-camera fades or dissolves. The tedious nature of this work, which can be time-consuming even for simple pan curves,

9-9 Neilson-Hordell aerial image stand and projector. (Courtesy of Neilson-Hordell, Ltd.)

adds greatly to the overall cost of the animated film production. The introduction of time-saving computer technology to control the stand compound, track zoom, and camera functions automatically has emerged as both a cost-effective and creative solution to the older manual methods.

Computer-assisted animation uses the computer to guide the compound mechanisms and operate the camera according to a specific program planned by the stand operator. This type of animation is not to be confused with *computer-generated* animation described earlier. The latter is imagery generated entirely by the computer display of pixels on a video screen.

An example of a computer-assisted animation stand is shown in figure 9-10. This is a Neilson-Hordell Nora System 1 digital computer control system mated to a large, fully motorized stand. This particular

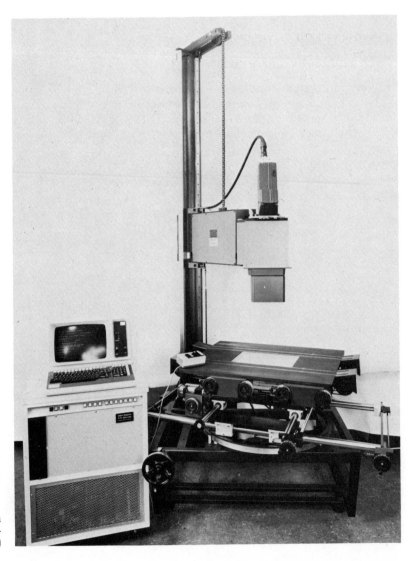

9-10 Neilson-Hordell Nora System 1. (Courtesy of Neilson-Hordell, Ltd.)

THE ANIMATION STAND

stand has a television camera on the camera carriage instead of the more usual motion picture camera.

Computer-assisted animation stands are designed to follow any movement command provided by the computer's program. Instructions for basic moves are in the form of code words typed directly on the computer terminal keyboard by the camera operator. The computer translates the instruction commands, which are stored on a magnetic disk, into electronic pulses. The pulses activate the animation stand compound motors, called *stepper motors*. A stepper motor advances by degree increments or steps unlike regular electric motors, which turn continuously whenever current is applied.

Each computer pulse turns the shaft only a fraction of a turn. Controlling the number of pulses allows the number of revolutions of the compound motors, and in turn, the length and direction of compound pan movements to be specified by the computer microprocessor.

Other stepper motors and relay controls adjust the camera lens focus and aperture, as well as shutter action and track zoom movements.

Once programmed, the computer can control the camera stand movements and compound shifts unaided by the operator. The automatic action can also be repeated exactly for any multiple exposure effects in-camera.

MOTION CONTROL

Motion control is a term used to describe visual effects produced by controlling the motion of a miniature or art graphic during a single frame exposure. The effect can be changed slightly or repeated for any number of repeat frame exposures to form a complete film strip. In most motion control camera systems the camera is also moved in relation to the subject being photographed to generate complex motion visuals.

The two basic motion control visual effects are *streak photography* and *slit-scan* photography.

Streak Photography (also called *Scan Photography*)

Streak photography is done by keeping the camera shutter open for a specific time interval of one to several seconds as the subject is moved across the field of view in lateral, vertical, or combined movements. This *time exposure* of the moving subject produces a blurred image of the subject in the film frame. This indistinct blur is the streak or smear trail of the subject movement.

A simple example of a streak effect applied to special visuals for film is the planet seen in figure 9-11.

The ring of the Saturnlike planet was created by streaking a sliver of white paper around the planet. The paper, attached to a motor via an L-shaped black wire support, took about three seconds to complete a single rotation. The camera shutter was left open during the rotation cycle with the lens set to a small shooting aperture. The resulting streak is in depth because of the normal perspective of the shot, i.e., the paper was moving at a near right angle to the camera image plane. Flat two-dimensional streaks can be done easily in a similar manner with flat and often backlighted artwork.

9-11 Planet with streak effect.

The entire procedure with the moving paper of figure 9-11 must be repeated exactly for every frame in a motion picture film strip. This requires a sturdy mounting of both the camera and the subject over the entire shot sequence.

Streak effects are used extensively in adding motion effects to title graphics, as in the title credit shots of the films *Superman I* and *II*. Streak effects photography also produced the famous *Star Wars* "jump into light speed" shot and the Starship Enterprise's "warp factor speeds" in all the *Star Trek* films.

Slit-Scan Photography

The "star gate corridor" of *2001: A Space Odyssey* is one of the early applications of the motion control technique known as *slit-scan photography*. The term is descriptive of the basic nature of the method: backlighted artwork is photographed through a narrow slit in an opaque mask. In a single-frame time exposure the camera, mounted on a special platform track, travels a long distance toward the slit very slowly. In an action synchronized to the camera approach, the artwork slides laterally to expose the entire artwork image over the course of the track movement. The vertical slit does not actually move during the entire shot.

However, as the camera moves forward, the slit appears to drift slowly from a midframe position to the extreme edge of the frame. This on-film movement is caused by the changes in the camera's field of view as it moves closer to the slit.

At each point along the dolly track the camera photographs only a small portion of the artwork—the areas exposed by the long slit. The combination of advancing camera, slit exposure, and shifting art work together to record a single whole image. The result on film is quite different from the expected shot: the camera appears to view the artwork from an extreme perspective. Figure 9-15 shows a slit-scan effect as it appears in a finished film frame.

In a film strip the cycle of movement between camera and artwork must be exactly repeated over hundreds of frames. When the film is

156   THE ANIMATION STAND

9-12, 9-13, 9-14 In this three frame sequence from the film *Superman—The Movie*, the credit line *"A Richard Donner Film"* is streaked toward the viewer and out of the frame. (Courtesy of R/Greenberg Associates. *Superman—The Movie* film titles. Client: Warner Bros./Dovemead Ltd.)

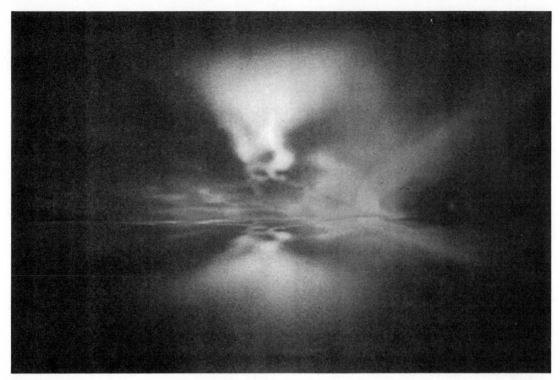

9-15 Slit-scan effect.

projected the slit is not seen at all in the individual frames. Instead, the artwork appears as a seamless sheet rushing toward the viewer at a surprising speed.

The slit-scan effect is an extremely popular visual technique for typographic effects, including advertising logos, title credits, and similar eye-catching displays of words in motion.

Motion Control Camera Systems

The use of the computer to automate the pan operation of the animation stand has found a similar application in camera systems designed for studio photography of spacecraft and flying miniatures.

The computer-assisted motion control camera systems are very similar to the computer-assisted animation stand. The camera, automated in a nodal mount, is attached to a motorized gimbal at the end of a long boom arm assembly. The boom in turn is attached to a motorized camera pedestal that rides on a precision track. The computerized tracking camera system made by Elicon is shown in figure 9-19. The camera has eight axes of motion control to do in-camera streak, slit-scan, and single-frame stop action cinematography.

Figure 9-20 is a motion control unit with an Acme process camera mounted on a computer gimbal support. It is equipped with a fully automatic directional control console.

The camera gimbal or geared support allows the camera to be turned, rotated, and tilted in any direction by the action of computer-driven stepper motors or servo drives.

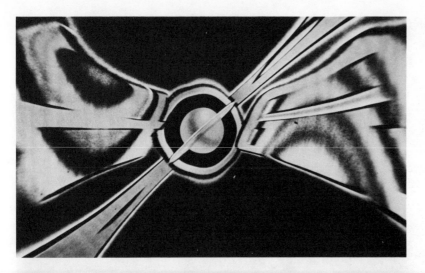

9-16, 9-17, 9-18 This three-frame sequence from the TV campaign for *Flash Gordon* shows a variation of the standard slit-scan. The words Flash Gordon flow toward the center planet and assemble on each side simultaneously. (Courtesy of R/Greenberg Associates. *Flash Gordon*: TV campaign. Client: Famous Films/Universal Studios)

9-19 Elicon computer tracking system. (Courtesy of Elicon)

9-20 Motion control unit with Acme process camera mounted on a computer gimbal support. (Courtesy of Elicon)

The robotlike boom arm support maneuvers the camera to any required position around a stationary model. The camera view of the miniature is from a motion perspective, but the optical result is that of a spacecraft or aircraft appearing to fly unaided across the field of view.

The camera repeats the programmed motion several times to expose the film to different lighting levels. The separate exposure elements of a typical space shot include:

1. the spacecraft surface details (first pass)
2. the spacecraft engine glow and exhaust trail (second pass)
3. the various port lights (third pass)
4. a starfield background coordinated to the apparent changes of perspective in the spacecraft motion (a separate camera pass over a backlighted star field [pin-hole sheet])

Each pass will be carefully exposed to adjust for the different intensities of light, light source balance, and any differences of scale among shot elements. Since the computer move of the original pass is recorded in the computer's memory, every subsequent move exactly duplicates the original. In this way several film exposures, either on the original in-camera negative or as separate rolls, can be assembled to form a matched whole image.

Motion control camera systems have contributed heavily to science-fiction and fantasy films. The many spacecraft dogfights of *Star Wars* formed the debut of the breakthrough camera system designed by the film's special effects director, John Dykstra. This early computer motion control system was dubbed the *Dystraflex* and established the potential of such cameras in modern visual effects.

Other prominent motion control cameras are the two advanced systems designed by the Walt Disney Studios: the *Aces* system and the *Matte Scan* camera crane.

Aces (Automatic Camera Effects System) was developed to generate space effects for the Disney production *The Black Hole*. It permits the camera operator to program a move without actually moving the camera through a pre-exposure trial run.

Matte Scan, also developed for *The Black Hole*, applies motion control to the photography of large matte paintings. The Matte Scan can be programmed to pan both horizontally and vertically and match a matte painting portion of a composite to the live action camera pan footage.

NEILSON-HORDELL ANIMATION STAND

This large animation stand is designed for the production of animation and special effects footage. The stand illustrated in figure 9-21 has a 35/16mm special effects camera, control console, and aerial image projection unit. The stand features an offset column design that gives an extra margin at the rear of the stand for large N/S compound moves.

9-21 Neilson-Hordell animation stand. (Courtesy of Neilson-Hordell, Inc.)

The Film Printer   10

A *print* is a film positive produced from an original or duplicate camera negative. It reproduces all the tonal values and colors of the negative image. Printing machines or *printers* are the devices used in studios and laboratories to copy the processed negative image onto raw or unexposed film stock.

In the preparation of special visual effects, the original camera negative is printed on three different types of film stock. They are:

1. *The intermediate duplicate,* a high-definition, low-speed emulsion used to copy the original camera negative. The intermediate is also used to make color separations of the original film—black-and-white versions photographed through color filters that, when printed through filtered light, re-create the original scene colors on a duplicate negative stock.
2. The matte *high contrast printing stock,* a black-and-white emulsion that reproduces an image with few or no intermediate values between the white highlights and black shadow values.
3. The *release positive,* a high-resolution, low-speed emulsion used for the final print seen in theater projection.

The printing films are used to create the duplicate positives and negatives that are required in the stages of a single composite shot.

The printer transfers the image frame of one film stock onto the unexposed image area on a different film stock. Printers are grouped according to purpose in one of two categories:

1. *The contact printer,* which copies the original or duplicate negative by exposing the film in contact as they pass under the printing light source.
2. *The optical printer,* which uses a lens system to transfer optically a projected image of the negative or duplicate frame to a new emulsion film stock.

Both types of printers are used in any single film production. However, special visual effects work is primarily centered on the capabilities of the optical printer.

THE CONTACT PRINTER

Contact printers are used to make direct 1:1 copies of the original image. The negative is pressed against a copy stock and the two are

10-1 Acme step contact printer, loaded and threaded. (Courtesy of Photo-Sonics, Inc.)

exposed to an overhead light source. The negative frame image is transferred to the new film by the tonal masking of the negative during the exposure pass.

A *continuous* contact printer runs an entire negative and duplicate positive roll paired in close contact at continuous high speed under the printing exposure light source. The print is not of the highest quality since inevitable slippage between the two films causes some loss in the resolution and clarity of the duplicate image.

The *step* contact printer improves the image copied from a continuous contact printer by using a camera-type intermittent movement to advance the two films frame by frame, one exposure per frame. Although not as fast as the continuous printer, the step printer has almost no slippage; it is a pin-registered movement. This produces higher image resolution in the duplicated image frame.

Optical effects such as fades and dissolves can easily be done with a variable light exposure during the printing of A-and-B rolls of edited film.

THE OPTICAL PRINTER

The optical printer is used to alter the image in various ways rather than simply to make a 1:1 copy. A versatile optical printer allows

10-2 An unsophisticated optical printer. (Courtesy of Century Precision Optics, Inc.)

10-3 Another simple printer. (Courtesy of Century Precision Optics, Inc.)

the original image frame to be enlarged, reduced, modified, or reversed during the copy rephotography. Typical optical printer effects from an original include: optical zooms of a stationary image, pans across the image frame, cropping or changing the field of view, split screen multiple exposures, and image transfer to a different film gauge, as from 16mm to 35mm.

A pair of somewhat limited simple optical printers for use on a standard production camera is shown in figures 10-2 and 10-3. They are both Duplikin printers manufactured by Century Precision Cine/Optics Company. The devices are designed to mount directly into the lens socket mount of a 16mm or 35mm camera. A 16mm film frame or 35mm slide positioned in the Duplikin end gate aperture is transferred by an internal process lens to the camera negative. Duplikins are useful for low-cost printing effects and film gauge transfers of a single frame image.

10-4 A sophisticated optical printer. (Courtesy of J-K Camera Engineering, Inc.)

The optical printer used for more sophisticated visual effects consists of a separate process camera, a pin-registered projector, and a high-quality flat field process lens between them. Figure 10-4 displays the essential parts in a 16mm optical printer. This printer is a Model K-104 J-K Optical Printer, made by J-K Camera Engineering, Inc.

The camera (left) and projector (right) operate together automatically and in complete synchronization with the projector running forward or in reverse. The individual components can also be controlled separately. The maximum copy speed for synchronized operation is 50 frames per minute.

The Optical Printer Camera

The optical printer camera may be designed for a particular line of printers or be one of a line of such cameras.

The optical printer camera employs a pin-registration movement to maintain the steadiest possible image for the transfer of the film frame. Most process cameras permit different film gauge components and movements to be interchangeable. These units, called *shuttles*, greatly increase the working range of the process camera. Three shuttles are shown in figure 10-5.

These three shuttles are for film sizes in Super-8, 35mm, and 16mm. Although these particular shuttles are designed for the J-K Optical Printer projector, similar shuttles are used in the camera movements of most standard process cameras.

The process camera is equipped with a variable shutter to produce in-camera fades and dissolves automatically at any frame rate by the use of an electronic control console. The 35mm/16mm Oxberry process camera, for example, has a 170-degree shutter for manual or automatic dissolve and fades of 8 to 128 frames.

10-5 Three interchangeable shuttles. (Courtesy of J-K Camera Engineering, Inc.)

THE FILM PRINTER

The Optical Printer Projector

The projector is the second major component of an optical printer. The term "projector" is misleading in that the projector unit does not transmit an image to a front screen, as do standard theater projectors. Instead the master film to be copied is advanced through a *printer head* aperture and illuminated from the back by a highly focused lamp beam from the *lamphouse*. The process camera lens is focused on the uniformly bright frame held stationary in the printer head aperture.

Most printer heads offer an accessory or builtin device for shifting the head a few inches or centimeters off the optical axis to the camera. This device is similar in function to an animation compound but operates in a vertical plane. It is used to shift the aperture in order to center a different portion of the frame in the camera lens field of view. By shifting the aperture between successive camera exposures, an effect known as *optical pan* can add a pan movement to an otherwise stationary shot.

The amount of light output by the lamphouse is controlled either by varying the lamp current supply with a rheostat control or by using an adjustable diaphragm aperture in front of the lamp called a *beam light valve*. The light controls enable the printer to compensate for exposure imbalances in the original camera negative. The shot-to-shot exposure compensation during the printing stage is called *grading* and assures a consistent level of image brightness throughout the entire reel of film. Grading is also known as *timing* the print. Likewise, color imbalances in the negative can be compensated for and balanced by using color-correction filters in the light beam. Two types of color lamphouses permit color control by altering the color mix of the light itself. The *additive color* lamphouse manipulates the mix of the primary colors red, blue, and green by using a separate light valve and lamp filter for each color. Equal mixing produces white light. Any weighting to one color shifts the color mix of the beam and creates a similar color cast in the photographed image frame. A *subtractive color* lamphouse uses a similar mechanical arrangement of three light valves but uses complementary filters instead of primary colors to shift the light output selectively.

The Printer Lens

The third important component in a basic optical printer is the process lens. The lens magnifies the film frame visible in the printer head aperture. Unlike an ordinary camera lens, the printer lens is a flat-field lens. The lens optics are designed for shooting two-dimensional surfaces such as the film frame rather than three-dimensional objects. The printer's lens gives the maximum resolution with an extremely sharp close-up focus of the entire frame from edge-to-edge over the field of view.

The lens is usually mounted in an adjustable bellows connected to the process camera. The bellows and separate movement controls enable the lens to be moved independently of the camera for enlargements or reductions of the image frame. The lens mount can be further adjusted with small hand wheel controls to move the entire lens up and down or left and right of the optical center. Large indicator dials mounted on the lens carriage show the exact placement of the lens in relation to the optical center of the camera frame aperture.

OPTICAL PRINTER SPECIAL EFFECTS

The optical printer offers a wide range of creative photographic effects. Each printer component is under the direct control of the operator. Almost any optical modification of the original image is possible by the combined and independent functions of the printer's projector, lens, and camera.

The basic printer controls are these:

1. *Printer Light Output.* The lamphouse light valves can be increased or decreased to adjust the beam's light intensity. The color of the light can also be altered by color filtration. The printer light valves permit fades to be made at the printer head aperture rather than in the camera. The standard printer light effects are the fade-in, fade-out, and lap dissolve. The printer light can also be varied to extremes for an overexposure or underexposure visual effect on the copied film.

2. *Frame Projection/Running Rate.* The projector and camera are electrically interlocked for routine synchronized printing. However, each part can be run separately at any required speed or single frame exposure rate.

   Several film rate visual effects are based on the number and frequency of master frames photographed by the process camera.

   A *freeze frame* (fig. 10-6) is the repeated printing of a single frame held stationary in the printer head aperture while the camera continues to run. The freeze frame is used to stop the flow of a scene action for a number of frames. For comparison, a standard frame printing is shown in figure 10-7.

   A *skip printing* (fig. 10-8) is the printing of only those frames at a specified interval, such as every second frame in a film strip. Skip printing is used to speed up the film action optically. The technique is also used in the frontlight/backlight traveling matte method.

   A *stretch printing* (fig. 10-9) repeats a selected number of adjacent frames to increase the screen time or stretch each action frame to simulate a slow motion visual effect.

3. *Lens Position.* The printer lens focuses the frame image illuminated by the printer head. Any change in the lens position on the focus track produces a related magnification or reduction of the image.

   A *blowup* is an enlargement of any small area of the film frame to fill the entire frame of the copy film. If the lens is moved during the actual photography, a continuous magnification of the frame produces an *optical zoom* into the copy film frame. The printer lens carriage is equipped with an automatic *follow focus* device to keep the frame in sharp focus as the lens is repositioned on the travel track rails. The device is uncoupled for a *soft focus* effect.

   Likewise, any lateral movement of the lens introduces a *pan* in either a horizontal or vertical direction.

10-6 Freeze frame printing.

10-7 Normal frame printing.

10-8 Skip frame printing (print one frame, skip two frames).

10-9 Stretch frame printing (each frame printed twice).

4. *Lens Attachments.* Lens attachments and filters creatively distort the frame image during process camera photography. By inserting prisms into the optical path, the image can be fragmented, multiplied, warped, or compressed.

A *ripple* effect is produced by placing a transparent sheet of ribbed or wavy glass between the lens and the projector. This effect is often used for the starting transition to a dream sequence.

Anamorphic or elongated images are produced by a cylindrical lens, as opposed to the standard round lens, that compresses or squeezes the image in only one direction of the frame.

A *kaleidoscope* attachment repeats the image in pie-shaped wedges.

A *dove prism* attachment permits the entire frame image to be turned upside down during the shot for a spin effect. Similar attachments can optically *flip* the image end-over-end.

A *wipe* attachment inserts a moving windowshade line transition by mechanical blades that slice across the projector's image aperture.

5. *Mattes and Bipack Printing.* Most professional film visual effects are achieved by the traveling matte process and bipack printing methods within the process camera. These have both been described in earlier chapters.

6. *Aerial Image Printing.* An aerial image projector in line with the printer head permits a superimposition of the printer head frame over a live action background. This technique is exactly the same as that described in the chapter on animation stands. The aerial image method is also used to insert a matte over a scene containing the subject element to be matted into the final composite shot. This use of the projector and aerial image projector reduces the number of times a duplicate negative will have to be run through the process camera.

A dual aerial image can be superimposed with a beam splitter by using two projector heads and two aerial images. This arrangement in the same optical axis with the process camera permits the entire composite background and foreground subject to be composited in a single camera pass of the duplicate negative.

THE MODERN PRINTER

An example of a modern optical printer is shown in fig. 10-10. It is a Pioneer/Trebes Model 7600 made by Pioneer Cine Corporation. The printer is a special effects step optical printer equipped with an aerial image projector. The sophisticated controls on the printer console give the filmmaker an almost unlimited range of printing effects.

This printer is extremely versatile. Many useful features are standard, while still more are available as options.

STANDARD FEATURES
electronic drive system
adjustable torque motors
subtractive Lamphouse
Acme Model 6 process camera
linear and logarithmic fades and
    dissolves
electronic skip frame
predetermined stops for frame
    lengths
footage counter alert system
presettable counters with
    electronic memories
precision dial indicators
all-purpose film takeup

16mm, 1,200 feet magazine
    (365.8m)
35mm, 1,000 feet magazine
    (304.8m)
16mm and 35mm shuttle
    components
high resolution Nikkor printing
    lenses
automatic lens aperture
    diaphragm control
automatic camera focus
projector compound, N/S, E/W
projector tilt control
camera tilt control

OPTIONS AVAILABLE
35mm bipack magazine
focusing prism for gate viewfinder
base for special effects devices
spin device
wipe device
flip device
color wheel for lens

2 × 2 slide holder
Anamorphic converter for lens
ripple device, motorized
AUTO-EFX motion control
    computer, 7 axes of movement
Super-8mm, Vistavision, and
    70mm components

2,000 feet (609.6m) projector takeup capacity
Spectra film gate exposure meter
Opcomatrix manual additive lamphouse unit
Automatic follow-focus for the aerial image projector

10-10 A modern special effects step optical printer. (Courtesy of Pioneer/Trebes)

SUMMARY OF OPTICAL PRINTER VISUAL EFFECTS

The optical printer is a key component in professional effects film production. It is required for the many duplicate negatives and positives, for fine grain plates, matte and countermatte footage, separations, answer prints, and release prints. Here is a brief summary of the opticals that can be created on a special effects optical printer.

exposure corrections
Bipack contact printing
color printing
color corrections
dissolves
double exposures
fades
dropped shadow titles
flipover image
forward and reverse action
frameline correction
freeze frame
multiple exposure
straight lines corrections
spins
tilts
moving flips and spins

out-of-focus shots
scene push-offs (wipes)
reductions
skip frames
split screen
titles
manual optical zooms
automatic optical zooms
off-center optical zooms
traveling matte
image size changes
aerial image
film gauge conversions
film image format conversions by
    anamorphic or Cinemascope
    widescreen systems

Mechanical Special Effects 11

When the term special visual effects is used in this book, the general meaning is that of photographic or optical effects such as mattes, animation, and process photography. However, the field of special effects also includes the two areas of *miniature* photography and of *mechanical effects*.

Miniatures are detailed constructions or models that represent a real or imaginary structure in a scene. Figure 11-1 shows a miniature of a space vehicle made from plastic sheeting and "junk," odd plastic pieces salvaged from commercial model kits rather than fabricated from stock plastic sheets.

Mechanical special effects comprise any nonoptical effects performed live on the location or set at the time of original photography. These mechanical effects or *physical effects* as they are sometimes termed, involve so many different types of materials and techniques that some film workers specialize in only one area, such as plastics or explosives.

One area of mechanical special effects that will not be discussed is that involving the use of *action props*. These are complicated working models, both large miniatures and full-size versions, that stand in for the real thing. The awesome shark in *Jaws* is an example of a full-scale action prop, a star in its own right. The lovable alien

11-1 Space vehicle miniature.

in *E.T.* is another ingenious action prop that often stole the spotlight from the live actors. Such props are elaborate constructions that incorporate hydraulic and pneumatic drives, motors, electronics, and advanced plastics for action, body, and skin details. Such topics require specialized knowledge that is beyond the scope of this book.

For a description of action props and a more detailed look at mechanical effects in general, there are two excellent books on the subject: Bernard Wilkie's *Creating Special Effects for TV and Film* and Frank P. Clark's *Special Effects in Motion Pictures*. Both books cover the many mechanical devices and chemical agents used in professional film productions.

A note of warning: many chemicals and all explosive materials are dangerous and regulated by federal and state laws. The spectacular explosions seen in action films are accomplished by skilled special effects workers with many years of professional experience. No student or amateur filmmaker should attempt to duplicate these effects with real explosive materials. Careless handling and improper detonation of explosive compounds, including those made in a home laboratory, can only result in needless injury. A lax attitude is extremely hazardous to everyone's health.

BREAKAWAY PROPS

Action-oriented films often entail the wholesale destruction of a set or its props. Chairs, tables, windows, and mirrors are routinely demolished or shattered by, say, a staged fistfight or saloon brawl. Whole buildings are sometimes required to collapse on cue in a single shot. In all cases the destruction is carefully planned by the special effects team. The usual device for achieving the desired mayhem is called a *breakaway*. The set props or structures are designed to be easily broken without endangering the actors or production personnel.

Breakaways are of four basic types:

TYPE	TYPICAL PROP	MATERIALS
glass and pottery	molded bottles, plates, ornaments, small statues	Thin (extended) plaster, wax, baked bread dough, cast sugar, polystyrene resin, Styrofoam, dense urethane
	windows	cellophane sheets, clear polystyrene
furniture	chairs and tables	glued balsa without nails, Styrofoam
hand props	spears, rocks, guns, knives, broom handles, small statues	soft carved balsa, bass wood, Styrofoam, flexible molded latex, papier-mâché, foam polyurethane
structural set pieces (collapsible)	doors, roof beams, window casings, bricks, timbers, walls	cardboard, laminated plastic sheets, vacuum-formed thermoplastic, Styrofoam, thinly braced fiberglass

MECHANICAL SPECIAL EFFECTS

The special effects worker designs the larger props and structural set pieces to break in a carefully determined way. Supports, posts, and panels are partially cut through to make the fall of the set predictable. Large areas of a set are destroyed by using cable release mechanisms to unhinge the pieces or by large air pumps called air cannons to simulate a blast shock-wave effect. All actors and production personnel in the breakaway line of sight destruction path are carefully briefed by the special effects team to avoid any injury from falling set debris.

PYROTECHNICS

Perhaps the most dramatic visual effects are those of explosions, fire, lightning, and smoke. These effects are called *pyrotechnics*.

The pyrotechnic worker is responsible for the transportation, preparation, handling, and detonation of explosive compounds and fireworks. Since such materials are regulated by law, the special effects worker is licensed by the state fire marshall as a qualified Special Effects Pyrotechnic Operator after a substantial apprenticeship. No unlicensed person is permitted to work with the pyrotechnic materials in a professional film production.

The basic pyrotechnic material is a crude gunpowder consisting of potassium nitrate, sulfur, and charcoal. The mixture burns rapidly, with the burn rate determined by the proportions of the components in the mixture. Ordinary gasoline and diesel fuel are also frequently used as liquid pyrotechnic material for burning and smoke effects.

Explosive powders are used in a range of strengths. The ratings index spans the high-power dynamite (used infrequently in films) to low-power black powder bombs that explode beneath a thin layer of earth and simulate the explosion effects of flying dirt, rocks, and other cannon-fire or rocket debris.

Bright flash effects are usually substituted for the more explosive materials. *Flash powders*, a mix of powered aluminum and magnesium, create a burst of ignition light and burn rapidly. The powders produce a display of bright spark streamers when steel filings are added to the basic mix. Flash powder is usually the only pyrotechnic material used on miniatures to simulate explosions and lightning effects. A variation of the powder is the *smoke flash paper* used by magicians. This paperlike material ignites readily and creates a large puff of white or colored smoke with only a small burst of light.

Explosive materials and flash powders are rarely ignited by a hand-held flame or match. A small electrical detonator or *squib* is used to maintain a measure of control over the timing and sequence of any explosions or flash effects.

The smallest and most common explosive device is the *bullet hit* that simulates the effect of a bullet striking an object or person. Different types of bullet effects are produced depending on whether a mechanical or pyrotechnic device is used. Mechanical bullet effects range from soft gelatin "blood"-filled capsules that are fired by slingshot at the actor, to drilled and plugged patterns in walls or ground that are forced out with compressed air.

The most commonly used bullet hit is the tiny charge, strapped to the actor's body and concealed by clothing, that is electrically detonated. Special precautions are taken to assure that no physical harm is done to the individual wearing the charge. The usual way is to anchor the charge in a grooved metal plate and back the plate with a thick leather pad that will cushion any shock and prevent a burn. Ordinary masking tape holds the charge pellet in place in the armor plate groove. Straps keep the pellet charge and plate in position beneath the actor's clothing during the scene. The charge is frequently used with a small plastic bag containing artificial blood liquid, the *blood sac* or *blood bag*. When the pellet ruptures the sac, the liquid soaks the shirt and exposed skin, simulating the effect of a bleeding wound. In films where gore is the main attraction, several bullet hits are covered with thin latex to resemble the actor's skin. The blood sacs not only contain liquid blood syrup but butcher scraps as well, which produce a vivid (and messy) bullet impact effect.

NATURE EFFECTS

The special effects worker is often called on to produce atmospheric nature effects in a studio set or on location. Such effects include fog, rain, snow, wind, and dust storms. Each effect can be achieved using specific mechanical devices.

Fog

An ordinary camera *fog filter* may be sufficient if mist is all that is called for in a scene. However, the appearance of true fog is created quite differently.

A light or heavy concentration of ground fog is easily generated by a *dry ice fog* machine. Dry ice is solid carbon dioxide, frozen under pressure to form a snowlike powder. Dry ice, unlike water ice, does not melt as a liquid but converts directly to a gas. This gas, extremely cold, acts as a refrigerant on any water vapor in the air to form cloudlike ice crystals above the melting ice. In the fog machine chunks of dry ice are warmed by air from a fan equipped with a heater coil. A dense white vapor is produced and fills the machine's reservoir tank, a 55-gallon (208.2-liter) drum. The vapor can then be vented to the floor by the machine operator using a hose, similar to a clothes dryer hot air hose. Since the drum's ice basket has a 100-pound (45.4-kg) capacity, a large amount of low-lying fog can be generated. The fog clings to the ground because the carbon dioxide gas is about 1.5 times as dense as air, thus heavier, and keeps the refrigerated water vapor down with it. Dry ice fog does not damage the stage floor, scenery, or actors' costumes. It leaves no residue after the fog disappears.

An alternate method of producing dry ice fog without a machine can be improvised at the time of shooting. The hundred pounds of dry ice are loaded into a large wire basket on the set floor. The ice basket may also be made of a large wooden box with an open lattice, such as the open slats of a vegetable crate. A quart of water or less is then poured slowly and directly onto the dry ice. A large amount of water vapor is immediately generated in the basket. Two or more fans are then placed around the box to blow the vapor through the open lattice out onto the set floor. As more vapor is continuously produced, a thick layer of vapor fog soon spreads out from the box.

A warning: Dry ice should never be handled with the bare hands or allowed to come in contact with skin or clothing. The extremely low temperature of solid carbon dioxide can cause severe burns.

A different type of fog is generated by a *smoke fog machine.* Usually small and portable, the machine creates a high-rising general smoke similar to natural fog conditions. One such machine can be seen in figure 11-2, an Alcone MF1 fogger. Like most machines of this type, it contains a heating coil that vaporizes a supply of petroleum distillate, a flammable liquid commonly called *fog juice.* Fog juice is separately ordered from theatrical suppliers in gallon or liter containers. Some types of machines substitute an aerosol pressurized container for the supply reservoir, and the fog juice is ordered in 16-ounce (473-ml) cannisters.

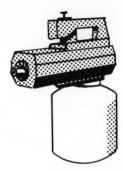

11-2 Handheld fog machine with one gallon of fog juice.

The fogger operates electrically by an extension cable to a wall outlet or power generator. After a short warmup period of a few minutes, the machine releases a dense white smoke whenever the activator button is pressed. The operator can then move anywhere on the set and spread the smoke fog by aiming the fogger's nozzle. The smoke rises to form a cloud or mist to simulate natural fog or, if used with appropriate scenery, an eerie, other-world effect. If a thicker, floor-clinging fog is desired, the smoke fog machine can be used at low ground level in front of a wire bucket of dry ice. As the smoke passes through the dry ice, it is cooled and stays near the floor as it spreads.

Any dense concentration of vaporized oil, such as that generated by a smoke machine, is highly flammable. Caution must be used when fogging a confined located set or closed room where a miniature is to be shot in fog. All flames must be extinguished prior to fogging. Any set lights, especially high-intensity units, must be kept outside the fog layer to prevent contact with oil vapor droplets. All technicians working within a dense fog should wear respirator masks to avoid inhalation of oil-laden air. Many of the problems associated with oil-based fog juice are relieved with a new and safer water-based fog juice offered by the Rosco Company. This juice is relatively odorless, leaves no film, and is not flammable.

Rain

Natural rain can be a delay-causing nuisance when it appears abruptly on a location during shooting. But rain effects are often used to establish mood in a scene. The special effects worker becomes an instant "rain-dancer," producing anything from a seasonal April shower to a tropical downpour.

On an outdoor location scene away from the studio, the easiest way to create rain effects is to jet water over the area from high-pressure fire hoses and water tanks or city hydrants. The nozzles are moved back and forth constantly to simulate the natural rhythms of rainfall.

Inside a studio building the set must be specially waterproofed. The rain area is bounded by plastic dropcloths or liners to keep water

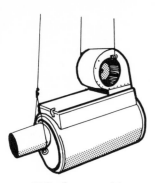

11-3 Snow machine on wire cables. Fan blows plastic "snow."

from spilling throughout the entire studio. Several plastic or metal water pipes are drilled with holes and suspended over the set. Water is pumped through hoses to the overhead pipes and emitted from the many holes in each pipe. Once again low-power fans help scatter the falling droplets to create the look of a realistic windswept storm.

A similar arrangement is used in miniature when only a single window-view of the stormy weather is needed. The pipes are mounted above the window casing and gravity forces the sprinkling flow of water across and down the glass, to a narrow trough at the base of the window. A small water pump and flexible piping channel the water in the trough back to the overhead pipes.

Snow

Snow in its natural form is nothing more than frozen water crystals. Unfortunately for the special effects worker, real snow melts too quickly under the hot stage lights for practical use in a studio scene. In some cases real snow is used in a special *refrigerated set*, built like a giant ice box, to allow realistic cold-weather vapor to come from the actors' mouths when they speak.

Shredded materials such as lightweight white polyethylene, paper punches, and Styrofoam pellets are often used to simulate falling snow. Low-power fans edging the set can easily blow these materials about. The actual "snowfall" is provided by a mechanical *snow machine* mounted above the set and suspended from wire cables. One such machine is shown in figure 11-3.

The snow machine contains a large snow-particle supply drum and an internal fan blower to spray the snow pellets out over the set. The machine shown in figure 11-3 can eject plastic snow up to 30 feet (9.1m) for blizzard effects.

Ground snow requires a denser material than that used for falling snow. Suitable ground snow materials are polystyrene shavings, pulverized Styrofoam, and rock salt crystals. These all have enough body to form large drifts against set pieces such as trees, fences, and walls.

Snow simulations in miniature sets are scaled down to keep the proper look. Household salt and baking powder have both been used as snow substitutes.

Wind and Dust

A *wind machine* is a large rack- or pedestal-mounted electric fan. Three and four blade fans give a strongly directional flow of air across the set or miniature. Large fans, approximately 18 inches (46cm) in diameter, are used to blow breeze and wind effects within a normal weather range. If hurricane-force winds are needed for a given shot, a huge airplane-type propeller and wire cage unit are required to generate heavy wind action and knock over any lightweight furniture used in the scene.

All fans require blade protection frame cages in order to avoid accidental contact by preoccupied production workers and spectators visiting the location or set.

Dust is easily simulated by groundup Styrofoam dyed to earth color, powdered chalk, or groundup cereals such as bran or corn flakes. This is added slowly into the fan's windstream and keeps the dust at a realistic optical density as it is blown out over the set.

Smoke

Smoke effects are similar to fog effects except that smoke usually fills the entire air space of the set. A foglike smoke is generated by a portable *smoke gun*, which is similar to a fog machine. The gun contains a heating coil or, in some designs, a butane or propane burner. Mineral oil or low-grade diesel fuel is vaporized to create the smoke.

Dense smoke is produced by a pyrotechnic type of chemical container called a *smoke pot*. These flat-bottomed bowls are available in several sizes for smoke of a particular density and burn. Colored smoke pots are also available in a wide range of colors and in the same range of sizes. The smoke is generally nontoxic, although a dense smoke in a confined area can make breathing difficult.

Smaller smoke-producing agents are available in packets called *smoke cartridges*. These cartridges measure only a couple of inches in length and are designed for use on props or moving vehicles where space is too limited for a smoke pot device.

Smoke grenades are small pressurized cannisters or grenades that plume approximately 12 seconds of a very opaque nontoxic smoke. They are activated by a pull ring and flip toggle release. The hand-tossed grenades are frequently used to simulate a tear-gas bomb or a military type of explosive phosphorus grenade.

Miniature Smoke Room

Smoke can be used to create a scaled-down dust-polluted atmosphere for miniatures. For example, if a miniature is reduced to a 1:10 scale, the atmosphere surrounding the miniature should also be in the same 1:10 scale density. Smoke simulates the way air particles diffuse distant details and increases the realism of the miniature. This diffusion effect is an optical phenomenon known as *atmospheric perspective*, and simply means that the more distant an object is from the camera lens, the more vague and diffused it appears.

A *smoke room* is a sealed room containing a miniature, a camera, and a smoke cloud generated by a smoke gun. The room confines the smoke only to the area of miniature photography and maintains the smoke density to a consistent level. A smoke room requires longer camera exposures to produce a clear image on film. Usually, the miniature is filmed twice, once for the smoke-diffused image of the model's surface details, and then a separate exposure for any running lights or pinpoint light sources. When used in a moderately dense smoke, the high-intensity lighting used on the miniature's *practical* or self-contained lighting lamps creates soft halos around the lamps as well as realistic light beams.

Because of the long exposures and small shooting lens apertures, a smoke room miniature shot requires a series of test shots prior to actual photography in order to determine the best smoke density/lighting/exposure values.

Clouds

Miniature cloud effects are achieved by using dry ice boxes or smoke guns. Such clouds overlaying a process screen and moving across the shot field of view are realistically transparent.

A different method uses water and thickened white paint in a *cloud tank.* The tank is a huge glass-walled aquarium-style structure that measures about $4 \times 8 \times 4$ feet ($1.2 \times 2.4 \times 1.2$m). Salt water fills about half the tank and fresh water fills the remainder. First the salt water layer is poured into the tank, and plastic sheeting is floated over the surface to prevent the fresh water from mixing into the salt as it is poured into the tank. The plastic sheeting is then gently pulled from the tank. After the water has stilled, there is an invisible boundary marking the separation between the two different densities of water. This boundary is called an *inversion layer* and it is where the clouds will be located. The camera outside the glass is focused on this thin layer.

Miniature clouds are produced in the water by injecting an opaque tempera or thinned latex into the inversion layer through a long tube inserted at the top of the inversion layer. The "cloud" is formed at the end of the tube. This cloud formation swirls out realistically into the water-filled "sky." The injection tube is moved gently through the water to avoid creating a violent ripple effect in the clouds. Figure 11-4 shows the arrangement and action of the water-tank clouds.

Cloud formations can be illuminated by arranging spotlights along the sides of the water tank. Color gels that filter the light sources bring interesting color and texture to the clouds as they drift across the tank. Flash strobe units above the tank or positioned behind cloud areas simulate lightning effects.

The cloud tank is a simple mechanical effects device, frequently used to create controlled cloud and, in space backgrounds, galaxy formations. The tank was used extensively in *Close Encounters of the Third Kind, Raiders of the Lost Ark,* and *Star Trek II.*

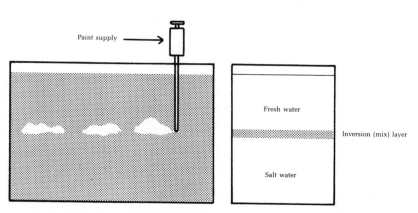

11-4 Cloud (water) tank.

Special Lenses and Camera Devices

12

This chapter covers a number of special purpose devices which are not directly related to visual effects but are frequently used to achieve various optical results. These devices are unique items that are available only in limited numbers from specific manufacturers. Many recent feature films have relied on the devices to aid in the creation of special visual effects. For this reason a brief summary of various devices is relevant here.

THE PERISCOPE LENS

A *periscope lens* (and its short version, the *snorkel*) is a long vertical tubelike optical relay. At one end of the tube is the camera body. At the other end is a tiny mirror or prism that deflects the line of sight 90 degrees. The tube's internal arrangement of lenses and prisms relays the light from the scene at one end of the tube to the other without distortion.

A basic periscope is shown in figure 12-1, this one designed by Laikin Optical Corporation. Its major components are diagramed in figure 12-2, and the light path through the internal optics is shown. Figure 12-3 is a schematic drawing of the actual arrangement of the lens system as defined by the light rays that pass through the many lens elements.

FOLDED PERISCOPE SYSTEM WITH ERECT IMAGE

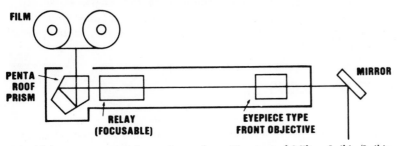

12-2 Major components of a periscope lens. (Courtesy of Milton Laikin/Laikin Optical Corp.)

12-1 Periscope lens. (Courtesy of Milton Laikin/Laikin Optical Corp.)

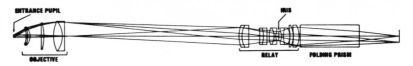

12-3 Optical schematic of a periscope lens. (Courtesy of Milton Laikin/Laikin Optical Corp.)

12-4 Snorkel lens. (Courtesy of Stephen Hajnal/F&B Ceco)

The short version of a periscope lens is called a snorkel. One is shown in figure 12-4. This snorkel, designed by Stephen Hajnal and distributed by F & B/Ceco Company, is a 12-inch (30.5cm) lightweight unit that enables the cinematographer to shoot handheld shots in restricted locations, such as inside an auto engine or inside machinery. The snorkel tube can be rotated in 90-degree increments with the image remaining erect at all times. Two models of this snorkel are available, one for 16mm camera mounts and the other for 35mm camera mounts.

The first periscope cameras were designed for use with a 16mm camera and intended for making film studies of tabletop architectural models. The camera was mounted in a mobile overhead scaffold rig that extended the periscope tube down into the miniature set. The periscope's end mirror maneuvered through the detailed miniature streets and alleyways to simulate the view of a person of scale size walking the route at ground level.

Modern periscopes and snorkels are used to shoot difficult angle shots of complex miniature sets. The periscope's unique perspective enables the miniature to stand in for full-size versions that would be impossible or too expensive actually to build. The periscope system has contributed to many special effects sequences, most notably the Death Star trench chase in *Star Wars* and the ice canyon pursuit scene in *Firefox*.

PITCHING LENS

A unique relay and lens system is the pitching lens system seen in figure 12-5. Designed and sold by Continental Camera Systems, the system is designed for deep-focus cinematography of tabletop miniatures and other special effects applications.

12-5 Pitching lens system. (Courtesy of Continental Camera Systems, Inc.)

12-6 Pitching lens system at work. (Courtesy of Continental Camera Systems, Inc.)

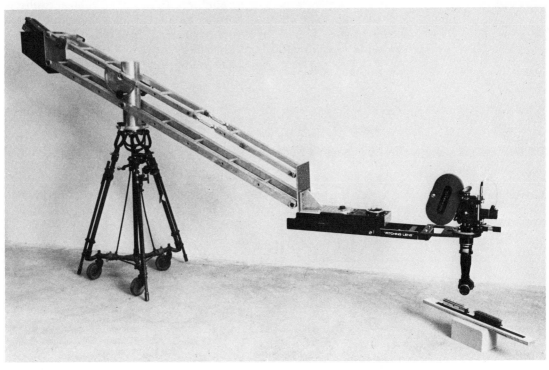

The outstanding feature of the pitching lens design is the motorized lens mount at the base of the periscope relay tube. The lens mount accepts a variety of prime lenses or a small focal length zoom lense. Any lens in the mount can be rotated for a 360-degree pan or tilted (pitched) 180 degrees. All movements are remote-controlled by an operator console nearby. The console features a joystick directional lever and a follow-focus control to keep a subject in sharp focus as it moves in the scene. A video tap on the periscope tube enables the operator to see the lens view of the shot on the console video black-and-white monitor screen.

The pitching lens attaches to a variety of studio cameras: the Arri IIC, Mitchell R35, 16mm Arriflex, Vistavision cameras, and the Norelco PCP-90. The camera and lens are usually mounted on a camera crane boom arm as seen in figure 12-6. The crane mount gives the camera operator maximum flexibility in placing the pitching lens in the midst of a miniature setup.

Because of the lens' wide f/3.9 aperture, only a minimum of light is required on the set to give a good exposure on film.

ASTROVISION

Astrovision is a special periscope system fitted to a Learjet. It creates an unusual airborne camera platform for air-to-air photography. Typical Astrovision shot maneuvers can be seen in figure 12-7. Unlike ordinary camera wing or helicopter camera mounts, the Astrovision system extends the periscope through the belly of the jet into the air below. This arrangement permits the periscope, a pitching lens, to rotate a complete 360 degrees or to pitch 46 degrees. The camera operator inside the plane observes the shot on a video tap television monitor and follows a flying subject anywhere in the sky below the plane via the directional joystick controls.

Astrovision was designed and built by Continental Camera Systems.

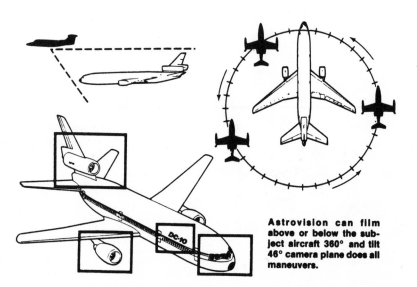

12-7 Astrovision. (Courtesy of Continental Camera Systems, Inc.)

Astrovision can film above or below the subject aircraft 360° and tilt 46° camera plane does all maneuvers.

The company has extensive experience with helicopter and aircraft camera systems. Astrovision was developed to meet the demand for a versatile high-speed camera plane to be used in shooting commercials and feature film sequences. The system is presently offered exclusively with Clay Lacy Aviation of California's specially modified Learjets.

Astrovision has been used to shoot air-to-air sequences and background plates for films such as *Capricorn I* and *Superman I* and *II*. The unique camera view offered by the jet's 600 miles per hour (967km) flight speed makes the Astrovision system a valuable special visual effects tool.

INCLINING PRISM

The *Samcine inclining prism*, shown in figures 12-8 and 12-9, is a lens prism attachment that allows the cinematographer to shoot a scene with the camera at a very low angle of view. The patented device can be used with regular production motion picture cameras without a significant loss of light in the lens image. The prism does not affect the lens depth of field or shooting aperture.

When attached to the front of a lens the prism deflects the optical path 51 degrees. It is superior to a simple front-surface mirror because the light passing through the prism is both reflected and refracted. This double action produces a correct-reading image, i.e., the right way up and with a proper left and right side. The optical path through the prism and lens is shown in figure 12-10.

Developed by Samuelson Film Service, Ltd., London, the Samcine inclining prism adapts to both standard and wide-screen Panavision and Vistavision formats. The prisms are leased by Samuelson throughout the world for use on feature films, television commercials, documentaries, and sports programs.

LOUMA CRANE

The *Samcine Louma crane* is a remote control modular camera crane that can make movements and swings usually associated with larger, heavier truck-mounted camera cranes. The lightweight and portable Louma crane, shown in figure 12-11, replaces the cumbersome bulk of the standard studio crane, the older cranes often weighing ten tons or more and needing plenty of space to maneuver on a studio set or location.

Designed by Jean-Marie Lavalou, Alain Masseron, and David Samuelson, the Louma won a 1981 Academy Technical Achievement Award for Excellence.

The Louma design mounts a remotely controlled camera at the end of a slender boom. The camera operator, located at ground level, uses a system of mechanical and electrical couplers to aim the camera, set the lens aperture, focus, and zoom. A television video tap and monitor provide the operator with a black-and-white rendering of the lens view.

The specification of the boom arm movement range is described in figure 12-12. At the end of the boom, the camera can continuously

12-8 Inclining prism. (Courtesy of Samuelson Group, PLC, London)

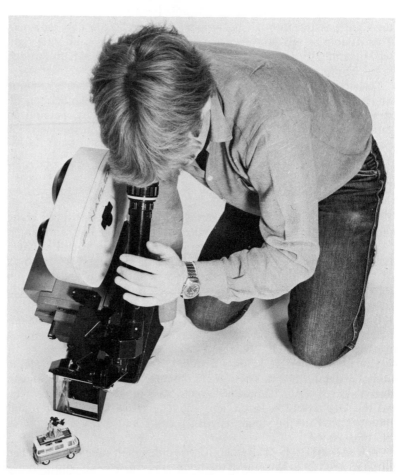

12-9 Inclining prism at work. (Courtesy of Samuelson Group, PLC, London)

SPECIAL LENSES AND CAMERA DEVICES

SAMCINE INCLINING PRISM

HOW IT WORKS

A. Optical axis set very much closer to a solid object than would be possible without optical assistance.
B. Tip of prism cut-away to lower optical axis.
C. Optical axis perpendicular to air/glass surface. Light passes through without deviation.
D. Rear surface of prism is mirrored, reflecting light at twice the angle of incidence.
E. Light strikes glass/air surface at an angle of incidence of 45° and is totally refracted.
F. Optical axis perpendicular to rear glass/air surface. Light passed through without deviation.
G. Camera lens inclined with optical axis 51° to the horizontal.

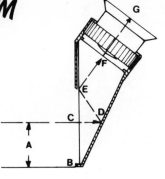

12-10 Inclining prism optical path. (Courtesy of Samuelson Group, PLC, London)

pan through 360 degrees and also do complete 360-degree roll tilts. This versatility gives the Louma camera fluid pan and tilt actions far superior to the traditional crane camera head.

The crane boom is mounted on a standard camera support, such as an Elemack Spyder Dolly or other suitable camera type support dolly. Unusual improvised crane platforms for the Louma have included a forklift truck and cherry picker industrial crane. The boom permits a continuous shot from a lens height of 4 inches (10cm) above the ground to a high of almost 45 feet (14m). The boom itself is made from a series of interlocking tubes that allows the boom to be extended from 4 feet (1.2m) to 26 feet (7.9m) simply by adding or removing tubes.

The Louma has been a major asset to creative camera effects in feature films such as *Raiders of the Lost Ark, Moonraker, 1941,* and *Wolfen.* The versatile crane can be leased from Samuelson's and from Filmtrucks.

STEADICAM

The *Steadicam* is a trademark for a motion-damping camera stabilizer that mounts to the camera operator's body. The Steadicam permits the operator to perform tracking movements over rough terrain without the need for a dolly or tracks.

Invented by Garret Brown, the Steadicam system is a highly stable nongyro camera support that uses a mechanical counterweight arrangement to keep the camera balanced in a floating position as the operator walks or runs through a scene with the camera. It removes the common problems that plague handheld camera footage: bounces, shakes, poor framing from jarring vibrations and an unstable camera support.

The Steadicam design places the camera at one end of a hinged metal arm. The camera is balanced to remain stationary unless moved by the operator. The hinged support arm is connected to a thick vest worn by the operator, which isolates the camera from any direct physical contact and further reduces the direct vibration of the camera

12-11 Louma crane. (Courtesy of Samuelson Group, PLC, London)

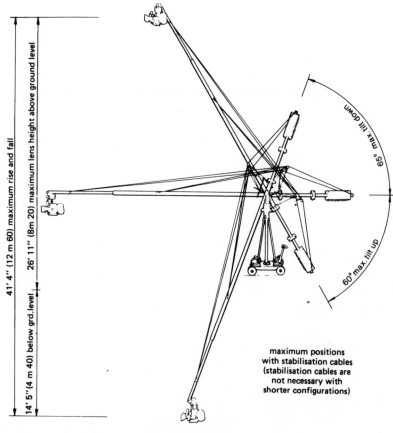

12-12 Maximum positions of Louma crane. (Courtesy of Samuelson Group, PLC, London)

    SPECIAL LENSES AND CAMERA DEVICES

body. Instead of using the camera's viewfinder, the camera operator composes the shot by watching a video tap monitor screen that is attached to the Steadicam support pole or lower sled section. All lens focus and iris adjustments are made through a servomotor mechanism linked electrically to the camera. The camera itself is not touched by the operator during Steadicam tracking moves.

The Steadicam operator usually is specially trained to use the device and is brought into a production for those specific types of shots. Often the Steadicam operator is required to do complex tracking

12-13 Steadicam. (Courtesy of Cinema Products Corporation)

shots, at times involving fast running, climbing stairs, walking backward and scrambling over rough terrain. Because the operator must keep an eye on the video monitor at all times to maintain a level and well-composed shot, a camera assistant handles the focus controls during a move and helps cue the operator for any upcoming turns or obstacles (especially during a backward track). When used properly, the Steadicam keeps the camera free of on-screen vibration and enables the operator to choreograph a smooth dollylike tracking of the subject.

The newest version of the standard Steadicam is the Steadicam Universal Model III, shown in figures 12-13 and 12-14. This design is lighter and more streamlined than earlier models. The film camera (or video camera as seen in fig. 12-14) can be rotated 180 degrees on the mount to permit unusual shooting angles or movements. The camera can also be pivoted up or down to meet a particular angle of view during a continuous pan action. The hinged arm swings 360 degrees horizontally for shooting behind the operator during a tracking shot. The lens aperture, focus, and zoom settings are adjusted by a wireless remote control unit. The Steadicam video monitor also electronically superimposes a white frame line on the screen to show

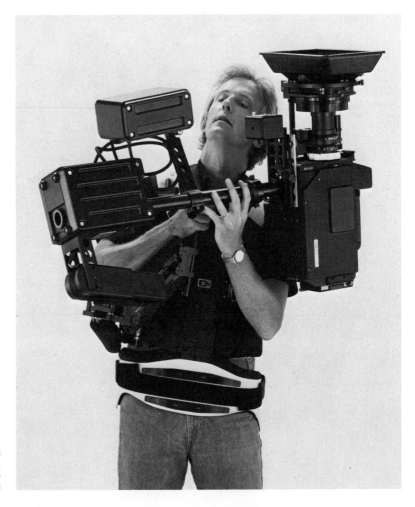

12-14 Video camera mounted on Steadicam. (Courtesy of Cinema Products Corporation)

SPECIAL LENSES AND CAMERA DEVICES

the cutoff area to match the camera format aspect ratio (35mm, 16mm, widescreen, and so on).

The Steadicam finds use not only as a stabilizer for a production camera, but also for process work as well. The most striking example of this is the use of the Model III Steadicam to shoot the forest background plates for the speeder bike chase in *Return of the Jedi*. Although the camera appears to jet through the maze of trees at high velocity, the shot was actually made at a single frame rate. The Steadicam camera was slowly walked through a previously determined path through the forest, one exposure per step. When projected at a normal speed, the footage simulates a high-speed background and is extremely smooth through the entire length of the shot.

The Steadicam camera stabilizer system is available through Cinema Products Corporation.

Two other camera stabilizer systems, the Panaglide by Panavision Corporation and the Camera Body Mount by Continental Camera Systems, are popular devices somewhat similar to the Steadicam. Despite the differences in mechanical design, all three are intended to give a camera operator unrestricted freedom of movement within a scene location during the photography.

PROJECTS

1: SCRIPTS AND STORYBOARDS

Project 1

Objective:
Seeing with a frame viewer

Materials:
Sheet of thin cardboard about the size of a standard notebook sheet
Right angle (90 degrees)
Cutting knife (X-Acto-type hobby knife)
12-inch ruler

Procedure:
Draw a 4 × 5-inch (101 × 127mm) rectangle in the center of the cardboard sheet.

Place the sheet on a cutting surface, carefully cut out the rectangle, and discard it.

The cardboard frame that remains is a viewing frame for composing and drawing a story board panel.

1. Look through the viewer at a nearby subject, with the viewing frame about 10 inches (25.4cm) from your eyes. This is approximately a Medium Shot if the subject is 15 feet (4.5m) from the viewer. Hold the viewing frame 2 inches (51mm) from your eye. This is approximately a Long Shot framing of the scene. Hold the viewing frame at about arm's length, or 24 inches (0.6m). This is approximately Close Shot framing of the scene.

Project 2

Objective:
To transfer a compositional frame to paper

Materials:
Pencil or dry marker (fine point)
Several sheets of typing paper
Viewing Frame

Procedure:
Trace the inner area boundaries of the viewing frame onto several sheets of paper. These lines will represent the *camera aperture* limits of a shot.

193

1. Repeat procedure number one of Project 1. Instead of cutting out the rectangle, this time scribble on it a rough sketch of the scene at each frame position. The sketch does not have to be artistic, only useful. The details of the scene are not important. The general relationship between the large shapes of the scene and the frame boundary are what is needed in the drawing.

2. After making a number of sketches of the interior of a room or of several subjects in a group, number the sketches according to the sequence in which they were drawn. Ask a member of the group or class to label each of the shot numbers as Medium Shot, Long Shot, or Close Shot, based only on your sketch. This exercise will help you to see how other people understand your drawings. If your sketches are to be meaningful as visual communication, they must be clear to everyone involved in a production. After the sketches have been labeled, see if you agree with the shot label. If not, why is it different than what you thought?

3. Write down the shot numbers and retrace the drawings on a photocopy of the blank story board art panel seen in figure 1-4. In the "Description" block write down the major elements of the scene viewed in the cardboard frame.

4. Give the story board drawings to someone else and have that person re-create the scene using different people from the original people in the shot. How well the "actors" are placed depends on how well the shot is described both in terms of the shot description and the art drawing composition. At each camera setup angle, verify if the camera person has correctly interpreted your original view or conception of the shot.

5. Write several paragraphs describing a scene and break the sentences into camera angles by jotting down the viewing frame views, such as Long Shot, Medium Shot, and Close Shot. This is similar to preparing a shooting script of the scene.

6. Using the viewing frame as a camera, draw a story board series that matches the paragraph breakdown.

7. Let another person arrange the scene using your shooting script and story board art panels. This action is the production stage of your pre-production work.

2: THE CAMERA AND CAMERA PROJECTS

Project 1

Objective:
To familiarize the reader with the essential parts of any camera.

Materials:
A 35mm single lens reflex still photographic camera (the SLR has a through-the-lens viewfinder)
A Super-8 or 16mm motion picture camera

Procedure:
Place both cameras on a table for a side-by-side comparison.

1. Identify the basic parts of a camera: Lens, Lens Diaphragm, Gate Aperture, Shutter, Movement, Film Supply, Viewfinder System, Film Counters, Speed and Exposure Controls.

Project 2

Objective:
To see how a lens forms an image on film.

Materials:
Several camera lenses of different focal lengths
  A simple hand lens
  An unlined 5 × 8 inch white index card to use as a small screen
  A darkened room with a window.

1. Hold an ordinary magnifying glass (a simple double-convex lens) in one hand and the white card in another. Bring the lens close to the card and focus an image of the window onto the card. What are the characteristics of the image: is it reversed, upside down? Are the boundaries sharply defined or fuzzy? Ask a friend to measure the distance between the lens and the card when the lens image looks the sharpest. This distance, in millimeters, is the approximate focal length of the lens. If you look closely at any edges within the focused image, you will see that every line is fringed by either a red or blue color along one side. This is caused by the different colors or wavelengths of the white window light being focused at different places on the card as light is bent or *refracted* as it passes through the lens. The simple magnifier lens is *uncorrected* for color. Corrected lenses focus the colors more closely together and produce a sharper image. *Achromatic* lenses correct for two colors. *Apochromatic* correct for three colors and provide an even sharper image than achromatic lenses. To correct for color, different types of glass, called crown glass and flint glass, are carefully ground into curvature and cemented together. This precision grinding and cementing of several pieces of glass contribute to the high cost of a top-quality photographic lens.
2. Have the friend hold the card at the best focus position while you make a square around the central image area with a marking pen. This area represents the way a film camera gate aperture makes a film frame out of a circular lens image.
3. Place two fingers in front of the lens. How does this affect the image? A lens diaphragm controls the image light by changing the size of the diaphragm opening. Your fingers act as a crude diaphragm to the simple lens. If you make several different-sized holes in a sheet of cardboard, these "apertures" for the simple lens will produce a better image depending on the size of the hole. Note that the smallest hole gives the sharpest but dimmest image.
4. Repeat step Number 1 with the different camera lenses set at full aperture. Where is the image formed on the card and how big is it, both in size of the frame and in size of the subject? Change both lenses to a smaller but identical aperture setting. How different is the image between them?

Project 3

Objective:
To make an in-camera special effect

Materials:
A Super-8 or 16mm movie camera
Film stock

Procedure:

1. Load the camera with film stock and mount the camera on a tripod. Stage an action scene such as a person walking across the field of view. Using the film counter, shoot this action, making a record of the start and stop positions of the frame/footage counter.
2. Make the same action go in reverse as an in-camera effect. This can easily be done by taking the camera off the tripod and holding it upside down as the scene is shot. This procedure is used for cameras without a reversing motor. When the finished processed film is projected, the sprockets will have been properly placed by flipping the film and splicing the length into the rest of the scene.
3. A side effect of step Number 2 is that not only the action is reversed, but the "geometry" of the shot as well. (Geometry refers to the left/right relationships). This reversal can be overcome by shooting with an upside-down camera at a mirror (a first surface-type) reflection of the staged scene action. When projected the film is edited into a normal but reverse speed order.

3: LENS FILTER EFFECTS

Project 1

Objective:
To make special effects filters

Materials:
Several sheets of various-colored acetates, either report covers or over-
    head projector transparencies
Several sheets of transparent colorless acetate
Fine sandpaper
Razor art knife
Metal straight edge
White spray enamel, small can
Nylon mesh (from nylon stocking)
Clear plastic sandwich bag
Several sheets of stiff cardboard
Compass and cellophane tape with a matte surface

Procedure:
Draw a circle about the size of a camera's lens aperture on each sheet of cardboard. Cut out the circle, leaving a hole in the cardboard. This is the filter holder. The plastic filters will be taped over this hole to make them easier to handle in front of a camera lens.

1. Make a single color filter by cutting a section of the plastic acetate and taping it to the frame.

2. Make a two-segment or dual color filter by cutting two pieces and joining them along the edges over the cardboard aperture hole. Butt the two strips straight across the center of the hole, but use no tape. The two filter pieces are centered in front of the camera lens, the midline at the horizon or center line of the frame.
3. Make a diffusion filter by taping a piece cut from a soft plastic sandwich bag. This material transmits nearly all of the light but diffuses the image to about a #2 grade diffusion factor.
4. Make a *fog* filter by lightly spraying white enamel paint over a sheet of clear plastic and taping it to the cardboard sheet. When placed in front of the camera lens, this fog filter produces a veil of gray diffusion that simulates a light mist. A denser fog can be produced by lightly sanding a clear sheet with fine sandpaper. A graduated fog filter can be made by sanding the edges of the aperture area at the top and lightening the pressure toward the bottom of the aperture, which should remain clear.
5. A different way of making a diffusion filter is to place nylon mesh—use a nylon stocking—over the hole. This produces a greater diffusion than the plastic bag material.
6. A star filter is made by lightly scoring a number of closely spaced grid lines across a clear plastic sheet. The star filter works best with bright points of light, such as moving auto headlights at night. A star filter can also be made by stroking coarse sandpaper in a horizontal and then vertical direction very lightly across the acetate. This action produces a " + " pattern of stars. By adding light strokes in other directions, any number of points can be added to the star pattern. However, care must be taken not to oversand the acetate sheet, as this will make the surface too opaque to see through. A single stroke in each direction is enough for a good effect.

4: ANIMATION I: TWO-DIMENSIONAL EFFECTS

Project 1

Objective:
To experiment with simple animation methods

Materials:
A tripod-mounted camera with a single frame release
500 unlined white index cards, 5 × 8 inches
Supplementary close-up lenses for the camera
Permanent-ink dry markers, various colors
A roll of leader film in any size format, preferably Super-8 or 16mm
1 cup fine-textured sand or an 8-ounce jar of popcorn kernels
Art construction paper, various colors, at least 5 × 7 inches
10 pieces of yarn or string, about 6 to 10 inches long
Two 500-watt lights, with reflectors and stands

Procedure:
Set up a simple animation stand by aiming the camera straight down at or at a slight angle to a floor or table top. Aim each light at a 45-degree angle so that the two beams overlap the area. A simple reg-

istration block can be made for the index cards by cutting an L-shaped piece out of cardboard and cementing it to a stiffer perhaps 4-ply backing board.

1. Draw a simple animated scene on the index cards. Both sides of the card can be used by holding the card against a window so that the image on the other side is visible; it can then easily be traced and changed slightly. Draw a number at the edge of the card with a light blue pencil, which does not show up too well on film. The numbers will help keep the cards in the correct shot order. To shoot the cards, postion the "L" frame just outside the area seen by the camera lens and place one edge of each card against the frame. Shoot each picture at one frame per shot.

2. Make a collage film by shooting photographs from magazines and newspapers. Move these photographs across the frame by shifting the picture slightly between exposures. By combining a single frame action to both the lens and the picture moves, a zoom and pan action is kinestatically animated.

3. Make a freeform frameless film by drawing or scratching directly onto the clear leader film. Ink can be applied to the line grooves to make etchinglike images. Color inks or dry markers that adhere to acetate add greatly to the kinds of images produced.

4. Animate tangramlike pieces of cut-out colored paper. Make a single figure out of separate pieces of colored paper so that they can come apart. Rearrange them into some totally different position at each successive single frame exposure. An animated figure film is the result.

5. Use pieces of string as individual puppets by moving several lengths across a background sheet made from art construction paper. Each piece of string need only be moved about one-quarter inch between frame exposures to look like swift snakes. The real challenge is in keeping track of which string has been moved and which has not prior to the frame exposure. Try to animate the snake strings in the following short scenes: the strings appear one-by-one in one corner of the frame and move in a follow-the-leader fashion along the four sides of the picture (seen through the view-finder). The train of strings then moves to the center of the picture area and forms a circle end-to-end. The circle suddenly changes to a square, then to a triangle, and finally a star. The strings then leave the picture area in a rapid follow-the-leader exit to end the short film. Although the action sounds easy, it requires concentration to keep all the short pieces of string moving smoothly.

6. Spread a handful of sand or popcorn kernels onto a background sheet made from art construction paper. Photograph the sand or popcorn in single frame exposures as you animate the loose material into a distinct shape. Try to make a standing figure by moving the sand with your finger into the right form. See if you can make the figure seem to walk by moving the individual grains or kernels that make the legs. These grains or kernels must all be moved as a group to keep the right action for each leg. The body does not have to move, but the walking legs should seem to move back and forth realistically. You can do amazing things with the loose material: the legs can jump away from the body and turn into a pair of wings; the legs can connect with the figure's arms to turn

the figure into a pair of wheels; the entire figure can magically turn into something else, such as a sailboat or flying saucer. The real fun of the sand or loose material animation is that it is so easy to create images as you shoot the film. Since each slight movement of the material is done between frames, the figure seems to change itself from one thing to another. If sand is used, a layer can be spread out and textured with a pencil end by making grooves in the sand. A comb can create a whole series of groove patterns at once. The sand layer can be used with a figure to make all types of scenes, such as a sailboat on the rough sea or trees popping out of the sandy ground.

5: ANIMATION II: THREE-DIMENSIONAL EFFECTS

Project 1

Objective:
To animate a clay puppet

Materials:
The camera arrangement of Chapter Four, Project 1, but with the camera at a level position
Enough colored modeling clay to make a puppet
Scissors
Tool kit pliers and screwdrivers

Procedure:

1. Animate a clay puppet figure by shooting at single frame release. Double-framing by shooting two frames instead of just one will make the shooting progress faster without affecting the animation. The puppet should be about six inches, large enough to photograph but not large enough to need an internal support or armature. Try to give your puppet "character" by exaggerating its features: big hands and feet, small eyes and big mouth, huge ears, even a lizardlike tail will help make your puppet unique. Animate the puppet by moving the limbs about one-eighth to one-quarter inch per frame exposure. To walk your puppet, use a sliding movement of the feet, rather than actually lifting the feet. This will keep your puppet balanced and make foot movements easier. Big feet help to keep the puppet from tipping over. Remember also that the larger the amount of movement between two adjacent frame exposures, the faster the move will appear in the finished film. Moving a leg one-half inch at a time creates a much faster walk than a one-eighth-inch spacing.

   Animate a short skit in which the clay puppet picks up the screwdrivers and throws each one like a spear into a tool box. You can use clear fishing line to "fly" the screwdriver spears by attaching a long piece to each end of the screwdriver. The line is then tied to a broom handle to make a fishpole aerial brace for the shot. By lifting the screwdriver with the fishing line, the puppet does not have to bear the weight of the screwdriver itself. The actual flight of the screwdriver into the tool box can be animated one frame at a time or filmed at normal speed to save time.

2. Transform the clay into a different figure during a single scene by modeling the changes between exposures.
3. Use wire on a simple broom fishpole between two chair backs to make an aerial brace. Wire or nylon thread is nearly invisible on camera and can be used to make the puppet suddenly fly out of the scene. Each upward move is, of course, shot at single frame exposures.

Project 2

Objective:
To make a simple three-dimensional animation with unusual puppets

Materials:
Same as Project 1

Procedure:

1. Animate ordinary household scissors to create a metal "beast monster" that endangers the clay figure. Open and close the blades of the scissors at a single frame rate. This exercise is also a good one for moving an entire figure (the scissors) while simultaneously animating an action (the opening and closing of the blades). The pliers and screwdrivers can also be used as ominous characters that engage in combat with the scissors while the puppet character heads for safety. This kind of complex interaction is quite demanding on an animator and requires that the intended movements be carefully planned prior to filming.
2. The entire contents of a tool kit spilling from an overturned tool box can be animated in a furious activity of "characters." This exercise is good to help the animator keep several "personalities" in mind as the various tool characters move about in the shot. The short film closes with the tools re-entering the tool box and the lid snapping shut.
3. An advanced version of the film in step Number 2 is one in which the camera movements are animated to coincide with action. This complex activity requires two people working closely together, one for the character tool animation, the other for the camera movement animation.

6: MATTES

Project 1

Objective:
To make a glass shot

Materials:
A sheet of acrylic plastic, ⅛ inch thick, 3 × 2.5 feet (3.2mm × 0.9m × 0.7m). This sheet is available at hardware, glass, or plastic suppliers as inexpensive glazing for "unbreakable" windows

An architectural magazine with color illustrations of unusual buildings
An X-Acto knife
Masking tape
Sheet of black paper about the size of the magazine page to use as
   backing
Spray cement (Scotch-3M Multi-Purpose Spray Adhesive is good)
Camera and tripod
Two adjustable stands, such as music or light stands

Procedure:
Cut out a page of the magazine that shows an unusual color photograph of a complete building, such as the Taj Mahal or Leaning Tower of Pisa. Place the page face down on a sheet of newspaper and spray it with adhesive. Quickly flip the page over and place it onto the sheet of black paper. (The black paper backing prevents the other side of the printed page from showing through during photography.) Take one edge at a time, rolling the paper to smooth out any wrinkles as they form. It is important not to have any wrinkles, folds, or bubbles in the glued sheet. Place the paper face down on a hard smooth surface and use a burnisher (the back of a spoon is fine) to rub the back of the black paper and firmly flatten the pasted-down artwork.

Now use the X-Acto knife and carefully cut out the complete building and its backing from the rest of the page. Be sure to use a thick piece of pressboard or cardboard as a cutting surface to avoid ruining a tabletop.

The cutout building will be used as a photograph *matte* instead of a painted glass shot.

1. Mount the acrylic sheet between the two stands. The easiest way to do this is to drill a tiny hole in each corner of the sheet, then loop a length of wire through the holes and around the stand to tie the sheet securely in place. Small C clamps can also be used to anchor the acrylic sheet between the two stand shafts.

   Place the camera on a tripod to shoot through the sheet, but with a field of view that does not include the stand supports. The acrylic sheet should be located just beyond the minimum focusing distance of the lens.

   Focus the camera at a somewhat distant landscape, with the horizon in the lower third of the frame. Lock the camera into position.

   Place a loop of adhesive tape with the adhesive on the outside on the back of the picture cutout. Attach the picture loosely to the acrylic sheet. Look through the camera and check the relative position of the cutout to the horizon line. Raise or lower the cutout's position and recheck the camera view. Do this until the cutout is properly on the horizon.

   When the cutout building matte is properly positioned, use additional tape to flatten it against the plexiglass surface. The finished setup is then ready to be photographed. The best matte shot is made on a bright day, when the camera lens can be set to a small lens aperture for the maximum focus of both the foreground matte cutout and the background scene.

Project 2

Objective:
To make a foreground miniature matte

Materials:
Broom handle or other rigid wooden rod 4–5 feet (1.2 to 1.5m) in
    length
Fishline monofilament
Two adjustable stands, such as music or light stands
Masking tape
Camera and tripod
Miniature, such as a model airplane or vehicle

Procedure:
Focus the camera on a relatively distant scene. The light stands are
set up at the minimum focus point of the shot, but out of the camera's
field of view. Bridge the broom handle between the two stands, and
raising it to a sufficient height to be out of the camera's field of view.
Wrap several winds of a masking tape around the broom ends and
stand poles to keep the broom rigidly in place.

1. Tie two or three strands of monofilament to the lightweight miniature. Each strand should be about 5 feet (1.5m) long.
2. Lift the miniature with a main strand and wind the strand several
   times around the broom handle. A piece of masking tape secures
   the loop for the time being.

   Check the camera view of the miniature in relation to the other
   elements in the background scene. If the miniature is too high,
   lower it by unwinding it or by adjusting the telescoping stand by
   collapsing a section into the stand. Properly aligned, the miniature
   appears to be in the same scene as the background from the camera
   lens view.

   Once the proper height is achieved anchor the miniature by
   attaching the other strands to the broom with tape. The extra
   strands stabilize the miniature in any light breeze and keep swaying
   to a minimum.

   The technique can be used to add an unusual miniature to an
   existing scene with a special script description, such as a flying
   saucer over a schoolyard.

7: REAR SCREENS

Project 1

Objective:
To make a simple rear screen composite shot

Materials:
Animation clay puppet or other figurine
A sheet of drafting Mylar or Lenscreen sheeting (available from Edmund
    Scientific Company; see list of suppliers) approximately
    20 × 24 inches (51 × 73cm)
A standard 500-watt 35mm slide projector

A 4-inch (102mm) projection lens
A 35mm SLR still camera
Wooden canvas stretcher frames used by artists to mount canvas; to
    be used for the rear screen sheet
Masking tape, 3 inches (7.6cm) wide
Camera tripod
Background slide

Procedure:
Arrange a rear screen projection setup as seen in figure 7-1. Placing
the projector about 90 inches (227cm) from the screen will provide
an image that will fill the screen.

1. Put a small table at the base of the screen. This is the stage for
the clay puppet or figure. Place the puppet close to the screen
and arrange the side lighting. Notice how the light beams spread
to cast shadows onto the screen and wash out the screen image.
Masks, such as gobo stands, or metal barndoors clipped to the
reflectors of the lamp units will permit the light to be carefully
focused only on the puppet and not on the screen. Adjust the
slide height by angling the projector. Position the slide behind
the puppet with regard to a ground level view (tabletop ground,
that is).

    Make several test exposures at different aperture lens settings.
Observe the effect of small and large apertures on the sharpness
of both the screen image and the puppet foreground. Also note
the different brightness levels between the background and foreground. The composite images require that the background image
be about the same intensity or brightness as the foreground. With
an automatic exposure meter reading, a too-bright screen causes
the foreground puppet to photograph dark. The composite rear
screen and puppet exposures should be graded by at least half a
lens stop between the different frame exposures of the test series.
The screen brightness can be decreased by inserting neutral density
filters into the beam or increased by moving the projector closer
to the screen.

    A greenish cast to the background colors in the processed film
is caused by ultraviolet light from the projector's lamp being passed
through the slide transparency to the screen image. A magenta
filter, which is a reddish color, will cancel the greenish cast when
placed over the projector lens.

8: FRONT SCREEN PROJECTION

Project 1

Objective:
To make a simple front projection composite shot

Materials:
Scotchlite 7615 cut to 2 × 3 feet (0.6 × 0.9m) mounted, following
    the manufacturer's instructions, on a hardwood panel (*Note:* If
    Scotchlite screen is unavailable or too expensive, the projects

can be completed with a high-quality glass-beaded screen or Kodak Ektalite projection screen to demonstrate basic front projection principles. For actual film photography, however, a Scotchlite screen is recommended.)

A beam splitter. A simple beam splitter is a thin sheet of transparent acetate (0.1 inch or 2mm), 12 inches square (0.3m). A better beam splitter is a semitransparent mirror such as a 5 × 7 mirror with 30 percent reflectance, 70 percent transmittance, available from Edmund Scientific (see list of suppliers).

A 35mm slide projector with background slide

A 35mm still camera SLR with exposure meter

A tripod with pan head

A free-standing puppet or figurine

Two studio lights, 300–500 watt bulbs with reflectors and barndoors

Work table, at least 3 × 7 feet (.9 × 2.1m)

Masking tape, ½ inch (1.3cm) wide

Procedure:

Move the large table near a wall and prop the Scotchlite into a vertical plane. Arrange the beam splitter and camera in alignment according to the positions seen in figure 8-2.

1. Insert a slide into the projector. If the beam splitter is properly in the projection beam the image on the screen appears intensely bright to the camera lens. Shift the angle of the beam splitter and note that any slight shift produces a large pan action of the screen image. In commercial front projection units the beam splitter is gimbal-mounted to allow swivel actions in a manner similar to this experiment.

2. Place a puppet in front of the screen. Notice that unless the side lights are very bright the puppet is simply a dark silhouette against the intensely bright Scotchlite-formed background image.

   The background brightness can easily outshine the set lighting, so the lights in front of the screen must be sufficiently bright to balance the output of the screen. An alternate method of balancing is to put neutral density filters in front of the projection beam to darken the screen image. Unless the screen light brightness is adjusted to match the in-front-of-the-screen lighting intensity, a proper composite of puppet and background cannot be made. Experiment with filters in the projection beam to dim and shift the background colors. With filtration and the light intensity, a great deal of exposure control is possible in the background and puppet composite shot.

Project 2

Objective:

To provide a motion picture background to a puppet composite shot

Materials:

Same as Project 1, but replace the slide projector with a 16mm projector and background film reel

Procedure:

1. Run the motion background footage with the same setup as for a

slide front projection composite shot. Note that the effect is that the puppet seems to be in motion, an illusion caused by the reference points in the moving background.

If the projector is equipped with a zoom lens, note how the zoom action causes the puppet to appear to shift position. This effect is most dramatic when the projector's zoom is manually synchronized to a similar camera zoom change, somewhat like the way the Zoptic system works to create the illusion of movement in depth.

2. Apply bits of Scotchlite materials to a miniature such as a space ship or vehicle. By arranging the mirror and camera-projector optical path as in figure 8-2, the effect of interior lighting is created where no lighting lamp exists. Even unusual things can be made to glow brightly in similar fashion, simply by applying the shaped piece of adhesive-backed Scotchlite. In the film *Superman I*, Jor-el's unearthly bright costume was actually a costume completely covered with highly reflective Scotchlite.

9 and 10: NO APPLICABLE PROJECTS

11: MECHANICAL SPECIAL EFFECTS

Project 1

Objective:
To make a cloud tank as a simple mechanical effect

Materials:
A 5-gallon (19-L) glass aquarium tank
A large thin plastic sheet, for example cut from a dry cleaner's bag
A plastic meat baster with squeeze bulb
A small bottle of white tempera (poster paint)
A 16-ounce (454g) box of coarse rock or sea salt
A large mixing container, such as an ordinary plastic water pail or
    bucket

Procedure:
Mix about a quarter of the salt or 4 oz. into 2 gallons (7.7L) of water and blend well. Pour this mixture into the aquarium tank. Next, gently place and float the plastic sheet over the surface of the water. This sheet will prevent the next water to be poured in from mixing with the first layer. Slowly pour into the tank about 2 gallons (7.7L) of fresh (unsalted) water. Let the water completely cover the first layer, then slowly slide out the plastic separator by gently pulling the sheet by one edge. Allow the water layers to settle for about fifteen minutes.

After the water is still, look closely for the hazy separation between the two layers. This is the inversion layer, which is something like a floor to the fresh water layer.

1. Prepare a mixture of white paint a bit thicker than for normal use. Fill the meat baster by squeezing the rubber bulb and then releasing pressure, with the nozzle in the paint. This release of tension causes a vacuum to suck up the liquid.

Wipe the nozzle of the filled baster clean with a soft cloth. Insert the tip of the nozzle into the water tank to the level of the inversion layer. Gently squeeze the bulb and observe the paint that is forced out of the tube. Instead of sinking to the bottom, the paint remains at the level of the inversion layer. Move the tube to another section of the tank and notice the different kinds of "clouds" that can be made by simply varying the squeeze pressure on the bulb. A sudden hard squeeze jets out a large amount of paint that can simulate an atomic mushroom cloud effect. When the water is completely hazy with floating paint, the tank must be emptied and two new water layers prepared.

2. To simulate a volcano in full eruption, make and paint a Styrofoam open-hole model of the volcano and invert it into the tank. On cue, the "eruption" is a half-pint of flat interior latex paint poured directly into the base of the cone. This will cause paint "smoke and ash" to spew from the open inverted crater of the volcano. This action should be shot in slow motion, with the camera at three to four times faster than normal speed. The camera must be turned upside down to make the volcano appear to be in a normal position. The inversion will also result in a reverse action of the paint flow, so the camera must be running in reverse when the shot is made to restore the original flow direction from the volcano. An optical printer can likewise print the film with the correct direction of flow. If a camera cannot run in reverse for filming the shot, the actual shooting can be done with a mirror to invert the volcano set-up. In this arrangement the camera is aimed downward at a mirror inclined 45 degrees to the volcano tank. The camera lens then photographs the reflection and not the volcano directly. The result is the volcano positioned properly at the base of the frame and the paint "smoke plume" drifting away from the crater.

GLOSSARY

aberration   Any defect in a lens or optical glass that causes a distorted image or flaw in reproduction.

Academy aperture   The standard aperture mask used in 35mm cinematography (except when a wide-screen anamorphic system is used) for theatrical presentations.

additive color process   A photographic method used to reproduce the natural colors of a shot. A black-and-white film exposed through a red, green, or blue filter records one primary as a color separation. Three separations are made, one for each primary color. Later, during printing, each separation is projected with a colored light matching the primary used to record the separation. When all three separations are printed in register on a single filmstrip with color sensitive emulsion, the original colors of the shot are accurately reproduced. This process is also used in televison to produce colors on the video screen. Close examination of a screen reveals the red, green, and blue phosphors that make up an additive color image.

angle, camera   The camera's position relative to the subject.

animatics   A film or video presentation of photographs or artwork that shows in condensed form what a longer film will contain in both story and visual style.

animation   The technique of creating the illusion of motion on film of a stationary object or drawings by means of single frame exposures.

animation camera   A camera used to animate artwork by shooting at a single frame exposure rate.

animation disc   A round aluminum plate with at least one set of peg bars; used by an animation artist to hold prepunched acetate or drawing paper.

animation stand   A metal scaffold for supporting an animation camera and artwork. The stand contains a movable table called the *compound* and motors or manual handwheels for moving the compound and camera.

answer print   The first print from the laboratory that combines the picture and soundtrack.

aperture   In a *lens*, the diaphragm opening expressed as a ratio of the lens focal length and the aperture diameter, preceded by an f, as in f/8. In a *camera*, the rectangular opening in the camera gate plate. In a *projector*, the rectangular opening that defines the projected screen image area.

ASA rating   The American Standards Association rating of the sensitivity of a film stock emulsion to light. The higher the ASA number the more sensitive the emulsion to light (a "faster" film).

aspect ratio   The proportion of a motion picture frame as expressed as a width-to-height ratio, as in 1.33:1 aperture for standard 35mm cameras.

ball and socket armature   A puppet support made of metal that has flexible joints made up of ball bearings sandwiched between drilled metal sockets to simulate natural hip and shoulder movements.

barndoor   A metal flap, usually used in pairs, fitted to a lighting unit to permit redirection or blocking of a light beam.

base   The plastic substrate that supports the film emulsion.

beam splitter   A semimirrored glass or plastic sheet that partially reflects as well as passes any light that passes through it. Beam splitters are used for many kinds of special visual effects and in front projection systems.

beauty shot   A camera shot that records the exterior of a detailed model or miniature, usually in connection with photography by computer-controlled cameras that shoot the model and all composite printing mattes in repeated camera moves.

bipack   A matte printing technique in which a roll of fresh film stock and a roll containing a master positive are run together in contact through a process camera for a contact printing exposure.

blowup   An enlargement of the film frame.

blue screen process   A traveling matte method that uses a screen of uniform blue as a backing to the foreground subject. In later optical printing, the blue screen is replaced with a separately filmed background by a series of masking films that conform to the blue screen area.

bottom pegs   The lower set of registration pegs on the animation stand compound table or animation disk.

cameraless films   Animated films made by drawing or painting directly on the film base as opposed to image-making by photographic means.

cel   A transparent acetate sheet used in cartoon animation and in title photography. The term is short for celluloid, an early film base.

close-up   A camera shot at a short distance from the subject.

color temperature   The index of the color quality of a given light using the Kelvin degree scale.

composite   A shot produced by two or more separately filmed elements optically combined.

compound   The animation stand assembly that permits the artwork to be moved in any direction on a flat plane parallel to the camera image plane.

computer animation   A general term for sequential images produced by a computer and usually displayed on a video screen to simulate 2-D or 3-D animation effects achieved by traditional hand methods.

contact printer   A printing machine that duplicates footage by an emulsion-to-emulsion contact between the original footage and a duplicating stock.

continuous step printer   A contact printer that employs an aperture frame registration and intermittent to hold a frame motionless as it is illuminated and copied onto a duplicating film stock.

cycle   A repetition of animation drawings to produce a continuous activity such as walking or running.

depth of field   The distance in front of a camera lens in which objects are in sharp focus.

dissolve   The overlapping of a fade-in and a fade-out for a scene transition.

emulsion   The light-sensitive layer on a film base.

establishing shot   A long shot that begins any series of shots to portray the basic situation of the scene.

exposure   The light striking the film emulsion and producing a latent image.

f/number   See *aperture, lens*

fade   An optical transition effect of a gradual lightening of the scene from full black (fade-in) or a gradual darkening to full black (fade-out).

fading shutter   A variable shutter on an animation camera that produces a fade by diminishing the amount of exposure over a number of preselected frames. The fading shutter is used to make in-camera fades and lap dissolves.

field   The area photographed by the camera.

field chart   A chart printed with a grid that defines the visual area covered by a camera lens at a given distance.

filter   Colored glass or a gelatin sheet that is used to modify light, control image contrast, or to correct for color differences in a film emulsion and light source.

filter factor   A number that indicates how much to compensate for the loss of light in an exposure when a filter is used.

floating pegs   The animation peg bars on an animation table that move independently in an east/west direction.

focal length   The measurement from the optical center of a lens to that point at which the image is in focus when the subject is positioned at the most distant point (infinity).

focal plane   The plane, perpendicular to the lens optical axis, where an image is formed when the lens is focused at infinity.

focal plane matte   Any matte located just in front of the film by means of a mask inserted into a slot in the camera aperture plate.

focus   The sharpest image produced by a lens as measured at the film plane of the camera aperture.

frame   The single picture area on a film strip or a single exposure on a length of film negative stock. Also a term for composing or arranging a camera shot.

freeform image   In cameraless animation a term for art areas on a film strip drawn without concern for limiting the art to individual frames. The opposite style is the registered frame image, which uses the standard frame interval of sprocket holes to define the boundaries and timing of the action art.

freeze frame   An optical effect created by repeated printing of a single picture frame for an extended number of frames to stop the flow of visual action in a scene.

front projection   A matte method in which an actor is composited to a background scene by projecting a scenery transparency to a large reflex surface screen that forms a backing to the actor. The actor is self-matting.

gauge   The film width in millimeters, i.e., 16mm, 35mm, 70mm.

generation   The number of successive printings that separate a given copy from the original camera negative.

gobo   An opaque sheet that prevents any unwanted light from striking an area of a set, miniature, or screen. Usually a gobo is mounted in an adjustable stand called a gobo stand, century stand, or C stand.

grain   The microscopic particles of silver suspended in the film emulsion gelatine that form the image, generally called "fine grain" or "coarse grain."

high-contrast film A special black-and-white film that has few or no intermediate tones of gray.

highlights The brightest parts of a subject or scene.

internegative A negative printed from an original color reversal print.

interpositive A special color positive with an orange-dyed base designed for printing opticals or duplicates.

key light The main light that establishes both the source direction and mood of the scene lighting.

kinestasis An animation method that pans or zooms the camera during photography of still photographs or artwork to add motion to the static images seen in the photographs or artwork.

latent image The exposed but undeveloped image on a light-sensitive film emulsion.

matte An opaque mask that blocks a portion of the scene being photographed or the area of the film emulsion being exposed.

matte box An adjustable bellowslike device that attaches to the camera lens to hold filters or mattes; also acts as a sunshade lens hood.

medium shot An intermediate camera position between a long shot and a close-up.

negative The processed camera-original film from which the positive projection print is made.

optical printer A machine consisting of a projector and camera that copies film footage for effects and manipulation of images.

opticals Any visual effect in a shot or scene, usually a dissolve, fade, or wipe effect, that is made by in-camera methods or on an optical printer.

pan A camera movement across a scene made by a horizontal rotation of the camera body.

panchromatic Sensitivity to all colors. Generally refers to a black-and-white film emulsion that reproduces the colors of a shot as a range of gray tones.

pantograph A rod pointer, interconnected to an animation compound and a field chart, that duplicates the area seen by the camera lens. When the pantograph pointer is moved to any field chart area, a similar and simultaneous move is made by the animation compound. The use of the pantograph enables the animation camera operator to map out any complex pan movements without mathematical calculations.

parallax error The degree of divergence, or error, between the image seen in a nonreflex viewfinder and the actual image recorded by the camera lens. When the two separate optical paths of viewfinder and lens are properly converged on the subject being photographed, there is no parallax error in the two views.

pass A single run of film through a camera or projector.

peg bars In animation, a flat metal strip with three fixed pegs used to hold drawings and painted cels in place on an animator's drawing disk or animation stand.

persistence of vision   A natural phenomenon of vision caused by a time delay between stimulation of the eye's retina by light and actual response to the cessation of the light. When images are projected rapidly at a rate of at least 16 per second, the eye sees no intermission between successive images. This phenomenon is essential to producing continuous movement on a screen when projecting a series of individual picture frames.

plate   In process projection, the film that is used to provide a background scenery to a foreground subject.

positive   The print produced from the original in-camera negative that has all the colors and tone values of the original scene.

print   Any positive film produced from the original or duplicate negative.

process camera   A camera with a film frame registration and single frame motor drive. Process cameras are used primarily on optical printers and animation stands.

process shot   Composite photography involving a projected background and a foreground live action subject.

raw stock   The unexposed film.

rear projection   A matte method in which a background is projected on the rear of a large translucent screen that forms a backing to an actor on the other side of the screen. The actor is self-matting in the composite image.

reflex surface   A surface that reflects nearly all the light projected upon it back along the projected beam optical path. Reflex surface screens are used in front projection systems.

register   An accurate superimposition of a frame or image over another frame or image.

replacement part animation   An animation method that uses a series of rigid puppets or parts of a puppet in sequential order during single frame photography. One puppet or part replaces the previous puppet or part for each frame exposure to create a fluid movement in the final print.

reversal stock   Film stock that is specially processed to produce a positive from the original in-camera negative exposure.

reverse angle   A shot that frames the subject from the opposite side of the previous shot.

rotoscope   A tracing of live action footage frames onto animation cels to simulate natural movements. The term also refers to the frame projection device that fits into an animation camera gate for projecting the frame image onto the table for tracing.

scene   (1) The script action and dialogue. (2) The subject being photographed by the camera.

Schüfftan mirror   A matte method invented by Eugen Schüfftan that uses a mirror reflection of actors conforming to a matte area on a miniature set.

Scotchlite   A trademark of the 3M Company for its brand of highly reflective sheeting commonly used in reflex surface screens for front projection process.

script   The written instructions that contain all dialogue, action, and camera directions used to guide a film production.

shooting script   The final version of the script used by the director and actors during shooting of the film.

shot   The image recorded by the camera in any continuous run of the film stock through the camera gate.

slit-scan photography A type of streak photography. The camera is mounted on a track and photographs a narrow slit behind which is a moving piece of artwork. The camera shutter is opened, then the camera is moved towards the slit. At the same time the back-lit artwork is moved laterally across the slit. When the camera reaches the point closest to the slit, the shutter closes. The cycle then repeats for the next single frame exposure. The result is a film frame image of the entire piece of artwork, seemingly at an extreme perspective. The artwork can be made to move if the artwork is advanced a bit from the last starting point prior to the last exposure. The slit-scan effect was first popularized by the film *2001: A Space Odyssey* in the famous "light corridor" stargate sequence.

special effects A general term for any shot that uses a shooting method other than standard studio or location camera shooting methods. Special effects encompasses mechanical devices for "live" on-location illusions (called physical special effects) and photographic illusions (or special visual effects) added in postproduction.

SPFX An abbreviation for "Special Effects." Also FX, EFX, and SFX.

splash lighting Light that strikes a projection screen other than the primary image supplied by the projector. Splash lighting is usually overhead set lighting and washes out the screen image considerably unless the lights are repositioned away from the screen; it can be diminished by the use of metal flaps called barndoors.

stepper motor A type of electric motor that is activated by a series of electrical pulses rather than a continuous alternating or direct current. By changing the polarity of the pulse or timing the pulse rate, the stepper motor can be accurately controlled. Stepper motors are usually an essential component of computer motion-control camera systems.

stop-action, stop-motion A general term for the animation of puppets or other objects achieved by shooting a single frame exposure after each new pose or movement of the puppet or object instead of shooting a normal continuous frame rate.

streak photography An optical effect created by keeping a camera shutter open as an object or graphic is moved across the field of view. The result is a blurred image. By planning the amount and direction of blurred movement, a large variety of complex images can be created in-camera.

subtractive color process A photographic method used to reproduce the natural colors of a shot. Similar to the color separation photography used in additive color processes except complementary, or subtractive, filters are used—magenta, cyan, and yellow. Subtractive filters subtract primary colors from white light: magenta subtracts green, cyan subtracts red, and yellow subtracts blue. All modern negative color film emulsions use the subtractive rather than the additive process to record primary color intensities. In film the filtration is achieved by multilayer coatings on the emulsion.

T/number The lens aperture in terms of how much light is actually passed by the lens at any given aperture diaphragm setting.

tiedown Any device used to anchor a puppet to the animation stage to keep the pupet from falling over.

tilt A camera movement caused by tipping the camera body up or down.

top pegs The upper set of registration pegs on an animation drawing disk or animation stand compound table.

tracking shot A camera shot that follows the subject continuously through a scene without stopping the camera. Also a commonly used alternate for the dolly shot, in which the camera is mounted on a wheeled platform called a dolly.

vignette A shading of the edges of a camera shot by use of a matte, filter, or matte box.

zoom In animation, the movement of the camera toward or away from the artwork on the table of the animation stand. Often called a *track movement*.

zoom lens A lens equipped with an adjustable optical assembly to provide a variable focal length range.

Zoptic A front projection method invented by Zoran Perisic that provides an effect of an actor moving in depth within an apparently stationary background scene. The method uses two synchronized zoom lenses, one on the camera and the other on the background projector.

BIBLIOGRAPHY

Agel, Jerome. *The Making of Kubrick's 2001*. Paperback. New York: New American Library, 1970.

Branston, Brian. *A Film Makers Guide*. London: George Allen & Unwin, Ltd., 1967.

Bulleid, Henry A. V. *Special Effects in Cinematography*. London: Fountain Press, 1954.

Bulluck, Vic, and Hoffman, Valerie. *The Art of "The Empire Strikes Back."* Paperback. New York: Ballantine Books, 1980.

Byrnes, Gene. *The Complete Guide to Cartooning*. New York: Grosset & Dunlap, 1950.

Campbell, Russel. *Photographic Theory for the Motion Picture Cameraman*. Paperback. London: Screen Textbooks, A. Zwemmer Ltd., 1970. New York: A. S. Barnes, 1970.

Caunter, Julien. *How to Produce Effects*. London and New York: Focal Press, Ltd., 1955.

Clark, Frank P. *Special Effects in Motion Pictures*. New York: Society of Motion Picture and Televison Engineers, Inc., 1966.

Clarke, Charles G. *Professional Cinematography*. Hollywood: American Society of Cinematographers, 1964.

Clarke, C. G., and Strenge, W. *American Cinematographer Manual*. Hollywood: American Society of Cinematographers, 1973.

Edmonds, Robert. *Scriptwriting for the Audio-Visual Media*. New York: Focal Press, Ltd., 1955.

Erickson, G., and Trainor, M. E. *The Making of "1941."* Paperback. New York: Ballantine Books, 1980.

Everitt, David, and Schechter, Harold. *Film Tricks*. Paperback. New York: A Harlin Quist Book, 1980.

Fielding, Raymond. *The Technique of Special Effects Cinematography*. New York: Hastings House, 1968.

Happé, L. Bernard. *Basic Motion Picture Technology*. New York: Hastings House, 1975.

Harryhausen, Ray. *Film Fantasy Scrapbook*. New York: A. S. Barnes, 1974.

Hoffer, Thomas W. *Animation, A Reference Guide*. Westport, Connecticut: Greenwood Press, 1981.

Holman, L. Bruce. *Puppet Animation in the Cinema*. New York: A. S. Barnes, 1975.

Ikuta, Mitch, and Seiler, Lee. *Building Beings, Creating Creatures, and Doing Dinosaurs*. Paperback. Elk, California: Cliffridge Publishing, 1979.

Lahue, Kalton C. *Photo Filters and Lens Attachments*. Los Angeles: Peterson Publishing Company, 1981.

Laybourne, K. *The Animation Book*. New York: Crown Publishers, 1979.

Levitan, Eli L. *Handbook of Animation Techniques*. New York: Van Nostrand Reinhold, 1979.

Lutz, E. G. *The Motion-Picture Cameraman*. New York: Arno Press & The New York Times, 1972.

Malkiewicz, Kris J. *Cinematography*. New York: Van Nostrand Reinhold, 1973.

Pittaro, Ernest M. *TV and Film Production Data Book*. New York: Morgan & Morgan, 1959. London: Fountain Press, Ltd., 1959.

Rovin, Jeff. *From the Land Beyond Beyond*. Paperback. New York: Berkley Publishing, 1977.

Russet, Robert, and Starr, Cecile. *Experimental Animation*. New York: Van Nostrand Reinhold, 1976.

Sackett, Susan, and Roddenberry, Gene. *The Making of Star Trek—The Motion Picture*. New York: Pocket Books, 1980.

Salt, Brian G. D. *Basic Animation Stand Techniques*. Oxford, England: Pergamon Press, Ltd., 1977.

Samuelson, David W. *Motion Picture Camera Data*. London and New York: Focal Press, Ltd., 1979.

————. *Motion Picture Camera Techniques*. London and New York: Focal Press, Ltd., 1978.

Titelman, Carol. *The Art of Star Wars*. New York: Ballantine Books, 1979.

Wheeler, Leslie J. *Principles of Cinematography*. London: Fountain Press, Ltd., 1965.

Wilkie, Bernard. *Creating Special Effects for TV and Film*. New York: Hastings House, 1977.

Wilson, Steven S. *Puppets and People*. New York: A. S. Barnes, 1980.

Magazines and Journals

American Cinematographer, International Journal of Film and Video Production Techniques. Vol. 59, No. 3, through Vol. 64, No. 4. Published by ASC Holding Corporation, Hollywood, California. Published monthly.

Cinefantastique, The Review of Horror, Fantasy and Science Fiction. Vol. 7, No. 2, through Vol. 11, No. 1. Published by Frederick S. Clarke, Oak Park, Illinois. Published quarterly.

Cinefex, The Journal of Cinematic Illusions. No. 3 through No. 6. Published by Don Shay, Riverside, California. Published quarterly.

Cinemagic, The Guide to Fantastic Filmmaking. No. 1 through No. 19. Published by O'Quinn Studios, Inc., New York. Published bimonthly.

Fantastic Films, The Magazine of Visual Fantasy and Science Fiction. Vol. 1, No. 3 through Vol. 3, No. 3. Published by Blake Publishing Corporation, Chicago. Published nine times a year.

Starlog, The Magazine of the Future. No. 7 through No. 59. Published by O'Quinn Studios, Inc., New York. Published monthly.

APPENDIX I
Suppliers

Many common items used in general photography and visual effects can be readily purchased at local stores and dealers. The suppliers given here are intended to provide a handy source when materials cannot be found locally.

The following is a selected list of both suppliers and manufacturers of visual effects materials and equipment. The companies offer a wide variety of materials and devices and should be contacted for updated catalogues and price lists before ordering. *Please specify your needs* when writing to a supplier.

Alan Gordon Enterprises, Inc.
1430 North Cahuenga Boulevard
Hollywood, CA 90028
Camera equipment rental

Alcone Company
575 Eighth Avenue
New York, NY 10018
Kryolan foam rubber, liquid latex, mechanical fog and smoke machines, theatrical lighting, and makeup supplies

Arriflex Corp.
500 Route 303
Blauvelt, NY 10913
16mm and 35mm production cameras

ASC Holding Corp.
P.O. Box 2230
Hollywood, CA 90028
American Cinematographer Manual

Bolex
250 Community Drive
Great Neck, NY 11020
16mm production cameras, matte boxes and equipment

Cartoon Color
9024 Lindblade Street
Culver City, CA 90230
Cel-Vinyl colors, animation art supplies

Century Precision Cine/Optics
10661 Burbank Boulevard
North Hollywood, CA 91601
Duplikins printers and camera lenses

Eastman Kodak
343 State Street
Rochester, NY 14650
Film stock and technical information

Edmund Scientific Co.
Edscorp Building
Barrington, NJ 08007
Optical lenses, screens, mirrors, and Lenscreen Rear Projection sheeting

F & B Ceco, Inc.
315 West 43 Street
New York, NY 10036
Camera equipment rental

Fax Company
374 South Fair Oaks Avenue
Pasadena, CA 91105
Animation stands and supplies

Fries Engineeering, Inc.
12032 Vose Street
North Hollywood, CA 91605
Special effects 35mm cameras and animation motors

Harrison & Harrison
P.O. Box 1797
Porterville, CA 93258-1797
Camera filters, diffusion, fog, special effects filters

J-K Camera Engineering, Inc.
5101 San Leandro Street
Oakland, CA 94061
Optical printers and animation stands

Jerry Ohlinger's Movie Material Store
120 West Third Street
New York, NY 10012
Film scripts (photocopies) and movie photos

3M Company
3M Center
Saint Paul, MN 55144
Front projection Scotchlite (write for local sales outlet)

L. S. Starret Company
101 Crescent Street
Athol, MA 01331
Surface gauges

Mitchell Camera Corp.
P.O. Box 279
11630 Tuxford Street
Sun Valley, CA 91352
16mm and 35mm production cameras

Ox Products, Inc.
108 East Prospect Avenue
Mamaroneck, NY 10543
Animation stands and supplies

Oxberry
180 Broad Street
Carlstadt, NJ 07072
Optical printers and animation stands

Polyform Products Co.
9420-T West Byron Street
Schiller Park, IL 60176
Modeling materials and paints

R & D Latex Corp.
5901 Telegraph Road
Commerce, CA 91141
Foam latex kit 318C and foam rubber supplies

Rosco
36 Bush Avenue
Port Chester, NY 10573
Color gelatin filters for cameras and lighting

Sculpture House
38 East 30th Street
New York, NY 10016
Hard plaster (HydroStone) and sculpture supplies

Stewart Filmscreen Corp.
1161 West Sepulveda Boulevard
Torrance, CA 90502
Rear screens, front screens, blue screens

Tiffen
90 Oser Avenue
Hauppauge, NY 11787
Camera filters of all types

Tri-Ess Sciences, Inc.
622 West Colorado Street
Glendale, CA 91204
Laboratory equipment and special effects pyrotechnics

Victor Duncan, Inc.
200 East Ontario Street
Chicago, IL 60611
Camera equipment rental

Windsor Hills Makeup Lab, Inc.
5226 Maymont Drive
Los Angeles, CA 90043
Schram foam rubber kit

Winfred M. Berg, Inc.
499 Ocean Avenue
East Rockaway, NY 11510
Steel stock, gears, bearings, and precision hardware

APPENDIX II
Animation Safety Hazards

Many animation chemicals and compounds are dangerous if precautions are not taken. Repeated exposure to various substances during the casting process create a serious cumulative danger to body organs and sensitive membranes. When used properly, with the correct preventive respiratory equipment, protective clothing, and gloves, the dangers to health are minimal. However, all serious animators respect the inherent risks of working with toxic casting resins, foams, and powders.

The following is a brief listing of common animation materials and problems. This list was prepared with the assistance of professional animator Rick Catizone of Anivision, Ltd.

Clay, Plastilina oil-base: Relatively harmless.

Epoxy: The catalyst and resin contain irritants and can cause slight skin burns if in contact with skin during the cure.

Fiberglass: Fiberglass should not be used by amateurs. Fiberglass resin is toxic if the working area is not adequately ventilated. Long exposure to the materials can lead to liver damage, lung damage, and severe irritations to skin and respiratory tissues.

Latex: Liquid is relatively harmless, but care should be taken to avoid getting the liquid into eyes or onto clothes. Cold foam is relatively harmless. Heat cured foam is relatively harmless.

Paints: Any paint with a toluene base should be used with adequate ventilation to avoid inhaling vapors.

Plaster: Plaster contains corrosive lime, which can severely damage the eyes. It may also irritate skin and the mouth lining. Plaster should not be used on a human being, as in making a facial mold, since burns can occur from the heat of the plaster as it cures. Suffocation is another possible danger, since plaster could plug the nose and mouth.

Resins: Most resins are toxic to some degree and must be used only in well-ventilated areas. Both resin and catalyst hardener can cause burns or severe skin irritation.

Rubber cement and rubber cement thinner: Benzene-based products (thinners) can damage internal organs after long exposure to the vapors. Use requires adequate ventilation.

Silicone rubber: The catalyst agent may burn skin and eyes on contact.

Urethane, polyurethane: Depending on the type of agent used to make the expanded foam, the urethane group can generate byproduct gases that cumulatively can lead to liver failure or collapse of internal organs.

Wax: Hot wax can cause serious skin burns.

Wood, balsa, patternmaker's wood, bass wood: Splinters can cause infections, dust can cause breathing difficulties, shavings can absorb flammable solvents.

A Cautionary Note: Mr. Catizone comments:

Carelessness, coupled with a lax attitude, can be dangerous or even deadly. Amateur animators (and professionals) can do a fine job with regular or foam latex, plaster, and other simple materials.

Professionals need speed and durability, so we sometimes go to the other more dangerous products. However, most of us do so with a very respectful attitude and handle the materials very carefully.

If we use these compounds a lot, then our *ease* with them makes others think that they are easy and safe for everyone. *Not* true!

Index